A LADY'S VOYAGE ROUND THE WORLD

For a lady to set off alone from Europe round the world in 1846 was so singular that it is no wonder Ida Pfeiffer's travels caused such consternation, admiration and even an insurrection at a Chinese tea factory. Her inquisitiveness and the economy forced on her by limited means made her travels no timid sampling of luxury ports, but rugged, often dangerous journeys by brig, junk, elephant, camel, horse, foot and Arab caravan to a world now utterly changed. Wonderfully forthright in all her opinions, she was imbued with little of the orthodox European arrogance of her times, and trenchant in her condemnation of unfeeling and cavalier behaviour on racial grounds.

Dressed as a man she was the first woman to walk round the walls of Canton and amazed the Persians by making her own way across the desert. She happily dined on monkey with the Puri Indians of Brazil and boa in Singapore, yet bemoaned the 'lamentable screeching of sylphs' at a Rajah's palace and 'the hideous yelping that represented a song' of South America. She was unruffled by the dangers of tiger hunting, warnings of strangulation by Thugs on the road to Bombay or false arrest by a Russian cossack. Yet she was also careful to report on the state of Bengali housekeeping and the fashions in a Pacha's harem.

A Lady's Voyage Round the World is the most delightfully well-rounded, exhilerating journey by a superbly adventurous traveller. In a gale off Cape Horn or at table with a sheik, one could wish for no more ideal companion.

Ida Pfeiffer (1792-1858) was born in Vienna and made two journeys around the world. She had saved for 20 years to enable her to undertake the first: 'In exactly the same manner as an artist feels an invincible desire to paint... so was I hurried away with an unconquerable wish to see the world'. In 1856 she went on an expedition to Madagascar, endured terrible hardships and came home to die.

Maria Aitken was born in Dublin. A graduate of Oxford University she was the first woman to be elected a member of the Oxford University Dramatic Society. She has played many leading roles for The Royal Shakespeare Company, the National Theatre and in the West End. She also directs in the theatre and produces television. She is the author of *A Girdle Round the Earth*, a biographical anthology of some women travellers of the last three hundred years. Her interest in women travellers prompted her to write and appear in a BBC drama documentary called *Lizzie*, based on the letters of Lizzie Hersel who travelled to the Amazon basin in 1896.

Recently published titles from Century Classics:

JERUSALEM by Colin Thubron
JOURNEY INTO THE MIND'S EYE by Lesley Blanch
A BACKWARD GLANCE by Edith Wharton
EVERY ROCK, EVERY HILL by Victoria Schofield
TOURING IN 1600 by E.S. Bates
UTTERMOST PART OF THE EARTH by Lucas Bridges
COUPS AND COCAINE by Anthony Daniels
LIFE IN MEXICO by Madame Calderon de la Barca
A SABINE JOURNEY by Anthony Rhodes
THE RIVERS AMAZON by Alex Shoumatoff
THE ISLAND by Anton Chekhov
THE WAITING LAND by Dervla Murphy
THREE ENGLISH WOMEN IN AMERICA by Una Pope-
    Hennessey
AT THE COURT OF KOREA by William Franklin Sands
PRINCESS by Vijayaraje Scindia with Manohar Malgonkar
TATIANA by Tatiana Metternich
A VANISHED ARCADIA by R.B. Cunninghame Graham
EXPLORATION FAWCETT by Col P.H. Fawcett
JOURNALS OF A LANDSCAPE PAINTER IN GREECE
    AND ALBANIA by Edward Lear
RAFFLES by Maurice Collis
WHEN THE RIVIERA WAS OURS by Patrick Howarth
THE INNOCENTS ABROAD BY Mark Twain
IONIA by Freya Stark
AROUND THE WORLD ON A BICYCLE by Thomas Stevens
INCIDENTS OF TRAVEL by John Lloyd Stephens
TALES OF TRAVEL by Marquess Curzon of Kedleston
MOGREB-EL-ACKSA by R.B. Cunninghame Graham

The cover painting shows *The Esplanade, Calcutta* by Thomas Prinsep (*by courtesy of Martyn Gregory*)

A

LADY'S VOYAGE

ROUND

THE WORLD:

A SELECTED TRANSLATION FROM THE GERMAN

OF

IDA PFEIFFER.

Introduction by Maria Aitken

CENTURY

LONDON MELBOURNE AUCKLAND JOHANNESBURG

First published by Longman, Brown, Green and Longmans 1851.
A selected translation from the German by Mrs Percy Sinnett.

This edition first published in 1988 by Century,
an imprint of Century Hutchinson Ltd,
Brookmount House, 62–65 Chandos Place, London WC2N 4NW

Century Hutchinson Australia Pty Ltd,
PO Box 496, 16–22 Church Street, Hawthorn, Melbourne,
Victoria 3122, Australia

Century Hutchinson Group New Zealand Limited,
PO Box 40–086, Glenfield, Auckland 10, New Zealand

Century Hutchinson South Africa (Pty) Ltd,
PO Box 337, Bergvlei, 2012 South Africa

British Library Cataloguing in Publication Data

Pfeiffer, Ida, *1797–1856*
   A lady's voyage round the world.
   1. Travel by single women – Stories,
   anecdotes
   I. Title
   910'.88042

   ISBN 0-7126-2427-9

Printed and bound in Great Britain by
Richard Clay (The Chaucer Press) Ltd, Bungay, Suffolk.

INTRODUCTION.

"ANOTHER journey,—and, moreover, into regions that everybody would rather shun than seek! This woman, it would seem, travels in order to attract attention! The first journey for a woman alone was tolerably venturesome, but it was possible that religious feeling might have something to do with it, and that will excuse much; but in the present instance, one can find no rational motive for such an undertaking."

Such, or, perhaps, still more severe, will be the judgments that will be passed upon me, and yet they do me great injustice. I am a harmless and well-meaning person enough, and certainly the last thought that would occur to me would be to do anything whatever with a view to attract attention. May I be permitted to say a few words concerning my character and circumstances, which may serve to remove whatever appearance there may be of eccentricity in my mode of action?

From my earliest childhood I had always the greatest longing to see the world. When I met a travelling carriage I used to stand still and gaze after it with tears in my eyes, envying the very postilions. till it vanished from my sight. As a girl of ten or twelve. I read with the greatest eagerness all the books of travels I could get hold of, and then I transferred my envy to the grand traveller who had gone round the world. The tears would come into my eyes when I climbed a mountain and saw others still piled up before me, and thought that I should never see what lay beyond. I afterwards, however, travelled a good deal with my parents, and subsequently with my husband, and did not reconcile myself to remaining at home, till my two boys required my attention and had to attend particular schools.

When their education was completed,—when I might, if I pleased, have spent the remainder of my days in quiet retirement, then my youthful dreams and visions rose again before my mind's eye. My imagination dwelt on distant lands and strange customs,— a new heaven and a new earth. I thought how blessed it would be to tread the soil hallowed for ever by the presence of the Saviour. I thought long; and at length formed my resolution. I had represented to myself first all the difficulties, obstacles, and dangers connected with the undertaking; and endeavoured to dismiss the idea from my mind, but in vain. I cared little for privation; my bodily frame was healthy and hardy; I had no fear of death; and as my birth-day dated from the last century, I could travel *alone.* With a joy amounting to rapture, I set out then on my journey to Palestine, and as I came home again in perfect safety, I trusted I had not acted presumptuously in following the impulse of my nature, and I determined to see a little more yet of the world.

These are Madame Pfeiffer's animated expressions in a preface to one of her works of travel. They are placed here by the translator as an introduction to the English public, and as giving a picture of her mental character, much in the way that a portrait is prefixed to a volume to give the reader some notion of the personal appearance of the author.

INTRODUCTION TO THIS EDITION

In her second book of travels, *A Journey to Iceland*, Ida Pfeiffer demurely excuses her 'love of adventure, which in the eyes of many does not accord with what is becoming in my sex'. But luckily for her readers, her whole life leading up to her first journey at the age of forty-five was a confusion of what was then considered appropriately feminine or masculine behaviour. Her upbringing might have been designed to provide the requisite intrepidity and the ox-like constitution demanded of the inquisitive nineteenth-century traveller.

She was born Ida Reyer in Vienna in 1797, the only girl in a family of six boys. She dressed as a boy and described herself as 'not shy, but wild as a boy and more forward than my elder brothers'. Her father was a wealthy merchant, but insisted on a spartan régime for his children. They ate a rigidly parsimonious diet and were only allowed to gaze on the rich delicacies consumed by the adults at the same table; even their reasonable requests were refused in order to accustom them to disappointment, and their father's word was law on all subjects. Ida seems to have flourished under this treatment; even her father's teasing that he would send her to military school only encouraged a pleasing vision of herself as officer material. Running free with her brothers, it never occurred to her that her horizons could narrow: 'From my earliest childhood I had an intense longing to go forth into the wide world... Tears often rose to my eyes if, after climbing a hill, I found others towering up beyond my reach, and I could not see what lay concealed behind them'.

But all the moral and physical certainties of her early life were overturned by the death of her father when she was thirteen. Her mother put an abrupt end to the boyish freedoms of the past and petticoats were instituted. Ida's diary ruefully records, 'how awkward and clumsy I must have looked in my long skirts, jumping and racing about and behaving generally like a wild restless boy!'

In the biographical memoir which was compiled from Pfeiffer's own notes, and which precedes her final book, she confers the anonymity of the initial 'T —' on the sympathetic tutor who 'changed me from a wild hoydenish creature into a modest girl'. Under his tutelage she channelled her exuberance into a passion for travel books, but not without pangs that she herself would never have the opportunity to be an explorer. 'I could not but repine at the happiness of every great navigator or discoverer who could explore the yet unrevealed secrets of the natural world.'

Perhaps predictably, Ida and her tutor fell in love. Their mutual admission of their feelings was accelerated by a proposal of marriage from a wealthy Greek when she was seventeen. The match was much favoured by Ida's mother. A tremendous battle of wills ensued, with Ida forced to renounce T —, but redoubtably refusing to marry the Greek. Three years later, Ida saw T — by chance in the street and was so overwhelmed by her emotions that she became desperately ill. Although her daughter nearly died of nervous prostration, Madam Reyer remained inflexibly opposed to the tutor. After Ida recovered, there were many other suitors, but she resolutely turned them all down. However, life at home was punctuated by so many terrible conflicts with her mother that eventually Ida began to see marriage as a preferable alternative. But so as not to betray the spirit of her commitment to T —, she declared she would only accept a much older man.

Dr Pfeiffer was the first suitable candidate. He was a distinguished lawyer twenty-four years her senior, and best of all, he lived at Lemberg, a hundred miles from Vienna and her mother. He was not a bad choice. He turned out to be tolerant and wise and a man of high principle. Sadly, it was his principles that ruined the Pfeiffer family financially. By exposing the corruption of some Lemberg bureaucrats, he earned the wrath of officialdom and was compelled to resign as a local councillor. His practice declined, so he moved to Vienna, but his reputation as an anti-establishment lawyer had preceded him there. The Pfeiffers moved back and forth within Austria and even to Switzerland, but his career never recovered. For eighteen years of her married life, Ida had a constant struggle against poverty. There were two sons to support and as her husband's spirit became progressively more crushed by events, it was Ida who, for the second time in her life, took on the dominant role. 'I performed household drudgery and endured cold and hunger; I worked secretly for money and gave lessons in drawing and music; and yet, in spite of all my exertions, there were many days when I could hardly put anything but dry bread before my children for their dinner... I might certainly have applied to my mother or my brothers for relief, but my pride revolted against such a course.'

With the death of her mother, after a long illness during which Ida nursed her selflessly, the Pfeiffers inherited enough to make ends meet. Ida and the boys settled in Vienna for the rest of their education, and Dr Pfeiffer remained in Lemberg. Once the boys' schooling was over, there was no longer any impediment to Ida's early dreams of travel. What is more, despite the restrictive views of her period, she could respectably travel alone. Her husband was too old to accompany her, her sons were starting work, and as she herself pointed out, she was no longer likely to suffer unwanted attentions; '... born in the last century, I need not fear to travel alone'. Schooled in self-reliance, as tough as old boots and used to practising a steely economy, she had undergone a perfect training for the rigours of travel.

Her first journey, to the Holy Land, Egypt and Italy in 1842, was not undertaken with a book in mind. She kept a diary to entertain her relatives, and every evening, whatever the exigencies of the day, she made notes in pencil, sometimes using a sand mound or the back of a camel as a table, while the rest of the caravan lay in exhausted torpor. Her publisher had to exert considerable pressure first to read and subsequently to print this record. 'My request to read our Authoress's journal was granted with some timidity... After much trouble, I succeeded in persuading the Authoress to allow her journal to appear in print.'

Then there was no stopping her. Inspired by the success of the book, which went into four editions, she prepared a journey to Iceland. With typical thoroughness, she studied English and Danish, researched and learned to take 'Daguerre-otypes' before setting off for Iceland and Scandinavia in 1845. The preface to the resulting book gave a clue to her further ambitions: 'Should death surprise me in any of my wanderings, I shall meet it with calmness, thanking God from my inmost heart for the blessed happy hours I have spent in admiring the wonders of his creation'. But she concealed the dangerous extent of her plans from her sons when she set off again in 1846, naming only Brazil as her destination. Two and a half years later, having travelled 2,800 miles by land and 35,000 by sea, she returned to write *A Lady's Voyage Round the World.*

The anonymous author of the short biographical memoir of Ida Pfeiffer makes it clear that her outward manner and appearance were very misleading. She seemed a staid, reserved creature of no obvious personality or attraction. But like many other women travellers of this period, it was when freed from the constraints of home and the expectations of society that she became most truly herself. So the biographer's conclusion that she 'may, indeed justly be classed among those women who richly compensate for the absence of outward charms by their remarkable energy and the rare quality of their minds' needs no stating to those who encounter her in *A Lady's Voyage Round the World.* She is a curious and highly beguiling combination of propriety and swashbuckle. Her independence is irresistible—'If I had attended to every advice, I should not have seen much'—and her resourcefulness is enviable. On an overcrowded ship from Bombay, she annexed a small space under the captain's table as her territory: 'I took possession of this place and threw my mantle around me so that I had a pretty secure position and no cause to fear that I should have my hands, feet or indeed my head trodden upon'. At mealtimes she had to creep away from her asylum to make way for people's feet. Five days of fever meant this was a painful imposition, but she does not complain and is typically courageous about the lack of any medicine. 'I trusted to Providence and my good constitution.'

But her courage is not born of insensitivity. A chilling description of a ride along the edge of a Turkish abyss culminates in a gory scene which continued to haunt her imagination: bloodsplattered rocks with two dead bodies lying far below. 'It was several days before I could free myself from the recollection of it.' Yet she resists hyperbole even in her detailed description of this macabre event. Her eye for detail is strictly truthful, whether it be for death in a Turkish crevasse, insurrection on a tea-plantation in Canton or hypocrisy at a Chinese funeral in Singapore.

She was free of most of the orthodox prejudices of the period and aired her dislike of them. Her indignation hums across the intervening years when a Memsahib aboard a ship from Madras to Calcutta orders a native mother holding a child with a bad cough to sleep on deck, in case her own child should catch the infection. 'Would that this rich English lady's child had only been ill and exposed with her to the foggy night air that she might herself have experienced what it is to be thus harshly treated!... No savages would have thus thrust forth a poor woman with a sick child, but would on the contrary have taken care of both. It is only Europeans, who have been brought up with Christian principles, who assume the right of treating coloured people as their whim or fancy may dictate.'

The shrinking violet of Vienna evoked by her biographer is nowhere evident. Instead we have the gallant tomboy of her youth merged with a formidable middle-aged woman. She is at her most vivid when she is at her most opinionated. Tahitian dancing evoked her violent disapproval — 'the more unbecoming bold and indecent their gestures, the greater the applause'—and the Russians released a torrent of spleen: 'The Russians and the Cossacks have stupid coarse features, and their behaviour corresponds completely to what their appearance indicates; I never met with a people so covetous, coarse and slavish as they are. When I asked about anything they either gave me a surly answer, or none at all, or else laughed in my face.'

Neither do the Europeans escape a lambasting, for she continues: 'This rudeness would not, perhaps have appeared so remarkable if I had come from Europe'.

Still strong and healthy after such a colossal journey, there seemed no reason for this indomitable woman ever to settle down, except lack of travelling funds. But articles were written on her behalf, such as this appeal by Mr A. Petermann which appeared in the *Athenaeum* of 6 December 1851: 'the resolute lady has at her command but very slender means for the performance of her journeys... Private resources has she none. It is to be regretted that the want of a little pecuinary assistance should deter the enterprising lady from carrying out her projected journey.'

Ida herself had never been slow to add footnotes to her work complaining of high costs, and now for the first time she received a small grant of 1500 florins (about £100) from the Austrian government. It was hardly generous, but enough to enable her to set off once more in 1852, and subsequently to produce *A Lady's Second Journey Round the World*, published in 1855. In a dizzying progress, she is the guest of the White Rajah of Sarawak; the first European among the cannibal Battas in Sumatra; thwarted by revolution in Lima; witness of a rare eruption of the volcano Cotopaxi in Ecuador. Finally, she falls into the alligator-infested

River Guaya, and when nobody comes to her assistance, she loses patience with South America and heads for home.

On her return to Vienna her worth was recognized for the first time. She had been neglected because she was not a scientist, but her observations were meticulous, she kept scrupulous meteorological records and had collected specimens establishing new *genera* for the British Museum and the Imperial Cabinets in Vienna. Now, at last, she was publicly admired by Alexander von Humboldt, elected an honorary member of the Royal Geographical Society in Berlin and given a gold medal for arts and sciences by the King of Prussia. Her efforts were acheived entirely by her own vision and energy: this was belated enthusiasm by the establishment.

Her next journey was to be her last. On a trip to Madagascar, aged fifty-nine, she contracted fever. Among its symptoms were long periods of lassitude. In her diary almost the last words she wrote were a characteristically indignant defence of her powers of resistance. 'This apathy ... is not peculiar to the persons of my age when attacked by this illness, but is felt by the strongest men in the prime of life.' But her health never recovered and she returned to Vienna to die in 1858 of cancer of the liver, a probable consequence of Madagascan fever. Her son, Oscar Pfeiffer, was too grief-stricken to prepare her papers for publication until 1861, when they appeared as *The Last Travels of Ida Pfeiffer*.

As strange as the neglect of her by contemporaries is the neglect, until now, of her books. While many lesser travel writers have had a renaissance, Ida Pfeiffer—for all her courage and her individual voice—has not, and one hopes that all her books will soon be back in print. Something of her freshness of eye brushes off on those of us who travel in her wake. By comparing her experience with ours we can momentarily push back the frontiers of tourism to become travellers again.

Maria Aitken
May 1988

CONTENTS

Introduction　　-　-　-　-　-　-　-　-　v

Introduction to this Edition　　　-　-　-　-　-　vii

At Sea off Rio de Janeiro.—Landing.—Description of the City.—The Blacks and their relation to the Whites.—Arts and Sciences in Rio de Janeiro.—Public Festivals.—Christening of the Princess.—Fête in the Barracks.—Climate and Vegetation.—Manners and Customs.—Emigrants.　　-　-　-　-　-　-　-　-　3

EXCURSIONS INTO THE INTERIOR.

The New German Colony of Petropolis.—Murderous Attack by a Maroon Negro.—Morroqueimado and Aldea do Pedro, Plantations of the Europeans.—Forest Conflagrations.—Primeval Forests.—Last Settlement of the Whites.—Visit to the Puri Indians.　　-　13

CAPE HORN.—ARRIVAL AT VALPARAISO.

Description of the Town.—Manners of the People.—The Restaurant o Polonku.—Little Angels.　　-　-　-　-　-　28

VOYAGE BY TAHITI TO CANTON.

Furnished Lodgings in Papeiti.—A Court Ball.—An Excursion.—Lake Vaihiria.—The Mountain Pass of Fantaua.—The Diadem.—Voyage across the Pacific.—Arrival in China.　　-　-　-　32

CHINA.

Macao.—Hong Kong.—Victoria.—Voyage in a Chinese Junk.—The Tsi-Kiang.—Whampoa.—Canton.—Mode of Life of Europeans.—The Chinese Manners and Customs.—Criminals and Pirates.—Murder of M. Vauchée.—Walks and Excursions.　　-　40

SINGAPORE.

The English Steamer from Hong Kong.—Singapore Plantations.—A Hunting Party in the Jungles.—A Chinese Funeral.—The Feast of Lanterns.—Climate and Temperature.　　-　-　-　67

CEYLON.

Departure from Singapore.—The Island of Pinang.—Ceylon.—Pointe de Galle.—Excursion to the Interior.—Colombo.—Kandy.—The Temple Dagoha.—Capture of Elephants.—Return to Colombo and Pointe de Galle.—Departure.　　-　-　-　-　-　80

BENGAL.

Calcutta.—Mode of Life of Europeans.—The Hindoos.—Things to be seen in the Town.—Visit to a Baboo.—Religious Festival.—Dying Houses, and Places for Burning the Dead.—Mahomedan and European Weddings. - - - - - - 92

BENARES.

Departure from Calcutta.—The Ganges.—Rajmahal.—Monghyr.—Patna.—Benares.—Description of the City.—Palaces and Temples.—The Sacred Apes.—The Ruins of Sarnath.—An Indigo Plantation.—Visit to the Rajah of Benares.—Martyrs and Faquirs.—Indian Peasants.—The Missionary Establishment. - - 102

ALLAHABAD, AGRA, AND DELHI.

Allahabad.—Cannipoor.—Agra.—The Mausoleum of Sultan Akbar, Taj-Mahal.—The Ruined Town of Fatipoor Sikri.—Delhi.—The Main Street.—Public Processions.—The Emperor's Palace.—Palaces and Mosques.—Old Delhi.—Remarkable Ruins.—The English Military Station. - - - - - - - - 118

JOURNEY FROM DELHI TO BOMBAY.

Thugs.—Departure.—The Cattle Market.—Kind Disposition of the Indians.—Kottah.—Description of the Town.—The Royal Castle.—Entertainments and Dances.—The Holy Town of Kesho Rae.—Patun. - - - - - - - - - - 137

CONTINUATION OF THE JOURNEY.

Meeting with the Burdon Family.—Women of the Lower Class in India.—Captain Hamilton.—Indor.—Presentation at Court.—Manufacture of Ice.—Industry of Women and Children.—The Rocky Temple at Adjunta.—A Tiger Hunt.—The Rock Temple of Elora.—The Fortress of Dowlutabad. - - - - - - - 148

BOMBAY.

161

FROM BOMBAY TO BAGDAD.

Departure from Bombay.—Smallpox on board.—Muscat.—Bandr-Abas.—The Persians.—The Straits of Kishma.—Buschir.—Entrance into the Shat al Arab.—Bassora.—Entrance into the Tigris.—Bedouins.—Ctesiphon and Seleucia.—Arrival in Bagdad. - 168

MESOPOTAMIA.—BAGDAD AND BABYLON.

Bagdad.—Climate, &c.—Festival at the English Resident's.—The Harem of the Pacha of Bagdad.—Excursion to the Ruins of Ctesiphon.—The Persian Prince Il-Hany-Ala-Euly-Mirza.—Excursion to the Ruins of Babylon. - - - - - - 178

MOSSUL AND NINEVEH.

Caravan Journey through the Desert.—Arrival at Mossul.—Things to be seen.—Excursion to the Ruins of Nineveh and the Village of Nebryanis.—Second Excursion to Nineveh.—Tel-Nimrod.—Arabian Horses.—Departure from Mossul.   -   -   -   -   191

PERSIA.

Caravan Journey to Ravandus.—A Kurd Family.—Continuation of the Journey.—Sauh-Bulok.—A Happy Family.—Oromia.—The American Missionaries.—Kutschié.—Three chivalrous Robbers.—The Persian Chan and the English Bongolo.—Arrival at Tabreez.   -   203

TABREEZ.

Description of the Town.—The Bazaar.—Behmen Mirza.—Anecdotes of the Persian Government.—Presentation to the Viceroy and his Wife.—Behmen Mirza's Women.—Visit to a Persian Lady.—The People.—Persecution of Jews and Christians.—The Departure.   -   228

ASIATIC RUSSIA.—ARMENIA, GEORGIA, AND MINGRELIA.

Sophia Marand.—The Russian Frontier.—Natchivan.—Caravan Journey.—A Night in Prison.—Continuation of the Journey.—Erivan.—The Russian Post.—The Tartars.—Arrival in Tiflis.—Residence there.—Kutais Marand.—Voyage on the Rione.—Redout-Kale.   -   -   -   -   -   -   -   -   236

EUROPEAN RUSSIA.

A Voyage on the Black Sea.—A Case of Cholera.—The suspected Vessel.—Kertsch.—The Museum.—Tumuli.—Continuation of the Journey.—The Castle of Prince Woronzow.—The Fortress of Sebastopol.—Odessa.   -   -   -   -   -   -   -   254

CONSTANTINOPLE AND ATHENS.

Constantinope.—Changes.—Conflagrations.—Journey to Greece.—The Quarantine in Egina.—A Day at Athens.—Callimachi.—The Isthmus.—Patras.—Corfu.   -   -   -   -   263

Bibliography   -   -   -   -   -   -   -   273

Bibliography of Introduction

Pfeiffer, Ida. *A Visit to the Holy Land, Egypt and Italy.* Trans. H.W. Dulken (Ingram, Cooke & Co, 1852)

Pfeiffer, Ida. *Journey to Iceland and Travels in Sweden and Norway.* Trans. Charlotte Fenimore Cooper (Richard Bentley, 1852)

Pfeiffer, Ida. *A Woman's Journey Round the World from Vienna to Brazil, Chili, Tahiti, China, Hindostan, Persia and Asia Minor.* Unabridged translation (Office of the National Illustrated Library, 1852)

Pfeiffer, Ida. *A Lady's Second Journey Round the World.* Trans. J. Sinnett (H. Bohn, 1855)

Pfeiffer, Ida. *The Last Travels of Ida Pfeiffer: inclusive of a visit to Madagascar.* Trans. H.W. Dulken (Routledge, Warne and Routledge, 1861)

A LADY'S VOYAGE ROUND THE WORLD.

At Sea off Rio de Janeiro.—Landing.—Description of the City.—The Blacks and their relation to the Whites.—Arts and Sciences in Rio de Ja- neiro.—Public Festivals.—Christening of the Princess.—Fête in the Barracks.—Climate and Vegetation.—Manners and Customs.—Emi- grants.

On the morning of the 13th of September 1846 I found myself on board a Danish brig, nearing the land of South America. I had been more than two months at sea, having left Hamburg on the 29th of June, and it was, therefore, with much satisfaction that, following the advice of the helmsman when I crept up on deck about daybreak, I stretched my head over the bulwark and drew in deep draughts of a sweet balmy land breeze. The land, however, to my surprise, was not yet in sight, though the sea was covered with the bodies of butterflies driven out by a gale that we had had for two days before, and which had cost us two sails. The sea had been so high, too, that we had had the greatest difficulty in getting our meals, as we had to hold our plates and the table with one hand, while with the other we made repeated efforts, some- times successful, to carry the food to our mouths. At night I had to pack myself tight in my berth with cloaks and clothes, to pre- vent my being beaten black and blue with the rolling of the vessel.

Longingly did our eyes now search the horizon for Cape Frio, which we were told was not far off. No Cape Frio, however, was to be seen, and the distance was covered with mists and clouds which the sun seemed to have no power to pierce. We hoped for what the next morning might bring us; but in the night came another gale, we had to go out to sea again, and were glad the next evening to be able to get back again to the same spot. We did really now catch a glimpse of the outlines of Cape Frio, but only for a short time, for the gale sprung up again, and again we lost sight of the wished-for land. On the 15th nothing was to be seen but sky and water except some sea-mews, which served to keep up our hopes by showing that it could not be far off, and affording us at the same time some amusement. They kept close to the ship, and swallowed eagerly every piece of meat or bread thrown to them. The sailors caught some and placed them on the deck, and they seemed hardly able to move a few yards, although they could rise quickly enough from the watery surface and fly very high. One of the passengers wanted to kill one for the sake of stuffing it, but the sailors protested, declaring we should have a calm directly if he did. They would often during a calm throw overboard empty casks or pieces of wood, probably, it seemed to me, as sacrifices to the gods of the winds.

In the morning we were really so fortunate as to be in sight of Rio de Janeiro, and by two o'clock we had entered the bay. Immediately at its entrance lie several mountains, some of which rise singly out of the water, and others are connected at the base. These sea-mountains, as one might call them, form by their combinations the most exquisite prospects, sometimes opening so as to show a singular ravine, sometimes a beautifully situated quarter of the town, and sometimes the open sea or a magnificent harbour. At that part where the city lies there are masses of rock which have served as foundations for the fortifications. On various conspicuous points are seen churches and convents—the public walk, with its two elegant pavilions, close to the sea—and the extensive villages, Praya Flamingo and Botafogo, with their beautiful villas and gardens,—these, with the many ships in the harbour, and the luxuriant vegetation,—all together formed a picture which my pen, at least, cannot describe.

We all went to bed that night rejoicing at the safe termination of our long voyage. There was one poor woman on board who had followed her husband, an artisan, all the way from Germany, and had spent all her little savings to do so. She rejoiced too, and the captain did not tell her till the following morning the news he had for her, namely, that her husband had quitted the place in company with a negress, and had left behind him nothing but debts.

On the morning of the 17th the captain accompanied us passengers ashore, warning us especially to make no attempt at smuggling, and to carry with us no sealed letters, for in no other place were the custom-house officers so rigid, or the punishment so severe. We felt, therefore, rather anxious when we saw the guard ship, and expected to be searched from head to foot, but instead of that, the captain simply requested permission to go ashore; it was immediately granted, and there was an end of the whole affair. As long as we continued to live in the ship, we went backwards and forwards as often as we liked, and were never subjected to any inquiry; only when we took chests and boxes with us we had to row to the custom-house, and there the examination was made pretty strictly, and the duty on books and other things was certainly very high.

We landed at *Praya dos Mineiros,* a dirty, disgusting looking square, with a no less dirty and disgusting population of negroes, who were crouching on the ground and offering for sale fruits and various dainties, the praises of which they were screaming in all possible discordant tones. Through this place we passed into the main street, the only beauty of which is its breadth. It contains several public buildings: the Exchange, the Post Office, &c., but all so insignificant looking, that you would not notice them at all but for the people standing before them. At the end of the street is the Imperial Palace, like a large private house, and without any pretensions to architectural beauty. It is adorned with a fountain of very dirty water, round which many poor free negroes take their repose for the night, and in the morning perform their ablutions very composedly in the presence of the public. One part of the space before the Palace is enclosed with a wall, and serves as a market for fish, fruit, and vegetables.

Of the remaining streets, the most interesting are the Rua Misericorda and Ouvidor; the latter has the largest and richest shops, but the best are not to be compared with those of a European city. I did not find much to admire in any, with the exception of the artificial flower shops, where was a splendid assortment of flowers made of birds' feathers, fish scales, and beetles' wings. From the Largo do Rocio, omnibuses run in all directions; here stand the government offices, and it also enjoys the distinction of being the very dirtiest square in the whole city. The first time I visited it there were dead dogs and cats lying about; and another time the carcase of a mule in a state of putrefaction. There is a fountain in it, but I do not know that that contributes much to its beauty, for since fresh water is somewhat scarce in Rio de Janeiro, the noble guild of washerwomen have established their head quarters in this square, which offers, at the same time, the advantage of a drying ground. Here, therefore, they wash and wring out and

dry, and carry on all their operations ; not to mention such a voci-
ferous exercise of tongues as made me glad to make my escape.

The houses are built much in the European style, but small and
mean, with only one or at the utmost two stories, and without the
terraces and verandahs found in other hot countries. Some tasteless little balconies hang against the wall, and the windows are
closed with clumsy wooden shutters which exclude every ray of
sunshine. You sit indeed, almost in darkness, but the Brazilian
ladies do not mind that, as they never have anything to do.

But if the streets of the city are little attractive, the people you
meet in them are still less so. Scarcely any one is to be seen but
negroes and negresses, mostly half naked, or clad in miserable rags,
or, what is almost as bad, in the worn-out European clothing of
their masters ; and the unpleasantness of their appearance is
greatly heightened by the numerous infirmities—elephantiasis
especially—to which they are subject. Even the dogs and cats,
which run about the streets in great numbers, are infected with
the general ugliness, as well as with diseases which manifest themselves in frequent sores.

I should like to bring to this city some of the travellers who
are frightened at the streets of Constantinople, and who expatiate
on the manner in which the impression made by the aspect of that
city from without, is destroyed by a sight of the interior. It is true
that the streets of Constantinople are narrow and dirty, the houses
are often small, the dogs unpleasant,—but every here and there
you come upon some magnificent memorial of former days, some
stately palace or wonderful mosque, and you may continue your
ramble into vast cemeteries and dreary cypress woods. Every now
and then you step aside before a pasha or high priest moving
onward in state, surrounded by a glittering throng of attendants,
or a Turk in his noble costume, or a Turkish woman with her
dark eyes flashing through her veil. You see Persians with their
high caps, the noble features of the Arab, dervises with their
conical head gear and flowing petticoats, and from time to time
heavy gilt and painted carriages, drawn by richly caparisoned oxen.

All these things make one some amends for what is ugly. But
in Rio de Janeiro there is nothing to offer compensation for the
disagreeable and repulsive sights that meet your eyes at every turn.
It was not till I had been several weeks in the city, that I could
find among the young negresses some pleasing figures, and among
the dark tinted Brazilian and Portuguese dames some handsome

expressive faces. On the male sex the gift of beauty seems to have been bestowed very sparingly indeed.

The animation of the streets I found by no means so great as I had often heard represented, certainly nothing to compare with that of Naples or Messina. The greatest noise is made by the negroes carrying burdens, and especially those who carry the bags of coffee on board the ships, singing at the same time a mono-tonous tune that helps them to keep time in their steps. All the heavy and dirty work of Brazil is of course performed by blacks, but many of them learn mechanical trades; and I have seen in the shops, black hands engaged in the preparation of fine gold and silver work, and delicate embroidery; but notwithstanding the many proofs they are constantly giving of skill and intelligence, there are among what we must call the educated classes here numbers who maintain that a negro is only a link between the races of man and monkey. The negroes are, I grant, far enough from the intellectual level of the whites, but I find the cause not in their want of capacity, but in their total want of education. There are in Brazil no schools for negroes, nor is the smallest attempt made to cultivate their intellectual faculties. Their lot otherwise is not so hard as many Europeans believe,—certainly not so hard as that of the Russian, Polish, or Egyptian peasants who are not called slaves. They are not overburdened with work, they have good nourishing food, and their punishments, except for running away, are not severe. One which I noticed was that of wearing a tin mask fastened behind with a lock, which is applied, among other offences, for that of drunkenness. The city of Rio de Janeiro is tolerably well lit, and even the environs to some distance, a measure which is to be ascribed to the fear entertained of the black population, which is four-fold that of the white. No slave is allowed to be seen in the streets after nine at night without a pass from his master. Should one be caught without this protec-tion, he is sent to prison, his head shaved, and he is kept till his master has ransomed him with a fine of four or five milreis; (a milreis is about 2s. 4d.)

One of the disagreeable characteristics of Rio de Janeiro is the entire want of drains. After a few heavy showers of rain every street is turned into a regular river, which one cannot cross on foot, but must be carried over by negroes. Almost all traffic is stopped; no invitation is accepted; nay, even bills of exchange are in such

cases not taken up.   One is not easily induced to make use of a
hired carriage, since the foolish custom prevails of charging as much
for the shortest drive as for the use [of a carriage for a whole day.
When you get them they are only half covered, and have seats for
but two persons, though a drive costs six milreis (14s. English).

For what concerns the state of the arts and sciences in this city,
they may be dismissed in very few words. The Academy presents
a few busts and figures, mostly in plaster, a few architectural plans
and drawings, and some old oil pictures ; the whole looking like the
refuse of some private gallery that had been cleared out. The pictures are so much injured that it is sometimes scarcely possible to make
out what they are meant to represent; but this is perhaps no great
matter, for their only claim to veneration is their age. A very
striking contrast to their faded dinginess is presented in some copies
made of them by the students, which are staring in all the fierce
intensity of red, yellow, and green, &c., with scarcely an attempt at
softening or harmonizing any tint. I had some doubts whether the
artists in question meant to found a new school of colouring, or
whether they intended to make the beholder amends for the dis-
colouration of the originals by the glaring brightness of their copies.
There were as many blacks and mulattoes among the students as
whites, but the number of the whole was very small. With music
the case is little if at all better than with painting. It is true that
in almost every family you enter the daughters both sing and play
the piano, but the style of their performance makes it difficult to
recognise any piece, even of the simplest and easiest character.
The church music is something better, though by no means what
could be wished; but the best certainly is the military band.

Considering, however, the generally feeble and languishing state
of art, one is rather surprised at the colossal proportions of the
Opera House, which has four tiers of spacious boxes, and is calculated to accommodate 2,000 people. I saw "Lucrezia Borgia" performed very tolerably by an Italian company, and the costume and
decorations were not amiss. But if this establishment on the whole
somewhat exceeded my expectations, I experienced the contrary on
visiting the Museum. In a country so richly endowed by nature,
I expected to find it large and well filled ; but though there were
many large rooms, I found them all but empty. The only department in any tolerable state of completeness was the collection of birds;
that of minerals is extremely defective, and that of the quadrupeds

and insects very poor. What most attracted my attention were the heads of four savages—two of the Malay race, and two New Zealanders, completely covered with the handsomest tattooing, and as fresh as if they had departed this life but yesterday.

Among other sights of Rio de Janeiro, I witnessed three public festivals, of which the best was the christening of the Imperial Princess. All the morning, carriages had been driving up to the Palace, with splendidly dressed ladies and gentlemen, and towards four in the afternoon the procession began to move. First came the band of court musicians, in crimson velvet, with three heralds in the old Spanish costume of black velvet and caps with waving plumes. They were followed by judges and official persons, chamberlains, courtiers, senators, deputies, generals, and clergy, and lastly came the tutor of the little princess, bearing her imperial highness on a cushion of white velvet, trimmed with broad gold lace, followed by the Emperor and the nurse, surrounded by the most distinguished cavaliers and court ladies. The Empress and her ladies, meanwhile, had reached the church by a private passage. She presented the most striking contrast to her husband, being little and sickly, while he, though not yet quite twenty-one, is six feet high, and very corpulent.

The moment of the baptism was announced by the firing of guns and the letting off of rockets and other fireworks; and when it was over the church was opened to the public. I went in with the rest of the curious crowd, and was really surprised at the magnificence and taste that appeared in the decorations. Costly silks and velvets, with gold fringes, clothed the walls; rich carpets covered the floor; on a table in the middle of the nave was set out the superb gold and silver plate belonging to the church; and amongst the massive vessels of the most elaborate workmanship stood splendid cut glass vases filled with flowers, and golden candelebras glittered with innumerable lights. In a little side chapel stood the cradle of the little princess, covered with white satin and gold lace and fringe. In the evening the public buildings were illuminated. But the most peculiar part of the entertainment consisted in a species of ballet, got up at the various barracks in honour of the occasion, in which all the parts, including those of the ladies, were performed by soldiers. The best of these was in the Rua Barbone, where, in a spacious courtyard, an elegant semicircular gallery was erected, in the centre of which was a small temple, with the busts of the imperial pair. The gallery was for the ladies, who appeared in full dress, and were received at the entrance by the officers. In front of the gallery was a stage, on each side of which were rows of benches for the less distinguished part of the feminine audience, and beyond these benches stood the men. The soldiers appeared in various costumes, as Scots, Poles, Spaniards, &c.; but what I most admired was the extreme propriety and decorum which the manly young ladies observed in all their evolutions.

Few armies are more splendidly equipped than that of Brazil. Every common man is fine enough for a lieutenant at least, but there is a total inattention to size and colour in their arrangement. You will see a black beside a white, and a boy of fourteen marching as the comrade of a robust man of full age, which makes the effect of the whole very odd and irregular. The army, I was told, is re-cruited by pressing, and the time of service is from four to six years.

I had heard and read much in Europe of the magnificence and luxuriance of nature in Brazil, of the constantly bright sunny sky, and the charms of perpetual spring; and it is true that vegeta-tion is here richer than in, perhaps, any country in the world, and that every one who wishes to see the operation of the forces of nature in their utmost activity should come to Brazil; but he must by no means expect to find every thing beautiful, or suppose that there will be nothing to weaken the charm of the first impres-sion. You may rejoice, perhaps, at first at the never-changing verdure, and the unfading splendour of summer; but with time this will lose its charm. You will be glad of a little winter, and find the revival of nature,—the re-animation of the plants after their apparent death,—the return of the fragrant breath of spring,—all the more welcome for having been deprived of them for a time. The climate and the atmosphere I found extremely oppressive and disagreeable; the heat, although at that season scarcely exceeding 24° (Reaumur) in the shade, very exhausting. In the hot months, that is, from the end of December till May, the heat in the shade often rose to 30°, and in the sun to 40°. But in Egypt I have borne a much higher temperature far more easily, possibly because there the air is very dry, whilst here it is extremely damp. Mists and clouds are in the order of the day, and highlands and moun-tains are often enveloped in impenetrable darkness, and the whole atmosphere impregnated with moist vapours.

The most agreeable season is the winter, when the temperature does not fall below 14°, and the air is dry and clear. This is the time usually employed for travelling. I really, however, do not understand what travellers mean by talking of the bright cloudless sky of Brazil.

Another enjoyment of temperate climates, that of the fine evenings, is lost here. The sun in the middle of the summer sets at three quarters past six; twenty or thirty minutes after it is quite dark, and with darkness everyone hastens home, since darkness and damp come together. Another annoyance is, of course, in the insects—mosquitoes, ants, and sand fleas, &c. Many a night have I passed in sleepless torment from their bites and stings. The ants especially often appear in innumerable swarms, and pass over everything that comes in their way.

At the country seat of a M. Geiger (the secretary to the Austrian consulate), who had been kind enough to invite me there for the recovery of my health, a swarm of this kind passed through the house, and it was really interesting to observe what a regular line they formed, and how impossible it was to turn them out of the direction they had chosen. Madame Geiger told me that she had once been awakened in the night by a terrible itching in her skin, and immediately springing from her bed, she perceived that a swarm of ants was passing across her bedstead. There is no help for it, and one has nothing to do but to wait quietly the end of the procession, which lasts from four to six hours. Still worse, perhaps, are the sand fleas, which fix themselves in the flesh, mostly in the toes under the nails, where they lay their eggs. Altogether Brazil, though for a traveller one of the most interesting countries in the world, is one of the last I should recommend for a permanent residence.

Of the state of morals in Brazil, the short duration of my stay there, not much over two months, gives me, perhaps, little right to speak. It appeared to me that the love of money, generally so striking a characteristic of the Americanised European, is very prominent here, and is much promoted by some peculiar customs. It is, for instance, usual for a husband not to make his wife any allowance in money, but to give her, for her own use, one or several male or female slaves, of whom she may dispose at her pleasure. She generally has them taught cooking, sewing, embroidery, and so forth, or various mechanical trades, and then lets them out by the day, week, or month to those who have no slaves of their own, or she allows them to do washing, or needlework, or make pastry at home and then go out to sell it. The profit accruing therefrom is of course her own, and is mostly spent in dress and amusement. Among tradespeople, the wife expects to receive payment for helping her husband in his business. The very defective state of morals in some other points is probably in some measure to be attributed to the children being left so much to the care of the negroes. Negresses are their nurses and their constant attendants; young negroes frequently attend the girls to school; and the dissolute manners prevalent among these people can hardly be otherwise than injurious to the young people with whom they are thus associated. Another cause I cannot but think is the want of religion, for though there are prayers, processions, and ceremonies in abundance, real religion seems to be entirely wanting. Considering these circumstances, the great demoralization, and the absence of religion, it is not surprising that murders are very common for revenge, as well as for robbery. Where the murderer is not inclined to execute the deed himself, he has it done by a slave, or for a trifle can hire some one to do it. Its discovery need give him little uneasiness if he is rich, for there are many ways of getting over such things with the help of money. I saw in Rio de Janeiro some men who I was assured had committed not one, but several murders, either by their own hand or otherwise, yet they not only went about freely, but were received constantly in society.

Before leaving this subject, let me entreat my own countrypeople to pause before they come to seek their fortune on the distant coast of Brazil. During my stay here several ships arrived with poor emigrants; the government, as it had not sent for them, gave them no support; money they had not, and could therefore buy no land; no planter would hire them as labourers, for they could not support the climate, and they had to go about the town begging, or put up with any kind of work and the worst conditions. When they have been sent for by the Brazilian government, for purposes of colonization, their case has, of course, been somewhat better; but even then, if they brought no money with them, they have been very miserable; and though skilled artisans get ready employment and good wages, the demand for them is every day becoming less, as the negroes are now continually brought up to trades.

Let none who leave their country delude themselves with false hopes, for terrible is the process of being undeceivèd, when they are here alone and in poverty.

EXCURSIONS INTO THE INTERIOR.

The New German Colony of Petropolis.—Murderous Attack by a Maroon Negro.—Morroqueimado and Aldea do Pedro, Plantations of the Europeans.—Forest Conflagrations. — Primeval Forests. — Last Settlement of the Whites.—Visit to the Puri Indians.

I HAD heard in Rio de Janeiro so much of the rapid growth and prosperity of a colony lately founded by Germans in the neighbourhood,—of the magnificent region in which it lies,—of the primeval forests through which a part of the road to it leads, that I could not resist the wish to make an excursion thither. Count Berchtold, who had been my travelling companion from Hamburg, was to accompany me, and we accordingly engaged two places in a vessel going to Porto d'Estrella, whence the journey must be continued on foot. The bay through which we passed was most picturesque, surrounded by beautiful hills and sprinkled with scattered islands, some of which were so thickly covered with palm and other trees that they seemed almost impenetrable, while others rose up abruptly as colossal rocks from the sea. Our crew consisted of four negroes and the captain; and as at first a favourable wind filled our sails, they took the opportunity to refresh themselves with a meal of boiled fish, roasted mullet, oranges, cocoa and other nuts. Even white bread was not wanting, and I was heartily glad to see them so well provided. After about two hours the wind left us, and they had to take to the oars, which is here extremely toilsome, for the rower at every stroke steps up on a bench before him and then throws himself back with all his strength. In another two hours we had left the sea, and turned into the river Geromerim, at the mouth of which lies an inn, where we stopped for half an hour, and where I saw an extraordinary kind of lighthouse, namely, a lantern hanging from a rock. The beauty of the country ceases here for a mere spectator, though a botanist would consider it glorious from the abundance of fine water plants. The shores are flat and low, and whatever houses are to be seen, though built of stone and with tiled roofs, have a deplorable appearance.

After a voyage of seven hours on the river we reached Porto d'Estrella, a not inconsiderable town, and the staple place for goods from the interior of the country, and which are thence forwarded to the capital of Brazil. It contains two handsome inns, a building much like a Turkish khan, and an immense tiled roof resting on strong pillars. The first is intended for goods, the latter for the ass-drivers, a party of whom had now encamped beneath it, and were preparing their supper over a merrily blazing fire. This kind of quarters would have served us very well, but we preferred going to the "Star" inn, where the clean beds and savoury dishes pleased us still better. From Porto d'Estrella to Petropolis we had still seven leagues. The distance is usually done on mules, for which you pay four *milreis* a piece; but since we had been told in Rio de Janeiro that there was a most beautiful walk to it through the woods, quite frequented and safe, as it formed the principal communication with Minas Geraes, we resolved to travel it on foot, and for this we had also another inducement, as the Count wanted to botanise and I to collect insects. The two first leagues led through a broad valley, for the most part covered with thick underwood and young trees, and surrounded by lofty mountains. The path was beautifully adorned on either side by wild pine-apples, not yet quite ripe, but of a glowing rose colour; but unluckily they are not quite so good as they look, and are therefore very seldom plucked. I was delighted too with the humming birds, of which I saw several of the smallest species. Nothing can be imagined more delicate and graceful than these little creatures. They get their food out of the cups of flowers, hovering about them like butterflies, for which, indeed, they may be easily mistaken. The trees rather disappointed me, for I had expected to find those of a primeval forest with thick and lofty trunks, but this was not at all the case. Probably the vegetation is too strong, and the large trunks are choked and rotted beneath the mass of smaller trees, shrubs, climbing and parasite plants. The two latter are so numerous and exuberant that they often completely cover the trees, hiding not only the trunks but the very leaves. We had made a rich harvest of flowers, plants, and insects, and were quietly pursuing our way, enchanted by the rich woods and the glorious prospects that opened to us from time to time over mountain and valley, sea and bay, even to the very capital itself, and the frequent troops of negroes, as well as other pedestrians, which we now met, freed us from any fear respecting the safety of the road, so that we took little notice of a negro who had been for some time following us, when, all at once, as we reached a rather lonely spot he sprang upon us. He had in one hand a long knife and in the other a lasso, and he signified, by sufficiently expressive gestures, that it was his intention to murder us and drag us into the wood.

We had no weapon with us, as it had not been thought necessary, and had nothing to defend ourselves with but our umbrellas. In my pocket, however, I had a penknife, which I managed to draw, firmly resolved to sell my life as dearly as possible. We parried a few of his blows with the umbrellas, but they were not strong enough, and besides, the negro seized hold of mine ; we struggled and it broke, leaving only a bit of the handle in my hand, but during the struggle he happened to let fall his knife, which rolled away a few steps. I darted after it, but he was quicker, and got hold of it again, striking me as he did so with both hand and foot, and giving me two deep cuts in the fleshy part of the left arm. I now gave myself up for lost, and only despair gave me courage still to make use of my knife ; I made two stabs at the breast of my assailant, but only wounded him in the hand, but in the mean time the Count sprang towards him and seized him from behind, so that I had time to get up again from the ground. All this had happened in less than a minute, and the wounds he had received now made the negro quite furious ; he gnashed his teeth, flew at us like a wild beast, and wielded his knife with terrible rapidity : but God sent us help at this last moment ; for we heard the steps of horses on the road, and the negro immediately left us and escaped into the wood, and directly afterwards two horsemen made their appearance round the turning. We hastened towards them, and our cut umbrellas, as well as our bleeding wounds, explained our situation : they enquired after the direction the fugitive had taken, sprang again on their horses, and endeavoured to overtake him ; but their exertions would probably have been in vain, had not two negroes come by and offered their assistance. He was soon brought back, tied fast, and when he refused to walk he received such a shower of blows, especially over the head, that I feared the poor creature's scull would have been fractured. He uttered no sound, however, but remained lying on the ground, and the two negroes had to carry him along—biting like an enraged beast—to the next house. The Count and I got our wounds bound up, and then continued our ramble, not without fear, however, especially when we met any negroes, but unmolested and in constant admiration of the lovely landscape.

The colony of Petropolis lies in the midst of the forest, 2,500 feet above the level of the sea. It was founded about fourteen years ago, principally for the sake of growing, for the supply of the capital, various kinds of European fruit and vegetables, which in tropical climates will only flourish at a considerable height. There is already a street of small houses, and on a cleared spot stands the wooden skeleton of a large building intended for an imperial pleasure palace, but which will hardly when finished have a very imperial aspect, for its little low doors contrast very oddly with its broad large windows.

The town is growing up round this castle, but there are also many houses lying scattered about in the woods. A part of the colonists, mechanics, storekeepers, and so forth, had small portions of land for building in the neighbourhood of the castle given to them; the cultivators got rather more, but still but a very moderate quantity—not more than two or three acres. Surely these people must have suffered much misery in their native land to have been willing to come to this remote part of the world for no more than an acre or two of land.

At Petropolis, as well as afterwards on our return to Rio de Janeiro, people wondered so much at the attack made upon us, that if we had not had our wounds to show they would certainly not have believed us. It was said, the fellow must have been drunk or mad, but we learned afterwards that his master had shortly before inflicted punishment upon him on account of some offence, and when he met us in the wood he probably thought it would be a good opportunity of revenging himself on the whites.

I did not allow this adventure to deter me from keeping the resolution I had previously formed of seeing before I left Brazil something more of the interior, and especially of paying a visit to the Indians—the original inhabitants. Count Berchtold again agreed to bear me company, and on the morning of the 2nd of October we set off for the port of Sampayo, lying at the mouth of the river Maccacu, and which consists of an inn, and two or three little houses. There we engaged mules to ride to the town of Morroqueimado, twenty leagues off, and according to a custom here, implying a great deal of confidence in travellers, we might if we liked, have taken no guides with us, but have agreed to leave the mules at an appointed place. As we knew nothing of the road, however, we preferred taking a guide, and were glad we did so, as we found it in many places closed with wooden bars, which had to be opened and shut.

In about three hours we reached the great sugar plantation or *Fazenda de Collegio*, which had the appearance of a considerable country seat. There were a spacious house, many domestic offices, and a chapel, all enclosed by a wall, and far around, the plains and the lower hills were covered with sugar plantations. The wealth of a planter is usually calculated by the number of his slaves, and this one had about 800—a considerable property, as every male slave is worth from six to seven hundred milreis. Not far from the fazenda to the right and left lay several others, by which the monotony of the road was much relieved. In the following day's journey the mountains approached more closely towards each other, and the woods became thicker and more luxuriant. Indescribably beautiful were the creeping plants, which not only covered the ground, but hung their splendid flowers from the highest branches of the trees, so that they looked like some wonderful blossom. There are indeed trees whose red and yellow blossoms equal the finest flowers, and others whose leaves gleam like silver through the green and flowery sea of foliage— such woods as these may be regarded as the giant gardens of the world.

After crossing a rather high ridge of mountains, we reached the town of Morroqueimado, or Novo Friburgo, which lies in a romantic valley, 3,200 feet above the sea. The night was far advanced, and we were heartily glad to find excellent quarters at the house of a German, Mr. Lindenroth, who made us beside a very moderate charge—one milreis a day for each person for lodging, and three good meals. We visited two other Germans of whom we had heard in Rio de Janeiro ; one, Mr. Beske, was a naturalist, with a better collection than that of the museum of the capital, and the other, Mr. Freese, a schoolmaster, with sixty scholars paying a good fee, and exhibiting considerable proficiency. We had not intended to make any stay at this place, but unfortunately the

Count's wound here became much worse, and as inflammation came on it was not possible for him to continue the journey. There remained, therefore, no choice for me but to go alone, or to give up the most interesting part of my excursion—the visit to the Indians. This I could not make up my mind to do, and I therefore made enquiries about the probable safety of the road, and as I obtained a sort of half and half assurance, and Mr. Lindenroth procured me a trustworthy guide, I armed myself with a pair of good double-barrelled pistols, and fearlessly set out on my ramble.

We soon descended from the mountains into the warmer regions; the valleys were mostly narrow, and the monotony of the woods was relieved by plantations, but these were not always beautiful; many of them are so full of weeds that it is scarcely possible to tell what has been planted, and little care is bestowed on anything but sugar and coffee. The coffee trees stand in rows on almost perpendicular hills; they reach a height of from six to twelve feet, begin to bear in the second or third year, and remain fruitful for ten. Blossoms and perfectly ripe fruit are found on the tree at the same time.

A spectacle which I here saw for the first time was that of the forest conflagrations, which are purposely kindled for the convenience of cultivation. At first I saw only volumes of smoke rolling up, and wished for nothing more earnestly than to come quite close to a fire; and my wish was fulfilled in the course of the same day, for our road lay between a burning wood and a tract of low bushes, called *Rost*, also on fire. We heard the crackling of the flames, and saw through the clouds of smoke huge tongues of flame darting up: from time to time there was a heavy sound like cannon, from the fall of some large tree. As I saw my guide turn in the direction of this flaming pass, I felt certainly some anxiety, but I reflected that he did not assuredly wish to throw away his life, and that probably experience had shown him the possibility of making the passage. At the entrance sat two negroes to warn the passenger of the direction he must take, and urge him to use the utmost speed: my guide translated to me what they said, and then gave his horse the spur; I followed his example, and we dashed into the fiery gulph. Glowing ashes flew all around us, and more oppressive still than the tremendous heat was the suffocating vapour and smoke, through which the animals could scarcely draw their breath. Fortunately the most dangerous part was not more than five or six hundred paces long, and we passed safely through it.

These fires never go to any great extent in Brazil, as the vegetation is too fresh ; the woods have to be kindled in several places, and even then the fire often goes out, and spots are left unconsumed in the middle of the burnt forest.

On the other side of this dangerous spot we came to an imposing rock, seven or eight hundred feet high; with large loose fragments lying about. To my great astonishment I was informed by my guide that we were to pass the night here, and he showed me the way to a lonely venda, or inn, in the thickest of the wood.

One of the things which most strikes a traveller in the inhabitants of Brazil is the strange mixture they exhibit of cowardice and courage. On the one hand every one you meet in the street is armed with pistols and long knives, as if the whole country were full of thieves and murderers ; and on the other, you see the planters living quite at their ease in the midst of a crowd of slaves, and the traveller fearlessly passes the night at one of these solitary little inns, hidden in the depth of impenetrable woods, with neither shutters to his windows nor locks to his doors ; the rooms occupied by the family are far away from those assigned to guests, and the servants (all slaves) are also a long way off, in the corner of some stable or outhouse. At first I felt very uncomfortable thus surrounded by the wild dark woods, and cut off from the possibility of any human help ; but as I was assured no one had ever heard of any one breaking into a house, I dismissed my superfluous fears, and went quietly to sleep. I know few countries in Europe where, under similar circumstances, in the midst of a thick forest, with no one to depend on but a hired guide, one would have felt equally easy.

The character of the country we passed through on the following day afforded little variety. There were still narrow valleys and hills, covered with boundless woods, and only a small fazienda here and there, or a purposely burnt forest, served to remind me that I was not travelling through a hitherto undiscovered country. My guide managed, indeed, in one place, to make a little variety for me by losing the way ; and in order to recover the path we had to break our way across the forest—a task of which a European can hardly form an idea. We got off our horses, climbed over fallen trunks, forced ourselves between others, and the guide hacked away right and left at the branches, and cut through the thick web of the countless creepers. Very often we were entangled up to our knees in them; and even now I can hardly understand how we got through such a thicket at all. We reached at length the little town of Canto Gallo, containing about eighty houses, and stopped at a venda, where I took my place near the hostess, in order that I might look as closely as possible into Brazilian housekeeping. But the good lady, unluckily, troubled herself very little about kitchen or pantry. The cooking was performed by a negress, assisted by two negro boys, and all her operations were extremely simple : the potatoes were mashed with a bottle and then squeezed into the pan with a plate, that they might take the form of a cake; a piece of pointed wood serving for a fork. For each dish prepared there was a large separate fire, and when the dinner was put on the table, all who could be considered whites took their places at it, the slaves being fed separately on beans, *carna secca*, manioc flour, and long flat strips of salt beef, dried in the air.

October 8th.—The woods we passed through to-day were more splendid than any I had yet seen. A narrow path led along the edge of a sparkling rivulet; palms with their majestic crowns rose proudly above the leafed trees, which formed with their foliage the most beautiful green bowers beneath. Orchidaceous plants, creepers, and ferns, shot up round the branches of the trees and formed perfect walls of flowers, which shone in the most gorgeous colours, and exhaled delicious fragrance ; delicate little humming-birds fluttered around ; the gaily-coloured pepper-bird flew upward ; parrots and parroquets rocked in the boughs, and many other superb birds, which I had known only in museums, animated these enchanted groves. It seemed to me that I was taking a ride in fairy-land, and that every moment some sylph or nymph would make her appearance. I was over happy, and felt every exertion I had made most richly rewarded. One thought alone clouded the sunshine of this enchanting picture—the thought that feeble man should venture to contend with this gigantic nature, and bow her to his will. How soon may the blows of the axe disturb the deep and holy tranquillity of these woods, and their glorious beauty be defaced to furnish the settler with the necessaries of life ! Of dangerous animals I saw only some dark green serpents, from five to seven feet long, and a dead ounce which had been skinned. Monkeys I did not see, they had probably hidden themselves deeper in the woods, where no human footstep could disturb them in their play.

At the village of St. Ritta, four leagues from Canto Gallo, there are some gold washings, and not far off diamonds are found. Since the seeking or digging for diamonds is no longer an imperial monopoly, every one can devote himself to this occupation, but it is nevertheless carried on with a great deal of secrecy. In order to deprive the State of its legal share in the profits, no one will confess to having been so engaged. The precious stones are dug out in certain places from the midst of the sand, stones, and vegetable soil, into which they have been washed by the rains.

After passing Canto Gallo, there were no more vendas in which I could find shelter, and I had to rely on the hospitality of the owners of fazendas. On arriving at one of these, etiquette requires that you shall remain outside the door and ask, through your servant, permission to enter, which is scarcely ever refused. At a fazenda, called Bona Esperanza, I received a particularly friendly reception, and as I came in just at dinner time, a cover was immediately placed for myself and servant. The dishes were numerous, and prepared mostly in the European fashion. At every fazenda there was of course always a good deal of wonderment at seeing me, a woman, come in with no other companion than a single servant. The first question was always whether I was not afraid to travel alone through these forests, and my guide was privately taken aside and interrogated as to what was really the motive of my journey; and since he often saw me collect flowers and insects he took me for a naturalist, and said that the object of my journey was a scientific one.

When dinner was over, the good-natured hostess proposed to me to visit the coffee plantations, &c., and I willingly accepted her offer, as it gave me the opportunity of seeing the preparation of coffee from beginning to end. After it is plucked, it is spread out in spacious places enclosed by a wall of about a foot high, with small drains to let off the rain water ; on these places the coffee is dried by the heat of the sun, and then shaken into large stone mortars, where it is struck lightly with wooden hammers, set in motion by water power. The whole mass then falls into wooden boxes fixed in a long table, at which sit the negroes, who separate the coffee from the husk, and put it into flat copper pans, where it is carefully turned about on a slow fire, till it is sufficiently dried —an operation which requires much care.

On the whole, the preparation of the coffee is not laborious, and the harvest far less so than our corn harvests. The negro in plucking the coffee stands in an upright position, and is protected by the tree from the heat of the sun. The only danger is of being stung by poisonous snakes, but that fortunately is of rare occurrence. The labour of a sugar plantation is said to be much harder, especially the weeding and cutting the cane.

At sunset the day's labour ends. The negroes then range themselves before the master's house and are counted, after which there is a short prayer, and then comes the evening meal, consisting of bacon, beans, *carna secca*, and manioc flour. At sunrise they all assemble again, are again counted, and then, after prayers and breakfast, go again to work.

In this as well as in many other fazendas, vendas, and private houses, I had occasion to observe that the negroes are by no means treated with the severity which we in Europe imagine. They are not overtasked; they go about it in an easy leisurely manner, and they are very well fed. Their children are actually the play-fellows of the masters, and they all romp and tumble about together. There may be cases where slaves are over severely or unjustly punished; but we have instances of injustice even in Europe. I am certainly an enemy to slavery, and should greet its abolition with infinite joy; but I must nevertheless repeat my assertion that the negro slave, under the protection of law, has a better lot than the free fellah in Egypt, or than many peasants in Europe.

The arrangement of these fazendas is extremely simple. The windows are without glass, and closed at night only by wooden shutters. It is not uncommon for the one ceiling to extend over all the apartments, which are then separated only by low partitions, so that you can hear every word and almost every breath of your neighbour, especially when he is asleep. The furniture is equally simple—a large dining-table, some divans stuffed with straw, and a few chairs. The clothes usually hang round the walls, and the linen only is put away in tin chests, in order to be preserved from the ants and barates. The children even of rich people go without shoes or stockings, but before they go to bed it is necessary to examine their little feet, and take out the sand-fleas that may have nestled in them—an operation which is commonly performed by the elder negro children with a pin.

I took leave of my kind hostess in good time in the morning, and she packed up carefully for me a roast fowl, manioc flour, and some cheese, so that I set out again well provided.

The next station, Aldea do Pedro, on the banks of the Parahyby, was four leagues distant. You pass through magnificent forests, and before you are half way to the station reach the river, which is one of the largest in Brazil, and has a very remarkable bed: it is covered with countless rocks and cliffs and little wooded islands, which in the rainy season are completely overflowed, so that the river appears of most majestic breadth ; but it is nevertheless, for this reason, only navigable by very small craft. As you reach the banks, the landscape changes — the foremost mountains sink into low hills, the higher retire, and the nearer you approach Aldeu do Pedro the freer and wider becomes the valley. My guide pointed to a rather bold conspicuous mountain in the background, and said that our road lay that way, behind that mountain; for there lived the Puri Indians.

About three leagues beyond Aldea do Pedro (a village where I was hospitably received by the priest) we reached the last settlement of the whites. On an open space, that seemed to be with difficulty wrung from the forest, stood a tolerably large wooden house surrounded by some wretched huts; the house served for the whites, the huts for the abode of their slaves. A letter which I brought from the priest procured me a good reception, but I found the housekeeping in such a style that I really thought myself already among the savages.

The house contained one large hall, from which opened four rooms, each inhabited by a white family, whose entire furniture consisted of some mats. The inhabitants were crouching on the ground and playing with the children, or mutually freeing each other from vermin. The kitchen was like a great barn, with a fire-place running nearly its whole length, on which several fires were burning; over them hung small kettles, and wooden spits were fixed to the sides on which pieces of meat were being cooked, partly by the fire and partly by the smoke. The kitchen was full of people ; there were whites, Puris, and negroes,—children of whites and Puris, or of Puris and negroes, in short, a perfect pattern-card of the various shades of these several races. The yard was swarming with beautifully-coloured ducks and geese, and I saw also enormously fat pigs and terribly ugly dogs. Beneath some cocoa-palms and tamarind trees, laden with splendid fruit, groups of white and coloured people were seated, mostly engaged in appeasing their hunger. Some had before them gourds or broken earthenware pans in which they were mixing with their hands boiled beans and manioc flour, and this thick untempting-looking mess they ate with great eagerness. Others were devouring pieces of meat which they tore with their hands and threw into their mouths alternately with handfuls of manioc flour. The children had to defend their dinners valiantly against sundry intruders, for now a dog would snatch a bit, then a hen would peck out something she took a fancy to, and occasionally a little pig would come waddling by, and by its joyful grunt as it hurried away I saw it had not come in vain.

While I was pursuing my observations there suddenly arose a loud and merry cry in the yard, and I looked and saw two boys dragging along between them a great snake, certainly above seven feet long, but dead. As far as I could make out what the people said they considered its bite mortal. This account made me a little unwilling to start again on my journey through the forest just as it was getting dark, as I must then necessarily sleep under a tree, and I therefore preferred putting off my visit to the Puris till the morning. The good people thought I was afraid of the savages, and assured me they were very inoffensive people; and as my stock of Portuguese did not extend beyond a few words, it was not very easy to make them understand the real cause of my fear, but at length, by means of gesticulations and a few drawings, I succeeded in explaining it. Among these semi-savages, therefore, I spent the night, and they treated me with the utmost kindness, indeed, almost overwhelmed me with attentions. A straw mat was, according to my wish, spread beneath a shed in the yard to form my couch, and for my supper they brought me a roast fowl and hard boiled eggs, with oranges and tamarinds for dessert. The women established themselves about me, and by degrees we got to understand each other very well. I showed them the flowers and insects I had been collecting, and they immediately came to the conclusion that I must be a very learned person, and of course possess a knowledge of medicine. They therefore begged my advice in various cases, and I gave it to the best of my ability, freely recommending soap and water. On the following day we started in search of the Indians, and after working our way for eight hours through an almost impenetrable thicket, we came to some Puri huts. I had seen many pictures of poverty in the course of my travels, but never anything like that. Their habitations consisted only of a roof of palm leaves supported on a sort of skeleton made with four stakes. It was open on three sides, a few mats were hanging up under the roof, their only weapon, the bow and arrow, leant against the wall, and a few gourds made up the whole stock of household utensils. Some roots and bananas were roasting in a glimmering fire.

I found these Indians still uglier than negroes : they have stunted-looking figures, broad compressed faces, and straight coal black hair ; their foreheads are low, their noses flat, their eyes small and cut out like those of the Chinese, their mouths very large with thick lips, and over the whole physiognomy is diffused a peculiar expression of stupidity, heightened by the constantly open mouth. They are mostly tattooed with red or brown colour, and both sexes are passionate smokers and lovers of brandy. Their only clothing was a few rags round the loins.

The whole number of Puri Indians in Brazil is calculated at not more than 500,000, and they live scattered far in the recesses of the woods. Not more than five or six families are ever found at the same place, and they leave it as soon as they have killed all the game near it, and consumed the roots and fruits. Many of these Indians have been baptized, and, indeed, they are at all times willing, for the consideration of a little brandy, to go through the ceremony again, and only regret that they have not more frequent opportunities, especially as it does not last long. The priest on his side generally makes his mind easy that by this holy action he has won the soul for heaven, and does not, therefore, give himself any superfluous trouble about the morals of his new Christians. The Puri seldom alters anything in his old customs concerning marriage and other points. Their language is extremely poor, and they have no method of expressing number but by repeating one two—one two, as many times as may be required. For yesterday, to-day, and to-morrow they have only one word, and they express the variety of meaning by pointing backward for yesterday, forward for to-morrow, and over the head for the passing day.

The Puri are said to have an extraordinary keenness of scent, so much so that they are employed to scent out runaway negroes, in which task, unless a stream of running water intervene, so that the fugitive can walk or swim, they scarcely ever fail. They will also for a very trifling reward perform very hard work, such as cutting wood; but there must be no attempt to constrain them, as they are conscious they are free men, and they can seldom be induced to work till they are half starved. I visited all the huts at this place, and as my guide trumpeted forth my praises as a woman of astonishing learning, I had soon a considerable number of patients asking for medical advice. Several of the women were afflicted with cancer, and with indurations and tumours on the breast, and one poor creature, whom I found groaning in a sort of hammock, made of a mat suspended between trees, had the entire breast eaten away by that terrible malady. I advised her to cleanse it with an infusion of Malva, a very wholesome plant that grows wild here, and then lay some boiled Malva leaves over it, and I trust that may have procured her some little alleviation.

After I had examined everything in the huts, I accompanied some of the Puris on a parrot and monkey hunt, and had an opportunity of admiring their skill in the management of their bows. They shot the birds even flying, and seldom missed their mark, but as soon as we had " bagged " three parrots and a monkey we returned to the huts. The poor creatures offered me the best of their huts for a shelter, and invited me to pass the night with them; I accepted their invitation willingly, for the heat, the exhausting foot journey, and the subsequent chase had greatly fatigued me. The day was drawing to a close too, and it would not be possible for me to reach the settlement of the whites before night-fall; I therefore spread my cloak on the ground, took a clump of wood for a pillow, and found myself magnificently accommodated. My hosts in the meantime were engaged in cooking our game, the parrot and the monkey, which they did by sticking them on wooden spits and roasting them, and in order to render the banquet still more complete they added some tuberous roots and some cobs of Indian corn. They then plucked some fresh leaves, tore the monkey to pieces with their hands, laid a good portion of it, as well as one of the parrots, upon them, and placed it before me.

My appetite was boundless, for I had eaten nothing since the morning, so I began at once with the monkey, and found it excellent; the parrot was not quite so tender and savoury.

After the completion of our repast, I begged the Indians to perform one of their dances for my amusement; they immediately complied, and as it was now dark they made a great pile of wood, and set light to it. The men formed a circle round me, and began to dance; they moved their bodies in a particularly clumsy manner from side to side, nodding their heads at the same time, and the women then made the same movements, but remained a little behind the men, who afterwards begun a hideous yelping that was to represent a song, and all distorted their faces in a most frightful manner, while some others stood by playing on a sort of stringed instrument made of the cane and fibres of the cabbage palm, and which gave a hoarse unpleasant tone. This whole performance was denominated a peace or joy-dance. Some of a wilder character were performed by the men alone; after they had armed themselves with their bows and arrows, and with stout sticks, they again formed a circle, but their motions were much more ferocious than the first time, and they laid about them famously with their cudgels. They then bent their bows, fixed their arrows, and went through all the pantomime as if they were shooting a flying foe, uttering at the same time such fearful yells that the whole forest resounded with them, and I started up in terror feeling as if I were surrounded with savage enemies, and no help near. Heartily glad was I when this terrible war-dance came to an end. When I once more lay down, and every thing was still around me, a fear of a different kind came over me; I thought of the many wild animals, the terrible serpents that might be lurking close to the open defenceless shed in which I was lying. For a long time I could not get over that fear, and I often thought I heard the leaves rustle as if one of these dreaded enemies was making his way to me. But at length my over-wearied body asserted its claims, I rested my head on the log of wood and consoled myself with the thought that there could hardly be so much danger as travellers would make us believe, or these savages would not sleep so composedly in their open huts, and without the smallest preparation for defence.

In the morning I took leave of the Indians, and presented them with some bronze ornaments, with which they were so delighted that they offered me every thing they possessed. I accepted a bow and arrows as a *souvenir*, and then returned to the wooden house, and after distributing some similar presents, mounted my mule and late in the evening found myself once more in Aldea do Pedro, where I took leave of the friendly priest, and in three or four days had made the journey back to Novo Friburgo, and again met Count Berchtold, now perfectly recovered from his wound.

CAPE HORN.—ARRIVAL AT VALPARAISO.

Description of the Town.—Manners of the People.—The Restaurant o Polonku.—Little Angels.

THE dangerous part of the passage round Cape Horn begins in the opinion of navigators with the Strait Le Maire, and ends on the west side of America, in the latitude of the Straits of Magellan.

Near this point, I found myself on the 3rd of February in the fine English barque " John Renwick," Captain Bell, with whom I had engaged for twenty-five pounds to carry me to Valparaiso. We had little to dread in the passage, for we had a good ship, large convenient cabins, as well as a most good tempered and complaisant captain, and such fare as none of us had ever seen equalled on a sailing vessel. Every day we had boiled or roast fowls, fresh mutton and pork, ducks and geese, plum puddings or pastry, besides fruit and side dishes. We were not, however, now to enjoy these good things without disturbance. As soon as we had reached the above strait, two sudden squalls from the icy ravines of Terra del Fuego seized the vessel, and violent storms afterwards drove us considerably too far to the southward, and all the while the motion was so violent that we could not attempt to dine at the table, but had to crawl with our plates on the ground. On one of these days the steward tumbled over me with a pot of boiling coffee, but fortunately only a small part came on my hand, so that the damage was not very great.

The extreme point of Cape Horn is a mountain about 600 feet high, but before it, and separated only by a narrow strip of sea, lies a magnificent group of black basaltic rocks. Near it we saw some whales and albatrosses, but no icebergs. We thought when we had passed this cape, and fairly entered the Pacific Ocean, it would have brought us weather that would do credit to its name, but for fourteen days we had to struggle with storm and sea, with rain and cold, before we reached the latitude of the Straits of Magellan, and after this came a tempest that lasted four and twenty hours, had carried away four of our sails. We shipped two such tremendous seas that a plank in the deck got loose, and the water penetrated to the cargo of sugar. The deck was like a lake, and it was necessary to make great openings in the bulwarks that the water might run off the quicker, and in the mean time we had got two inches of water in the hold. No fire could be made, and we had to content ourselves with bread and cheese, and raw ham, which indeed we had no little difficulty in carrying to our mouths. The last cask of lamp oil too became a sacrifice to the storm, it broke loose and was dashed to pieces, and the captain began to be apprehensive that we might not have oil enough left to light the compass till we reached Valparaiso. All the lamps in the ship were therefore replaced by wax lights, in order to save what remained. In spite of all these disagreeables, however, we kept up our spirits, and during the gale could not help laughing at the comical positions we involuntarily assumed whenever we attempted to rise.

The first view of Valparaiso is dreary and monotonous. The town consists principally of two long streets, which stretch round the foot of bleak hills, looking like gigantic sand heaps, but which are really rocks, thinly covered with sand ; some houses are also scattered about them, which somewhat improve the prospect. Seen from within, the streets look tolerably animated from the number of fine horses ; and every Chilian is born a rider.

The more modern houses are in the European style, with flat Italian roofs, and tastefully arranged in the interior. A broad flight of steps leads up to the first floor, and into a lofty hall, serving as an antechamber to the reception-room, which is the pride not only of European settlers, but also of the Chilians who often spend considerable sums in fitting it up. Heavy carpets cover the floor, the walls are hung with rich paper, the most costly furniture and looking glasses decorate the rooms, and on the tables lie magnificent albums and engravings. Very elegant fire-places suggested to me also that the winters are not quite so mild as many of the inhabitants would have had me believe.

The dwellings of the poor are extremely miserable-looking huts of wood and clay, that mostly look ready to tumble in ; I scarcely ventured to enter them, but when I did so found to my great astonishment not only good beds, tables, and chairs, but often little domestic altars very prettily decorated with flowers. The dress, too, of the people was far better than might have been expected, and the linen that I saw hanging up to dry before these hovels was often superior to what I had seen in towns in Sicily, hanging before the windows of elegant mansions.

To make one's self acquainted with the manners and mode of life of the people, there is no better way than to go among them on Sundays and holidays in the quarter of Polanka, and visit the cooks' shops. I will introduce my readers to one of these.

In a corner on the ground a great fire is burning, surrounded by pots and pans, and spits with pieces of pork and beef; and such a cooking and roasting and boiling is going on, that you see there will soon be a famous meal ready. A rough wooden tressel, on which is placed a long broad plank, stands in the middle of the room, and is covered with a table cloth, the original colour of which might be hard to guess. This is the table round which the guests place themselves. At dinner, not only do all the guests eat out of one dish, but every thing is served in one and the same; beans and onions, beef and rice, potatoes and fruit, all lie comfortably together, and are eaten in silence with abundant appetite. At the end of the meal, the jug, whether it contain wine or water, is passed from hand to hand, and after that, the company begins to talk, and there is often a good deal of dancing to the guitar. Unfortunately it was fast time when I was there, but people are not immoderately strict, and for a few reals they agreed to perform in a little back room their national dances, the Sammaquecca and the Refolosa, to the best of their ability. I soon had enough of it. The movements of the dancers were so extremely indecorous that I could not but grieve for the young people whose natural delicacy must be so early corrupted by the sight of such things.

I was not much better pleased with a strange custom that prevails here of considering the death of a young child as a festival and an occasion of rejoicing for the parents. The deceased child is called an angelito, or little angel, and dressed out in all the finery that can be mustered. The eyes are not closed, but on the contrary opened as widely as possible, the cheeks rouged, a garland of flowers put on the head, and it is then placed on a small chair in a niche, also adorned with flowers. The relations and neighbours then come in, and wish the parents joy on the possession of such a little angel, and on the very first night after the death there is feasting and dancing and all kinds of merriment. Not long before my visit to Valparaiso, a case occurred of the landlord of a public house having bought one of these angelitos for two reals from the man who was carrying it to the churchyard, and then stuck it up in his house, and made it the occasion of a merrymaking.

Of the uncommon honesty of the Chilians, of which Captain Bell had spoken to me in a flourishing style, rather customary with him, I am sorry I cannot speak so confidently. He said I might leave a purse full of gold in the street over night, and be sure of finding it the next day; whereas the expression of many of the faces I met was so decidedly sinister, that I should have been rather sorry to meet them in a lonely place, with money even in my pocket; and as I saw a great number of prisoners in chains, working on the roads, and found the doors and windows barred in a way I have scarcely ever seen in any town in Europe, I incline to the opinion that my own impression was nearer to the truth than the account of the captain. At night there are placed in every street, and on all the hills that are built on, police patrols, who challenge one another like the sentinels in war time; mounted policemen also traverse the town in various directions; and it is very common for people coming from the theatre, or from parties, to get some of them for an escort;—all this does not look as if robbery were a very rare occurrence. I was not a little surprised in this country, where no regular communication is established with any place, and where there is not even a regular post, to hear mention of a railroad, the surveys for which, I was told, were already made. It is in the hands of an English company, and is to run to Santiago ; but the country is extremely mountainous, and the expenses must be far greater than the present traffic can support. It was the general opinion, whether well-founded or not, that the railroad was undertaken principally with the view of thoroughly exploring the country for gold and silver mines, as the conditions are here extremely favourable to discoverers. They have the fullest right of property in the discovery, and need do nothing more than notify to the Government their taking possession. These privileges are carried so far, that if you can show any tolerably plausible reason for supposing that a mine exists under a house or a church, and can give security for making good the damage, you have a right to pull it down.

VOYAGE by TAHITI to CANTON.

Furnished Lodgings in Papeiti.—A Court Ball.—An Excursion.—Lake Vaihiria.— The Mountain Pass of Fantaua.—The Diadem.—Voyage across the Pacific.—Arrival in China.

THE announcement, that the ship in which I had taken my passage to China was about to sail, arrived at a moment when it was extremely unwelcome, since I had been for some days suffering from diarrhœa, and that was not likely to be improved by the sea diet and the exposure to weather; but as I had already paid my two hundred dollars I was obliged to go on board, and take my chance. The most effectual remedy I found was a cold sea bath, which I used to take in a cask, remaining a quarter of an hour at a time in the water : besides this, cooling drinks—such as buttermilk, sour milk, orangeade, and so forth—were very beneficial when this malady attacked me in warm countries.

On the thirty-ninth day after leaving Valparaiso we came in sight of Tahiti, where we were to touch, and soon after saw the entrance to the harbour of Papeiti, surrounded by coral reefs as by a fortification. A strong surf was beating upon them, leaving only a narrow entrance open; but we got a pilot, and though the wind was unfavourable, he carried us safely in. We were, however, congratulated on our escape, for the people on shore watching us had thought that from the turn the wind had taken, we should certainly have run on one of the coral reefs—an accident that had really happened under similar circumstances some months before to a French ship, which was still here repairing her damage.

The anchor was scarcely let fall before we were surrounded by half a dozen canoes, with Tahitians, who climbed on the deck from all sides, and offered us fruit and shell fish—not as formerly, for glass beads and baubles, those golden days for travellers are over, but for hard cash, which they are just as eager after as the most civilized Europeans. I offered one of them a brass ring; he took it, smelled it, and then shook his head and returned it to me, giving me to understand that it was not gold. He then remarked a ring on my finger, and after smelling it also, signified that he would accept of that one. I am told they can always distinguish real gold by the smell.

On landing, I went in vain from house to house to procure some kind of lodging ; but as the town consists only of a row of little wooden cottages round the harbour (with the woods immediately behind them), and even officers of rank have to put up with a wretched lodging in Indian huts, I was for some time unable to find a place where I could lay my head. At length I procured it, in the most literal acceptation, in the house of a carpenter,— a house consisting of one room, in which his family of four persons already lived ; I obtained leave to deposit myself in a corner behind the door, in a space exactly six feet long and four broad ; the floor was not boarded, the walls were only palisades, and of chair or bedstead there was no question.

Tahiti, as is known, is now under the protection of the French, who are building a handsome house for Queen Pomare, and allow her a yearly pension of 25,000 fs. ; but she is not allowed to receive any stranger without their permission. There were several of their ships in the harbour, and the place was full of French soldiers ; a circumstance which, as far as I could perceive, did not seem likely to improve greatly the morals of the inhabitants. The people have acquired a number of new wants, in consequence of which the eagerness for money has greatly increased among them ; and what is worse, as they are by no means fond of work, they make their wives, daughters, and sisters earn money for them. The women have no objection, for they get dress and ornaments on what they consider easy terms ; and the house of almost every French officer is a rendezvous for these native beauties, who are to be seen going in and out at all times of the day, and even joining them in public.

As a woman of advanced age, I may be permitted to speak of these things ; and I must declare that, much as I have travelled in the world, I have nowhere seen behaviour in this respect so shameless.

On the 1st of May the French officers gave a public entertainment, at which her Tahitian Majesty was present. She was very showily dressed in sky-blue satin with flounces of rich black blonde, a wreath of flowers in her hair, and in her hand an embroidered handkerchief trimmed with broad lace, and, moreover, for this

D

grand occasion she had crammed her feet into shoes and stockings
—a restraint to which they are but little accustomed. Her husband,—whom the French call "Prince Albert of Tahiti," not only
because he is one of the handsomest men in the island, but because
he is not king but only the consort of the queen, wore a French
General's uniform, in which he really looked very well, if you did
not see his feet. Besides these illustrious personages there was a
neighbouring potentate, a King Otoume, from one of the other
islands, whose costume was somewhat singular. He had short
white breeches, a coat of brimstone-coloured calico, and bare feet.
Some of the elder Tahitian ladies wore old-fashioned European
bonnets, and some of the younger ones brought their babies with
them, and when they could not otherwise keep them quiet sat down
very composedly and suckled them.

In some small matters the behaviour of Queen Pomare was
rather peculiar. Her Majesty retired during the evening to enjoy
the solace of a cigar, and at table she called for a plate to put by
some nice things to carry home with her ; but her husband and the
brimstone-coloured prince paid me all the usual European table
attentions with punctilious politeness.

The island of Tahiti is intersected throughout by beautiful
mountains, and in the centre rises a singular mass of rock, called,
from the form in which its many peaks are arranged, the Diadem.
Around this mass runs a girdle of five or six hundred yards breadth
of the finest woods, in which the bread-fruit, mango, orange, and
guava grow to perfection. The bottom of the sea, too, vies with
the land in beauty. The water is clear as crystal, and as your boat
glides over its transparent depths you see groups and combinations
of coloured corals and madrepores of incomparable splendour. It
is like looking into enchanted gardens ; there are gigantic flowers
and leaves, arabesques formed of sponge, strange shells lying scattered on the sand, and little bright-coloured fishes darting about like
butterflies ; these delicate creatures were scarcely four inches
long, some of pure sky-blue, others light yellow, and again others
of transparent green.

One of my excursions was to visit a singular lake lying among
some mountains at the height of 1,800 feet. To reach it I had to
make a journey on foot of eighteen miles ; and in Tahiti, on account
of the abundance of streams to be waded through, foot journies are
very troublesome. I dressed myself in a suitable manner in

trowsers, men's shoes, and a blouse, which I could tuck up to my hips, and, thus prepared, I set forth in company with a guide. The first part of the way led along the sea coast, and I counted thirty-two brooks which I had to walk through. We then turned inland through some ravines, and halted at a Tahitian hut for a meal of fish and bread-fruit, for which the inhabitants were quite willing to receive compensation. After this we continued our journey and came to a broad stream, which, from its frequent windings, it was necessary to cross sixty-two times: at dangerous places the Tahitian took hold of my hand and drew me often half swimming after him. The water reached to my waist, and when I came out it was, of course, no use to think of drying myself. The foot-path, also, was very toilsome and difficult. We had to climb over rocks and stones so covered with the large leaves of the oputu, that we never knew where we could safely set our foot. I got many a wound in my hands and feet, and frequently fell in attempting to cling to the treacherous stem of a pisang that broke under my hands. It was really a break-neck expedition, and probably never before undertaken by a woman.

In two places the ravine narrowed so much that there was no other path than the bed of the river; and at these places the Indians had, during the war with the French, carried up stone walls five feet high, as a defence against the enemy if he should attack them from this side.

After eight hours toil we had ascended a height of 1800 feet, and then we saw the lake lying in a hollow of the mountain. It has, at the utmost, a diameter of not more than 800 feet; but it has a very strange appearance, being so closely surrounded by a girdle of deep green hills as not to leave space for the narrowest foot-path or margin. It is probably the burnt out crater of a volcano which has filled itself with water; and this conjecture is strengthened by the masses of basalt that lie in the foreground. It is said, however, to be full of fish, and even to possess some of a peculiar kind, also to have a subterranean outlet, but this has never yet been discovered.

Whoever wishes to cross the lake must either swim or make use of a very fearful kind of vessel, which every Tahitian can make in a few minutes. Curiosity induced me to try this mode of navigation, and I signified to my guide that I wished to cross. He immediately tore down some stalks of the pisang, fastened them together by means of some long tough grass, laid a few leaves upon them, and then, signifying that my boat was ready, pushed it into the water and invited me to take a seat upon it. I felt a little afraid, but I was ashamed to say so. I took my seat, and my guide followed swimming, and pushing me before him. We made the voyage across and back in perfect safety, but I must own, on my side at least, not in perfect comfort; the thing was so small, there was nothing whatever to hold by, and I thought every moment I should have been over. I would not advise any one who could not swim to make a similar venture.

When we had remained long enough contemplating the lake and its singular environs we turned back for some hundred paces, till we came to a place where there was a roof or bower of leaves. Here my Tahitian guide soon kindled a cheerful fire in the Indian fashion : he cut one piece of wood to a sharp point and made a hole in another, in which he rubbed the pointed piece till smoke began to rise from it ; he had before prepared some dry grass and leaves, and he now threw the smoking splinters into them, and then moved them backwards and forwards in the air till they burst into a flame. The operation scarcely lasted two minutes. For our evening meal he plucked some bananas and laid them on the fire, by which I now also made some attempt to dry my clothes by sitting down before it and turning one side when the other was done; but at last, feeling pretty well tired out, I went to bed,—that is, I lay down on a heap of dry leaves.

Fortunately for me in this remote wild neither men nor beasts were to be feared ; the first are extremely peaceful and inoffensive, —of the latter there are none at all dangerous, except a few wild hogs. The island is so favoured by nature that it harbours no poisonous or even injurious reptile or insect ; even the scorpions are quite harmless, and may be taken in the hand with impunity. The mosquitoes only, as in all southern regions, are troublesome.

In the night, unluckily, it began to rain, and in the morning there was not the smallest prospect of its leaving off ; on the contrary, the clouds became thicker and thicker, rushing on from all sides and pouring themselves down in streams upon the country. There was nothing for it but to resign myself to their displeasure, and go on my way as best I might. In the course of half an hour the water was streaming from every part of my clothing, and as I could not now be wetter I could continue my journey in peace.

Mr. ———, at whose house I stopped, frequently receives visits from travelling French officers and their Tahitian female friends, whose behaviour is not always of the most decorous. Thus it was on this occasion, and I took refuge with my book in the room where the servants sit; *their* jokes, at least, were not such as I was ashamed to listen to.

Somewhat comical was it to hear one of these gentlemen boasting of the gratitude, attachment, and fidelity of his Tahitian lady; considering what I saw of her behaviour in his absence, I could not help once hinting my opinion on this point, and expressing my surprise at the universal attention and devotion with which these covetous mercenary creatures are treated; but the reply was that if they were not, they would run away, and that even the best treatment only served to keep them faithful for a short time. The Tahitian people in general — I cannot but think from what I saw of them—are not very capable of any noble feeling, and have no aspiration after any thing better than enjoyment. In this nature seems to encourage them, for they have no need to earn their bread by the sweat of their brow. Their island is superabundantly rich in delicious fruits, in edible tuberous roots, and in wild pigs; the people have really nothing to do but to kill the pigs and pluck the fruit, and it is consequently very difficult to get any of them to work. The poorest day labourer will not engage under a dollar a day, and for washing twelve articles of linen you have also to give a dollar, and find the soap into the bargain.

One of my most interesting excursions was to Fantaua and the Diadem mountain. Fantaua is a point which the Tahitians considered impregnable, and which nevertheless the French took in the last war. As I wished to see it, the Governor, M. Bruat, was so kind as to lend me horses, and send a subaltern officer with me, who could explain every position of the French and Tahitians. The road for two hours led through savage ravines, rushing mountain torrents, and thick woods. The mountains often approached so closely that, as at the pass of Thermopylæ, a small band of determined men might keep back whole armies. The entrance to Fantaua is the key to the whole island, and in order to take it, it was necessary to climb one of the steepest mountain sides, and advance along a narrow ridge, in order to attack the enemy in the rear. For this dangerous service M. Bruat called for volunteers, and had soon more than were necessary. Out of them he chose sixty-two men, who stripped themselves to their trowsers and shoes, and took with them nothing but a musket and a cartridge box. After twelve hours hard climbing, they succeeded, by means of ropes, bayonets, and sharp irons, in reaching one of the mountain tops, where they made their appearance so unexpectedly to the Tahitians that they were struck with terror and threw down their arms. They thought that mere men could never have climbed that point; "they must have been assisted by spirits, and against them they were not able to fight." A small fort is now built on Fantaua, and on one of the highest peaks is a guard house. This is reached by a foot-path along a narrow ridge falling on both sides into measureless abysses. People who are subject to giddiness could scarcely venture to proceed along it; but they would lose a splendid prospect if they did not—mountains, valleys, and ravines without number, of the latter, especially the colossal rock of the Diadem, woods of palm and other gigantic trees; and, beyond, the mighty ocean breaking on a thousand cliffs and reefs, and, in the remote distance, mingling with the clear blue sky. Near the fort a cataract plunges down a perpendicular wall of four hundred feet high. The body of water is not great, and the bottom of the fall is, unluckily, concealed by rocks and advancing hills, or it would deserve to be counted among the grandest in the world. The view from the Diadem is still more extensive than from the fort, as on two sides you look over the island to the sea.

This was the last of my excursions, for on the following day, the 17th of May, I had to return on board the ship. The cargo was discharged, the ballast taken in; for Tahiti produces no article of export, and the flour, salt, meat, potatoes, wine, &c., for the use of the French, have all to be imported. In the morning we got out of the harbour of Papeiti. A fine wind carried us clear of the coral reefs, and in seven hours we had lost sight of the beautiful island, which I should have left with still more regret, had it not been for my desire to see the strangest of all countries—China.

The first days of our voyage were very agreeable. Besides the favourable breeze, we had the company of a fine Belgian brig, that had run out at the same time with us. We seldom indeed came so near as to be able to have any verbal intercourse, but those who are aware of the exceeding monotony of long voyages will know what a pleasant, nay, joyful feeling, it is to be within reach of human society.

It was intended that we should keep together as far as the Philippines; but, alas! on the third morning our companion had disappeared, without our being able to discover whether we had out-sailed her, or she us; and we were now again alone on the measureless waste of waters.

On the 23d of May we came near the low island of Penrylm. Some dozens of the inhabitants, half naked savages, appeared to intend paying us a visit in canoes; but we were sailing too quickly for them; many of the sailors and the captain declared that we had had a lucky escape, for that with these people the name of "savage" was by no means a misnomer. I believe I was the only one who regretted not to have made a nearer acquaintance with them.

On the 1st of July we again saw land — the coast of Luzon — the largest of the Philippines, on the south coast of which is the harbour of Manilla. In the course of the day we came to the island of Papua, and to several colossal rocks which rose like towers out of the sea. Four of them formed a particularly picturesque group, and afterwards we saw two more.

On the 2d of July we reached the western point of Luzon, and sailed into the dangerous Chinese Sea. I was heartily glad at length to bid farewell to the Pacific Ocean, for a voyage upon it is excessively tedious: you very seldom meet a ship, and the water is so smooth that you seem to be sailing upon a river; not seldom I started from my writing-table, actually thinking for the moment I was in some tiny room on shore — a delusion so much the more natural as we had on board three horses, a dog, some pigs, geese, and canaries, and there was a perpetual neighing and barking and grunting and cackling, as if it had been a farm-yard.

The first days in the Chinese Sea presented little change from what it had been in the Pacific, and we moved slowly and calmly on. On the 6th we saw the coast of China, and towards evening we were not a hundred miles from Macao. With considerable impatience I awaited the following morning, hoping now soon to tread the long wished for Chinese shore, but in the middle of the night the wind changed, and before the next we were driven nearly 400 miles off. The barometer too fell so rapidly that we feared the typhoon, and made on board all preparations for the reception of this dangerous guest. But the hurricane did not come after all, or it passed at a great distance from us, and we had nothing more than a trifling storm of very short duration.

On the 9th we cast anchor in the roads of Macao. The town is delightfully situated on the sea-shore, surrounded by fine hills ; and the palace of the Portuguese governor, the convent of Guia, the fortifications, and some other handsome buildings have a picturesque appearance from the sea.

CHINA.

Macao.—Hong Kong.—Victoria.—Voyage in a Chinese Junk.—The Tsi-Kiang.—Whampoa.—Canton.—Mode of Life of Europeans.—The Chinese Manners and Customs.—Criminals and Pirates.—Murder of M. Vauchée.—Walks and Excursions.

A YEAR ago I should have little thought there was any chance of my becoming acquainted with this remarkable country, not merely from books but in my proper person ; that the shaven heads and long tails and cunning little eyes, as we see them in pictures and on tea chests, would have presented themselves in living forms before me. But scarcely was our anchor dropped before several Chinese already stood upon our deck, whilst numbers of others appeared in boats surrounding us, and displaying in pretty order fruits, pastry, and various kinds of beautiful works, so that the space round the ship looked like a fair. Some among them lauded in broken English the treasures they had brought, but after all they got but little for their trouble, for our crew bought only fruit and cigars.

Captain Jurianse now hired a boat and we rowed ashore, but on landing the first thing we had to do was to pay half a Spanish dollar each to a mandarin. I heard that this abuse was shortly after abolished. We had to go to one of the Portuguese houses of business, and in doing so passed through a great part of the town ; for Europeans, women as well as men, can now go about freely here, without as in other Chinese towns being exposed to the danger of being stoned. In those streets which are exclusively inhabited by Chinese, things looked very lively and bustling. The men were sitting in groups playing dominoes in the streets, and in the shops of the locksmiths, tailors, shoemakers, &c., there was working, gossiping, gambling, and dancing going on at once. I was greatly amused at the Chinese mode of eating with two little sticks, which they manage with great adroitness ; it is only in eating rice that they seem to labour under difficulties, as it will not hold together. The plan is therefore to bring the vessel containing it as near as possible to the mouth, which is held in readiness wide open, and then dexterously shove a heap into the expectant aperture. In performing this operation it happens of course often that a portion falls back again into the dish, but that is of no consequence ; with fluid food they make use of China spoons. My stay at Macao proved to be an exceedingly short one, for as our captain found there was no chance of doing any business there, he resolved to go to sea the next day, but he kindly offered to take me with him as a guest. His invitation was so much the more welcome to me, as I had not a single letter of introduction to Macao, and the opportunities of going to Hong Kong are not at all frequent.

Our vessel, on account of the shallowness of the water, lay rather far from the land, by no means out of the reach of the pirates, who are here so numerous and audacious, that it was found necessary at night to take all possible precaution, and set a double-watch, especially as a year or two before a brig had been plundered by them on this very spot, and the crew killed. In the middle of the night, a shampan (a smaller vessel than a junk) rowed up to the ship, and the leader delivered a note to the watch, saying it came from the captain, who was not on board. As the sailor advanced to the lantern to read it, the pirate struck him a blow on the back of the head that felled him to the ground. The rest of the gang, who had been concealed in the shampan, then climbed up on all sides of the deck, and soon made themselves masters of the sleeping sailors.

The distance from Macao to Hong Kong is about sixty leagues, and as you are continually passing bays, gulfs, and groups of islands, the voyage is varied and interesting.

The English obtained the island of Hong Kong from the Chinese in 1842, and founded upon it the seaport of Victoria, which already contains many palace-like buildings of freestone. Merchants receive land gratis from the government, on condition of building upon it, and many on the first occupation of the island began buildings on a grand scale, which they would now gladly sell for half their cost price, since trade has been far less profitable than was expected ; nay, in some instances, they would be willing to give up their land and the foundations laid upon it, merely to be released from the necessity of completing the buildings. The situation of Victoria is not very pleasing, as it is surrounded by naked hills ;

it has a decidedly European aspect, so that if it were not for the Chinese workmen and small dealers in the streets and booths you could hardly believe yourself on Chinese ground. No Chinese woman was to be seen in the streets, so that I was not sure it might not be unsafe for me to wander about as I did. I never experienced, however, the smallest insult, and even the curiosity of the people was by no means troublesome.

In Victoria I had the pleasure of becoming acquainted with the celebrated Mr. Gutzlaff, and with four other German missionaries. They were studying the Chinese language, allowing their heads to be shaven, and wearing the Chinese costume, long tails included. It happened after a few days that an opportunity presented itself for me to go to Canton, but in a Chinese junk. Mr. Pustan, a merchant of Victoria, who had received me in a very friendly manner, strongly dissuaded me from trusting myself without any protection to the Chinese, and thought I should either hire a boat for myself or get a place in the steamer; but for my limited means these plans were too expensive, as neither would have cost less than twelve dollars, while the price on the junk was only three. The appearance and manner of the Chinese too was not such as to occasion me any fear, so I put my pistols in order and went quietly on board the junk. It was raining violently, and just getting dark, and I therefore went down into the cabin, to amuse myself by looking at my Chinese fellow voyagers. The company was certainly not select, but not at all indecorous in behaviour, so that I had no fear of remaining among them; some were playing at dominoes, and others on a sort of mandolin with three strings, which uttered most dismal music, and nearly all were smoking and gossiping, and drinking tea without sugar out of little cups, which were offered to me from all sides: no Chinese, either rich or poor, drinks either water, or anything stronger, but constantly unsugared weak tea.

I did not go into my cabin till rather a late hour, and then I made the unpleasing discovery that it was not water tight, and that the rain was coming in. Immediately, however, that the captain of the junk was made aware of this, he found me another place, in company with two Chinese women, who, as well as the men, were smoking tobacco, and out of pipes not larger than thimbles, which required to be stuffed afresh every four or five whiffs. My neighbours soon remarked that I had no *head-stool*, and they would not desist from their entreaties till I accepted one from them. These stools, made of bamboo or strong pasteboard, and about eight inches high, are made use of instead of pillows, and are really more comfortable than might be supposed.

Early in the morning I hastened on deck to see the entrance into the mouth of the Yang-Tsi Kiang, (also called the Tiger River,) but we were already so far up that there was no more mouth to be seen; I saw it, however, on my return: it is one of the largest rivers of China; and at a short distance from its entrance into the sea it has a breadth of nearly eight miles, but at the actual mouth it is so hemmed in by rocks that it loses half its breadth. The country is beautiful, and some fortifications on the summit of a hill give it a very romantic effect. At Hoo-man, or Whampoa, the stream divides into several arms, of which the one leading to Canton is called the Pearl river, and here ships drawing much water have to anchor. Along the banks of the Pearl river extend immense rice plantations, intermingled with fruit trees and bananas: the latter often form beautiful arcades; but they are planted more for utility than ornament, as they consolidate the ground, and prevent its being entirely washed away by the abundant irrigation required for the rice. Pretty country houses, in the true Chinese style, with fantastic jagged and •peaked roofs, and coloured tiles, come into view from time to time, lying in the shade of groups of trees; and various kinds of pagodas, from three to nine stories high, rise on small hills near the villages, and draw attention from a great distance. There were many fortifications, but they looked more like great unroofed houses than anything else.

As you advance towards Canton, the villages begin to follow each other very closely; but they have a miserable appearance, and are mostly built on stakes close on the river, and lying before them are numerous boats, many of them also serving as dwellings. The river now becomes more and more animated, and covered with vessels of all sizes and of the strangest forms. There were junks, the back part of which rose two stories above the water, and which looked like houses with lofty windows and galleries, and covered by a roof; they are often of immense size, and several thousand tons burthen. Then came the Chinese ships of war, flat, broad, and long, and carrying twenty or thirty guns: mandarins' boats, with their painted doors and windows, carved galleries, and coloured silk flags; and, best of all, the flower boats decorated with wreaths and garlands, and pretty arabesques. The interior of these flower boats consists of a saloon and several cabinets, furnished with looking glasses, silk hangings, glass lustres, and coloured lanterns, between which are suspended ornamental baskets filled with fresh flowers, so that they have quite a fairy-land aspect. The flower boats remain at anchor night and day, and serve for places of entertainment; plays are acted in them, and dancing and conjuring tricks performed. Women of good character are never to be seen in them; the entrance of Europeans is not exactly prohibited, but they would not be likely to receive a very flattering reception, should they make their appearance, and might even meet with serious ill-treatment. Besides all these, there were thousands of shampans, some anchored, some cruising, and darting about; fishermen casting their nets; people of all ages bathing and swimming; and children romping and tumbling about in the boats, so that one dreaded every moment to see them fall overboard: but careful parents tie the little ones to hollow gourds, or bladders filled with air, so that if they fall into the water they may not sink. All these varied occupations, this unwearied life and activity, affords such picturesque effects as can hardly be conceived without being witnessed.

Since these few years past, the entrance into and residence in the factories of Canton has been permitted to European women, so that I did not feel much hesitation in landing from the junk. It required consideration, however, by what means I was to reach the abode of Mr. Agassiz, to whom I was recommended. I could, as yet, speak no Chinese word, and had to make myself understood by signs; I succeeded, however, in making my captain comprehend that I had no money with me, but that if he would take me to the factory I would pay him, and he agreed to accompany me thither.

When Mr. Agassiz saw me come in in this unceremonious manner, and heard the mode of my journey, and of my having walked from the junk to his house, he appeared excessively surprised; and it was then that I first learned how much risk I had run in venturing into the streets of Canton, in company only with a Chinese: I was told I might regard it as quite a peculiar piece of good fortune that I had not been grossly insulted, and even stoned by the populace, and in such a case my Chinese escort would infallibly have taken to flight, and left me to my fate.

I had certainly remarked that on my way from the ship to the factory, that old and young had called and hooted after me, and pointed their fingers,—that the people had run out of the shops, and that by degrees we had quite a procession following us. But there was nothing to be done but to put a good face on the matter, and I therefore marched fearlessly on; and it may be that precisely because I showed no fear, no harm happened to me. Since the last war with the English the hatred against Europeans has been on the increase, and it has been embittered against the women by a Chinese prophecy, which declares that a woman shall one day conquer the Celestial Empire. I feared, therefore, that it would be to little purpose for me to remain in Canton, and was beginning to consider whether I might not do better to go to the north of China, where the people and the nobles are easier of access; but I fortunately became acquainted with a German, a Mr. Carlovitz, who had passed some years in Canton, and who offered to become my mentor, if I would only wait with patience for the arrival of the European post, which was expected in a few days: during this period the minds of merchants are so excited that they have not leisure for any other thought than that of their correspondence. I had to wait eight days—until the steamer arrived and again departed—but the reception I met with was so very kind and cordial, that the time did not appear at all long; especially as I had thus an opportunity of studying a little the mode of life of the European residents.

Very few Europeans bring their families to China, and fewer still to Canton, where women and children live almost as prisoners, and can at the utmost only leave the house in a closed litter. Besides this, everything is so excessively dear that you might live as cheaply in London. An apartment of six rooms and a kitchen costs from seven to eight hundred dollars. Servants require from four to eight dollars a month, and female servants nine or ten, for no Chinese woman will serve a European without being very highly paid for it. Since, too, custom requires a separate servant for every different kind of work, you have to keep a great number.

A family of not more than four persons will need twelve or more. In the first place every member of the family must have one servant exclusively to himself,—then there must be cooks, waiting women, nurses, and coolies for the commoner kinds of work, such as cleansing rooms, and carrying wood and water; and with all this crowd you are badly served, for if one goes out, and you happen to want his particular branch of service, you must wait till he comes back, for no other will supply his place.

The whole household is under the guidance of an officer called a comprador, to whom all the plate, furniture, linen, &c., is given in charge, and who engages the other servants, feeds them, and is answerable for their fidelity.   In consideration of this he deducts for himself two dollars per month from the wages of each.   It is the comprador who makes all the purchases of provisions, pays the house bills, and at the end of the month gives you in the total sum, without troubling himself too much with details.   In some houses the comprador, besides fulfilling all these domestic duties, is also cashier for the house of business.   Hundreds of thousands of dollars pass through his hands, for the goodness of which he must vouch, and for paying or receiving large sums he has his assistants, who examine every piece with unexampled rapidity.   They will take a whole handful of them, and tossing up every piece ring it with the thumb and middle finger, and examine the reverse side as it falls back into their hands.   In a few hours they will thus examine many thousands of pieces, and this care is necessary on account of the many false dollars in circulation.   On every piece found good, the house stamp is struck, so that at last the coins become so broad and thin, that they fairly fall to pieces, but the separate pieces lose nothing of their value, being always estimated by weight.   Besides dollars, pure silver in ingots is in circulation, and the practice is to cut off larger or smaller pieces, as they are wanted. Europeans seldom carry any money about them, but it is all kept in the room of the comprador, who has a per-centage upon all money transactions, and knows very well how to make them for himself out of the house bill—a matter of course, as he receives no salary.   Allowing for this, he is usually trustworthy, and indeed a mandarin high in office (to whom he has to give security) is answerable for him.

The daily manner of life of the Europeans settled here is the following.   A cup of tea is taken immediately after rising, then a cold bath.   About nine follows the more substantial breakfast, consisting of fried cutlets, cold roast meat, eggs, bread and butter, and tea.   Every one then departs to his employment till dinner, which is generally at four o'clock.   The general dishes are turtle soup, highly seasoned curries, roast meat, ragouts, and pastry. All the dishes, curry and rice excepted, are dressed in the English mode by Chinese cooks. Cheese and fruit are taken after dinner, pine-apples, mangoes, *long-yen*, and *lytschi:* which latter fruit the Chinese esteem as the most delicious in the world; it is about the size of a nut, has a reddish brown rough shell, very white and tender pulp, and a black kernel. The *long-yen* is something like it, but rather smaller, and somewhat watery in flavour; I did not think either very good. The pine apples are larger than those reared in European forcing houses, but inferior I thought to them in sweetness and aroma.

The liquors drunk are Portuguese wine, and English beer. Ice broken into small pieces and wrapped in a napkin, is offered with both; though this is rather an expensive article, as it is brought from America. In the evening tea is again drank.

A large punka is kept constantly going during the meals by a cord carried through the room like a bell wire, by means of which a servant works the punka in an ante or lower room.

Living is very dear for Europeans—for the cost of a small establishment cannot be reckoned at less than 6,000 dollars yearly—a large sum considering what is got for it; neither carriages nor horses are kept, there are no public amusements; the solitary recreation of many gentlemen consists in a boat, for which they pay seven dollars a month, or in a small pleasure-garden laid out by the Europeans of Canton, where they walk occasionally of an evening. It lies opposite the factory, surrounded by a wall on three sides, the fourth is washed by the Pearl river. The Chinese on the other hand live at very small expense; a man can subsist very well on 60 cash a day—(1,200 cash make a dollar.) He can hire a boat for half a dollar a day, which will bring him in enough for a family of from six to nine persons to live on. It must be confessed, however, that the Chinese are not fastidious in the matter of eating; they devour dogs, cats, rats, and mice, the blood of every animal, the entrails of birds; and even, I have been told, silk-worms, grubs, and animals that have died a natural death; but rice is their chief article of food, and serves them not only as a dish, but as bread. It is very cheap, from one and three-fourths to two and a half dollars the pikul, of 125 pounds.

The dress of both sexes, of the lower classes, consists of wide trowsers and a long upper robe, generally disgustingly dirty; indeed a Chinese is no friend to washing either his garments or his person, and generally wears his trowsers till they fall to pieces. The upper robe is made of silk or nankeen, dark blue, brown, or black. In the colder season, they put one summer garment over another and bind them together with a girdle.

As great pride is taken in the length and thickness of the tail of hair, it is often increased by false or black silk interwoven. When they are at work, the tail is coiled round the neck, but it must always be let down on entering a room, as it is contrary to all Chinese notions of propriety to appear with it twisted up. The women comb their hair back from their foreheads, and bind it round their heads in a very artist-like style ; it must take a good deal of time to construct the edifice, but is seldom done more than once a week. Both men and women cover their heads occasionally with hats of thin bamboo, often three feet in diameter, which are admirable protectors from the sun and rain, excessively light and almost indestructible. The poorer classes go barefoot ; their houses, of brick or wood, are miserable hovels, and the inside is worthy of the out—a wretched table, a few chairs, and bamboo mats, head-stools, and old coverlets form the whole furniture ; a few flower-pots, however, are never wanting. The cheapest of all dwellings is a boat : one half of which is reserved for the family, and the other let out either as a ferry or excursion boat, generally under the management of the wife. Notwithstanding the limited space, for the whole boat is scarcely twenty-five feet in length, it is usually kept extremely clean. Every nook is put to use, and place for a diminutive altar always found ; all the cooking and washing for the family is done in their half of the boat, yet no disagreeable sight shocks the temporary possessor of the other half, and rarely is a whimper from the poor little ones heard. The mother steers with her youngest child tied to her back ; the elder children have often similar burdens with which they climb and jump about without taking any heed of the unfortunate infants. I was often pained to see the head of a newly born baby flung from side to side with every caper of its juvenile nurse, or exposed wholly unsheltered to the burning sun. One who has not seen can hardly form an idea of the poverty and privations of a boat-dwelling Chinese family.

The Chinese are accused of putting many of their children, especially the weakly ones, to death. It is said that they either suffocate them immediately after birth, throw them into the river, or expose them in the street. The latter is the most cruel of all, as the wretched babes become the prey of the numerous swine or masterless dogs. It is generally the girls who are thus sacrificed, as the boys are bound to support their parents in their old age, and in case of the father's death the eldest son is bound to supply his place, and has the same claim to unconditional obedience from all his brothers and sisters. The Chinese esteem it an honour to be a grandfather, and make known this dignity to the world by wearing a moustache ; these scanty grey decorations excite the more notice as the young men wear neither moustache or beard.

It is exceedingly difficult, almost impossible, for a foreigner to give any very accurate information of Chinese habits and customs, but I saw all I possibly could, never missed an opportunity of mingling with the people, and carefully noted down all I saw. One morning, as I was going out, I met fifteen criminals all bearing the *Cang-gue*, or wooden yoke, in which they are led about the streets as a spectacle to the people. The *Cang-gue* consists of two large pieces of wood fitting into each other and having one to three openings, through which the head and one or both hands are drawn, according to the greatness of the crime. Such a yoke weighs from fifty to a hundred pounds, and weighs so heavily upon the back and shoulders that the poor criminal is unable to feed himself, and must wait till some compassionate person lifts the food to his mouth : such a punishment is inflicted for periods varying from a few days to several months, and in the latter case it is almost always fatal.

Another punishment, beating with a bamboo stick, if given on a tender part of the body, often causes death after the fifteenth stroke. Some of the punishments are of such hideous severity that our capital punishments of strangling or beheading seem mild in comparison : the Chinese endeavour to obtain the ends of justice by flaying alive, crushing the limbs, cutting the sinews of the feet, &c., and I was told that in certain cases criminals are sawed in two or starved to death. In the first case the poor wretch is pressed between two planks and sawed lengthways, in the second buried up to his chin in the earth and so left till death puts an end to his sufferings, or the *Cang-gue* is put on him and from day to day less and less food given him, till at last it is reduced to a single grain of rice.

In the year 1846 *four thousand* men were beheaded in Canton ; it is true they were the criminals of two provinces which together

E

reckon nineteen millions of inhabitants, yet it is a frightful number. Were the criminals really so many, or is the punishment of death so lightly inflicted, or is both the case ?

I came once by chance upon the place of execution and saw, to my unspeakable horror, a long row of bleeding heads set upon poles. The relations are permitted to remove the bodies.

The population of China consists of many and very different races, whose characteristics I am, unfortunately, unable to give, on account of the shortness of my stay in China. The people whom I saw in Canton, Hong Kong, and Macao were of middling stature; the countryman, the porter, the workman, is much sunburnt; the upper classes, generally white skinned. The face is broad, the eyes small, oblique, far apart, the nose broad, and the mouth wide. The fingers of many I found to be extraordinarily long and thin. Aristocratic nails are generally half an inch long; one man I saw who had them above an inch in length, but only on the left hand: with this hand he was unable to lift a flat object without laying the hand flat upon it and clutching it between the fingers. Women of rank are generally inclined to corpulence, which is greatly admired in man or woman.

Although I had heard so much of the little feet of the Chinese women, the first sight of one excited my highest astonishment. The sight of these feet *in naturâ* was procured me by a missionary's wife, Madame Balt. The four smaller toes seemed to me grown into the foot; the great toe was left in its natural position. The fore part of the foot was so tightly bound with strong broad ligatures that all the growth is forced into height instead of length and breadth, and formed a thick lump at the ancle ; the under part measured scarcely four inches long and an inch and a half wide. The foot is constantly bound up in white linen or silk and strong broad ribbons, and stuck in a very high-heeled shoe.

To my surprise these crippled fair ones tripped about with tolerable quickness ; to be sure they waddled like geese, but they did manage to get up and down stairs without the help of a stick.

The boat dwellers being the poorest are the only class of Chinese who do not cultivate this peculiar species of beauty. In families of rank all the girls are condemned to it, in the lower classes only the eldest daughter. The value of a bride depends upon the smallness of her foot.

The crippling process is not begun before the completion of the first, sometimes not till the third year : and the foot is not pressed into an iron shoe, as some have asserted, but only tightly bound with very strong ligatures.

Although the religion of the Chinese permits several wives, they are far behind the Mahometans in their use of the privilege; the rich have seldom more than from six to twelve, and the poor are content with one.

I visited in Canton the workshops of the different artists and artisans as much as possible. My first visit was to the painters, and I must admit the vivacity and splendour of their colouring : of perspective they are wholly ignorant; the figures and objects in the back emulate those of the foreground in size and brightness of colour, and rivers and seas often hover at the top of the picture among the clouds. On the other hand they are excellent copyists, especially of portraits : I saw portraits so well drawn and admirably coloured, that European artists of reputation need not have been ashamed of them. The extraordinary skill of the Chinese in carving ivory, tortoiseshell, and wood is well known. I saw little work-tables of the value of 600 dollars. The mats, baskets, &c., of bamboo, are equally excellent. The beauty of the Chinese porcelain too, is undeniable; tea-cups and other objects of small size are exquisitely fine, transparent as glass, and with brilliant colours, but the drawing is stiff and bad : some vases, four feet high, which I saw, were not transparent. The goldsmiths' work I thought clumsy and tasteless; but their silk and crape stuffs I consider unsurpassable, the latter, especially in beauty and substance, are far superior to either French or English manufacture.

In music the good Chinese are scarcely above the level of savages. They have instruments, but not the skill to use them; violins, guitars, lutes (all with metal strings), wind instruments, cymbals, drums, and kettle-drums, but they are ignorant of melody, harmony, and execution : and they scrape, scratch, and beat their instruments in a style that has all the effect of a regular cat's concert. I had the pleasure of hearing many such from the mandarins and flower boats on the Pearl river. In the arts of trickery and deceit of all kinds, however, the Europeans certainly cannot come near them. Honour seems an unknown thing among them. If their roguery is found out they simply observe, " Such a one was cleverer than I was !" I was told that when they sell living animals, calves, swine, or the like, whose value is determined by weight, it was a common practice to make the animals swallow large quantities of water and even stones. The flesh of dead birds they have a way of so puffing up as to give them the appearance of being perfectly fresh and fat; and lying and cheating are not confined to the lowest classes, for these estimable qualities may be found amongst the highest officers.

It is well known that the seas of Canton swarm with pirates, yet nothing is ever done either to punish them or diminish their numbers, as the mandarins do not think it beneath their dignity to go shares with them. The commerce with opium is forbidden, yet so much is smuggled into the country every year that its value exceeds that of the tea exported. The merchants come to an understanding with the mandarins and public officers, a certain sum is paid for every pikul, and not unfrequently the mandarin will bring the whole cargo to land under his own flag.

It is said that an extensive establishment for coining false money is known to exist near Hong Kong, which carries on its operations quite undisturbed simply by paying tribute to the mandarins in authority. A short time ago some pirate ships ran aground near Canton and the commanders were captured. Their companions wrote to the government to free them, and threatened, in case of refusal, to set some towns on fire: every one was convinced that a sum of money had been sent with the letter, for shortly after it was announced that the pirates had escaped.

An affair that took place while I was at Canton, and caused me great alarm, was proof enough of the weakness and wickedness of the Chinese government.

On the 8th of August, Mr. Agassiz went with a friend to Whampoa intending to return in the evening. I was left alone in the house with the Chinese servants. Mr. Agassiz did not return; at last about one o'clock in the morning I heard loud voices without, and a violent knocking at the house-door. At first I supposed Mr. Agassiz had returned, and only wondered he should make so much noise; but I soon became aware that the noise was not in our house, but in one opposite. It was easy to make such a mistake, as the streets are very narrow, and the windows stand open day and night. I soon heard people exclaim, "Get up and dress yourself—it is horrible, it is dreadful—good God! where did it happen?" I sprang out of bed, and threw on my clothes, thinking there must be a bad fire or an insurrection broken out. A report that such a thing might be daily expected, and that no mercy would be shown to Europeans, was very current at this time—and I was alone, surrounded by Chinese !

Seeing a gentleman at a window near, I called out to him, and begged him to tell me what had happened. He said that news had just been brought him that two of his friends, who had gone to Hong Kong, (Whampoa lies on the road to Hong Kong,) had been attacked by pirates ; that one was murdered and the other wounded. He left the window directly after, without mentioning the name of the unfortunate man, so that I was left the whole night in terror lest it should be Mr. Agassiz. Happily this was not the case ; at five o'clock he returned home, and I then heard that the victim was a M. Vauchée, a Swiss, who had frequently spent the evening with us. I had seen him the very day before in the house of a neighbour, where he had entertained us with some beautiful songs and quartettes. This was about eight in the evening ; at nine he went on board the boat, it sailed at ten, and about a quarter of an hour after he met his tragical end, though hundreds of shampans were on the river at the time. Vauchée had intended to go to Hong Kong, and there embark in a larger vessel for Tschang-hai, a new port opened by the English in 1842. He had Swiss watches with him to the value of 40,000 francs, and had been telling his friends how careful he had been in packing that none of his servants should know anything about them. Unfortunately that was not the case, for the pirates have their spies in every household, and they were only too well informed.

A day seldom passed on which I did not hear of some act of violence, and an attack upon all Europeans was hourly expected. Many of the merchants were prepared for flight, and almost all had a formidable provision of muskets, pistols, and sabres in their counting-houses. Happily the Chinese populace did not put their threat in execution.

The Chinese are in the highest degree cowardly ; they talk big indeed when they are in no danger, but where resistance may be expected they will be in no hurry to attack : I believe a dozen good European soldiers might at any time put hundreds of them to flight. A baser, falser, crueller people than the Chinese I never met with ; and one proof of this is, that their greatest diversion consists in tormenting animals.

In spite of the ill-will of the people I ventured upon many excursions, in which Mr. Von Carlovitz had the kindness and the patience to accompany me, and exposed himself to many dangers on my account ; he bore with the greatest indifference the abuse of the mob, when they followed us and gave vent to their wrath at the boldness of the European woman ; and I saw, under his kind protection, more than any woman ever saw in China before.

Our first visit was to the celebrated temple Honan, said to be one of the finest in China. This temple with its numerous subsidiary buildings and extensive gardens is surrounded by a high wall. We entered a large outer court, at the extremity of which a colossal gate led into an inner court : under the arch of this portal stand two statues of war-gods, eighteen feet high, in threatening attitudes and with frightfully distorted faces ; they are to guard the entrance from evil genii. A second similar portal, under which the four heavenly kings are placed, leads to a third court, in which is the chief temple, 100 feet long, and of equal width. The flat roof, from which depend a multitude of glass lustres, lamps, artificial flowers, and coloured ribbons, rests on rows of wooden pillars. The numerous statues, altars, censers, vases of flowers, candelabras, and other ornaments, reminded us involuntarily of a Catholic church.

In the fore-ground stand three altars, behind which are three statues, representing Buddha as the past, the present, and the future, of colossal size, and in a sitting posture. By chance a service was going on when we entered,—a kind of mass for the dead, celebrated at the charge of a mandarin for his deceased wife. Before the right and left altar stood priests, whose robes, as well as the ceremonial observance, strikingly resembled those of Roman Catholics. The mandarin himself was praying before the middle altar, attended by two servants armed with large fans. He kissed the ground repeatedly, and every time he did so three perfumed wax tapers were put into his hand, which he first elevated in the air, and then handed to the priests, who placed them before the images of the god, without lighting them however. The choir consisted of three men, one of whom scraped a stringed instrument, another struck upon a metal ball, and the third played the flute.

Beside this chief temple there are a number of small ones, all decorated with statues of gods. The twenty-four gods of mercy and Kwanfootse, a demi-god of war, seemed to enjoy particular reverence. The former have four, six, and even eight arms. All these divinities, including Buddha himself, are made of wood, gilded and painted in gaudy colours. In the Temple of Mercy we had like to have met with a disagreeable adventure ; a Bonze offered me and my companions a couple of wax tapers to light in honour of their god ; we were about to comply as a matter of civility, when an American missionary, who accompanied us, snatched them out of our hands angrily, and gave them back to the priests, declaring that our compliance would be an act of idolatry. The priest took up the affair seriously, immediately closed the door and called to his brethren, who came flocking from all sides, and abused us terribly, all the while pressing upon us in an alarming manner. With considerable difficulty we fought our way through the crowd, and got out of the temple.

When the scuffle was over, our guide led us to the house of the Sacred Swine, a handsome stone hall ; but in spite of all the care bestowed upon these singular objects of reverence, their odour was so offensive, that we could only approach them with compressed noses. These creatures are fed and cherished so long as they live, and are suffered to die a natural death. We saw only one pair of these fortunate grunters, and were told the number rarely exceeded three pairs. The dwelling of a bonze which we visited pleased me better than the swine-palace ; there were but two rooms, a sitting and bed-room, but they were neatly and conveniently arranged. The walls of the sitting-room were ornamented with wood carving, the furniture was old and elegantly wrought, a small altar stood against the further wall, and the floor was paved with large stone slabs.

We found here an opium smoker ; he lay stretched on the ground on a mat, and had beside him some tea-cups, some fruit, a small lamp and several pipes, the heads of which were smaller than thimbles; out of one he was imbibing the intoxicating vapour. I was told that there were persons who smoke from twenty to thirty grains a day. As he had not yet reached the unconscious state, he dragged himself up with some difficulty and laid his pipe aside ; his eyes were fixed and vacant, his face deadly pale—it was a depressing and pitiable spectacle. In conclusion, we were taken into the garden, where the bodies of the bonzes are burnt after death—a particular distinction, other persons being simply buried.

A plain mausoleum about thirty feet square, and a few small private monuments, is all there is to be seen ; and neither were handsome. The large one contained the bones of the consumed bodies ; in the smaller, rich Chinese were buried, whose friends must pay enormously for the honour of such a burial place. At a little distance stands a tower, eighteen feet high, and about eight in diameter, in the floor of which is a small hollow where the fire is kindled ; over the hollow stands an arm-chair, wherein the deceased bonze is placed in full costume. Wood and dry twigs are then heaped round, kindled, and the door fast closed. After some hours it is re-opened, the ashes scattered round the tower, and the bones laid aside till the mausoleum is opened, which is only done once a year.

The beautiful water rose or lotus (*Nymphæa Nelumbo*), of which China is the native land, is the greatest ornament of these gardens. The Chinese are such lovers of this flower that they often make ponds in their gardens on purpose for it. The flowers have a diameter of six inches, and are generally pure white ; sometimes but very rarely of a pale rose colour ; the seeds resemble the hazel nut in size and taste, and the roots when boiled are said to have the flavour of artichokes.

Above a hundred bonzes have their dwelling in the Temple Honan. In their house-dress they are only to be distinguished from the common Chinese by their wholly shorn heads ; and none of the priests seem to rejoice in the smallest respect from their countrymen.

Our second excursion was to the Halfway Pagoda, so called by the English, because it is situated halfway between Canton and Whampoa. We went thither by the Pearl river. The pagoda stands on a little eminence in the midst of extensive rice fields, has nine stories, and a height of 170 feet. The circumference is not great, and the size all the way up being nearly the same, it has the appearance of a tower. It was formerly one of the most celebrated in China, but has been long disused : the interior was quite empty, and no intermediate ceiling prevented the eye from losing itself at the summit of the building. On the outside, narrow balconies, without any kind of balustrade, and attainable by excessively steep stairs run round each story. As these projecting balconies are formed of coloured tiles, and floored with brightly painted clay, the effect is very pretty. The edges of the tiles arranged obliquely in rows, with each edge raised about four inches above the next, have, at a distance, the effect of fret-work ; and from the beauty of its colour, and fineness of the clay made use of, they might easily be mistaken for porcelain.

Whilst we were looking at the pagoda the people of the village gathered about us, and as they seemed tolerably quiet, we ventured upon a visit to the village itself. The houses, or rather huts, were built of a kind of brick, with flat roofs, but had nothing peculiar in their construction. There was no interior ceiling ; the only covering was the roof of the house, the floor of beaten clay, and the partition wall chiefly composed of bamboo matting ; there was very little furniture, and that little exceedingly dirty. In the midst of the village stood some small temples, with a few dim lamps burning before the chief idol.

The most remarkable thing about this village was the enormous number of domestic birds in and about the houses. It really required considerable care to avoid treading on the creatures as they walked ; they are artificially hatched, as in Egypt. As we were leaving the village, we saw two shampans approach the shore, out of which leaped a number of brown, half naked, and mostly armed men, who rapidly traversing the rice-fields, came straight towards our party. We took them for pirates, and awaited their approach with some anxiety : if they meant mischief we were lost ; for here, at a distance from Canton, and surrounded by Chinese, who would unquestion-ably have lent them a helping hand, it would be easy to despatch us, if they were so inclined.

But the leader, accosting us in broken English, announced him-self as the captain of a Siamese ship-of-war. He said that he had brought over the Governor of Bankok, who was going thence to Pekin, and by degrees we recovered from our fright, so far as even to accept the captain's invitation to go on board his ship. He took us into his boat, which he steered himself, and did the honours of his vessel in person. There was nothing very attractive in it : the crew were a rude, wild-looking set, and all alike so ragged and dirty, that it was impossible to distinguish officers from men. The ship mounted twelve guns ; the crew was sixty-eight in number. The captain entertained us with English beer and Portuguese wine ; and it was late in the evening when we reached home.

The farthest excursion it is permitted to make from Canton extends to about eighty miles up the Pearl river. Mr. Agassiz

was so good as to procure me this pleasure. He hired a handsome
boat, furnished it amply with provisions, and requested a missionary, who had made the voyage several times, to accompany
me and Mr. Von Carlovitz. A missionary is the best escort one
can have in China ; for they speak the language of the country,
become acquainted with the people, and, within certain limits, go
about in tolerable freedom and security.

About a week before we ventured on our excursion, some young
men had made a similar attempt, but were fired upon from a
fortress on the river's bank, and compelled to return. As we
approached this fortress, our boatmen would not proceed till we
compelled them, and we too were favoured by a discharge from the
fort, but, fortunately, not till we had nearly passed it ; and
receiving no damage, we pursued our way without further hindrance, landed at several villages, entered the so-called " Lord's
Pagoda," and looked about us to our hearts' content. The country
was very beautiful ; extensive plains with fine groups of trees,
rice, sugar-cane, and tea plantations, and graceful hills ; the view
bounded in the distance by lofty mountains. On the declivities of
the hills we observed many upright monumental stones.

The Lord's Pagoda consists of three stories : the roof is peaked,
and the exterior much decorated with sculpture ; and round each
story winds a triple wreath of foliage. In the first and second
story, which were reached by excessively steep narrow steps, we
saw some small altars with carved idols : the third we were not
allowed to enter, under the pretence that there was nothing to
be seen in it.

The villages were all more or less like those we had seen in the
neighbourhood of the Halfway Pagoda.

In this excursion I had an opportunity of observing the manner
in which the missionaries manage their peculiar business. The
gentleman who had been so obliging as to accompany us, made use
of this voyage to scatter some of the good seed. He had packed
five hundred tracts in our boat, and as often as another boat
approached ours, which happened pretty frequently, he leaned as
far over the side as he could, held up his hand, furnished with
half a dozen tracts, and shouted and gesticulated for the people to
come nearer and receive the prize. If they did not comply with
the invitation, we rowed close to them, the missionary showered
down his tracts by dozens, and rejoiced in anticipation at the good

that was to result from this proceeding. When we reached a village the business was done on a yet more liberal scale : the servant was laden with a whole pack of tracts ; in a few minutes we were surrounded by curious lookers-on, and as quickly the cargo was discharged amongst them.

Every Chinese took what was offered—it cost him nothing ; and if he could not read (the tracts were written in the Chinese language) he had at least a stock of paper. Our friend returned home glowing with satisfaction. He had distributed 500 copies of his book among the Chinese! What delightful intelligence for the Missionary Society! what a splendid announcement for the religious periodicals!

Three months later, six young Englishmen made the same excursion up the Pearl river, stopping also at the villages and mixing with the country people ; but, unhappily, they all fell a sacrifice to Chinese fanaticism. The whole six were murdered under circumstances of horrible cruelty !

My wish to take a walk round the walls of Canton, an attempt no woman had ever yet ventured to make, was gratified by the kindness of the missionary ; but under the condition that I should put on male attire. We passed through a number of narrow streets, paved with broad stones. In every house we saw in some niche a small altar, from one to two feet high, before which lamps were burning : the quantity of oil wasted in this way must be enormous. By degrees the shops were opened, which resembled pretty little booths, as the front wall was entirely removed. The goods were contained partly in open chests, and partly displayed on tables, behind which the owners sat at work. In one corner a small flight of steps led to the upper part of the house.

As in the Turkish towns, each trade has a street to itself, the dealers in glass in one street, the silk merchants in another, &c. : the physicians, who are also the druggists, have their street apart also. Between the houses we saw many little temples, of which, however, the gods contented themselves with the ground floor, the upper ones being occupied by ordinary mortals.

The life and movement in the streets were very great, especially in those where provisions were sold. Women and girls of the lower class were walking about, making their purchases as in Europe. They were all unveiled, and many waddled like geese ; for, as I have before observed, the custom of crippling some of the women prevails in all classes. The throng was greatly increased by the number of porters carrying huge baskets laden with provisions on their shoulders, and shouting continually, now in praise of their wares, now bidding people get out of their way; sometimes the way will be stopped by the sedans of the wealthier inhabitants, which take up the whole width of the streets.

The care with which the Chinese cultivate every spot of earth is well known; as they have few cattle it follows that they have little manure, and hence the extreme care with which they seek for the article furnished by any and every living creature. The most disagreeable incident of the streets is meeting, as you do in every street—I had almost said at every step—persons bearing vessels full of all sorts of ordure.

All these little streets were built along the wall; and low doors, closed in the evening, lead into the interior of the city, which no foreigner dare profane.

Some few sailors and others, in their rambles about the wall, have passed through these doors without knowing whither they were going, till made aware of their mistake by a shower of stones.

After we had walked at least some miles, forcing our way through these close alleys, we emerged again into the open air, and from a small elevation near the wall gained a tolerable view over the town. The wall is about sixty feet high, in many places overgrown with grass, bushes, and parasite plants. The town looked, from the hill, a confused mass of little houses, with a few trees growing among them, for we could discern no wide streets or squares, nor any building of architectural importance, with the exception of one pagoda of five stories.

The road led us over a hilly but fertile country, and well cultivated fields and meadows. Many of these hills serve as cemeteries, and are covered with mounds, against which were laid gravestones about two feet high: some had inscriptions, and there were also family vaults excavated in the hill side, and marked out by masonry in the form of a horse-shoe.

The Chinese do not bury all their dead. The coffins are sometimes placed on wooden benches, two feet in height, within small stone buildings, consisting of two side walls and a roof, the other two sides being left open. The coffins are hollowed trunks of trees, and very massive.

All the hamlets we passed through were populous, but the inhabitants looked very poor and very dirty. In passing through some of the streets we were obliged to hold our noses, and would willingly have closed our eyes also, so nauseous were the disgusting sights of sick people, whose bodies were covered with eruptions, boils, and tumours.

In every hamlet we saw swine and domestic fowl in abundance, but only three horses and one cow buffalo ; both horses and cow were of particularly small race.

When we were nearly at the end of our walk we met a funeral procession. Its approach was announced by horrible discordant sounds, intended for music ; and we had hardly time to get out of the way when the train came by, in as much haste as if they had been running away from something. First ran the worthy musicians, then followed the mourners, then two empty sedan chairs, and lastly came the coffin,—a trunk of a tree hollowed,—the priests, and a crowd of idlers.

The high priest wore a sort of white fool's cap, with three points ; the mourners, all men, had each a white cloth, either wrapped round the head or the arm,—white being the mourning colour in China.

I was fortunate enough to see some of the summer palaces and gardens of the upper classes ; that of the mandarin Hauquau was the handsomest. The house was tolerably large, with very broad stately terraces : the windows were turned towards the interior, and the roof like those of Europe, except that it was somewhat flatter. The projecting roofs, with zig-zag edges and points, with the numerous little bells and painted tiles and bricks, are used for pagodas and summer pavilions, but not for dwelling-houses. On the principal door two figures of gods were painted, to guard the entrance from evil spirits.

The fore-part of the house contained several reception rooms, with one side entirely open to the garden on the ground floor ; in winter these sides are hung with matting ; the upper one opened on a magnificent terrace, adorned with flowers, and commanding a splendid view of the thronged river, the country around, and the suburbs of Canton.

The saloons were surrounded by pretty little cabinets, from which the only partitions were transparent pictures, painted with flowers, or beautifully written moral sentences on bamboo, fine and delicate as a gauze veil.   By the number of chairs and sofas placed against the walls, we concluded that the Chinese are no strangers to large parties.   There were arm-chairs formed of a single piece of wood, very richly carved, others of which the seats were slabs of marble or porcelain ; European looking-glasses, table-clocks, vases, and console tables of Florentine mosaic, or coloured marble.   The number of lamps and lanterns suspended from the ceiling was amazing : they were of various materials,—glass, transparent horn, coloured gauze and paper,—and decorated with beads, fringes, and tassels : some lamps were also hung against the wall, and when all is illuminated the effect must be magical.

As we had been so fortunate as to reach the house without being stoned, we took courage to visit the extensive pleasure-grounds belonging to the mandarin, situated about three miles from the house, on a canal connected with the Pearl river.   We had scarcely entered the canal, however, than our boatmen attempted to turn back, for they saw a mandarin-boat lying within with all its flags flying—a sign that the mandarin himself was on board ; and they were afraid of incurring punishment from him, or being stoned by the people, if they rowed past with Europeans. However, we would not hear of such a thing, but boldly passed the mandarin's boat, landed, and pursued our way on foot.   In a few minutes we had a crowd after us, and the people began to push the children against us, in order to irritate us.   But we armed ourselves with patience, quietly walked on, and succeeded in reaching the gardens, the gate of which was instantly closed behind us.

The gardens were in perfect order, but laid out with very little taste.   On all sides, pavilions, kiosks, and bridges were to be seen ; and every path and corner was encumbered with pots of all sizes, containing flowers and dwarfed fruit-trees of various kinds.

The Chinese are masters in the art of crippling trees, which they prefer thus treated to the finest in a state of nature.   The taste that called forth these Lilliputian woods is not to be admired ; but the quantity and beauty of the fruit their miniature branches bore was really something remarkable.   Amongst these dwarfs we found playthings of another kind : plants tortured into the shapes of fish, birds, ships, pagodas, &c., the eyes of the animals being represented by eggs stuck in their heads, with a black spot in the middle.

There was no want either, of rock-work, singly and in masses, all crowded with figures of birds, beasts, and flower-pots, which can be removed at pleasure, and formed into different groups —a favourite amusement of the Chinese ladies ; another, an equal favourite with both sexes, is flying kites, which they divert themselves with for hours together : and the garden of every Chinese of rank contains one or more open spaces for the pursuit of this pastime.

We saw here abundance of water in streams and ponds, but no waterworks.

As we had been so successful in all our attempts hitherto, Mr. Von Carlovitz proposed we should visit the garden of the mandarin *Punting-qua ;* in which I was the more interested because it was the birthplace of the first Chinese steam-boat, built by order of the mandarin and by Chinese workmen. The mandarin had gone through his studies in North America, where he remained for thirteen years.

The work was so far advanced that the boat was to be launched in a few weeks. The head builder exhibited his work to us with evident satisfaction, and was well pleased to hear its praises from our lips. He seemed to value himself especially on his knowledge of the English language ; and when Mr. Von Carlovitz spoke to him in Chinese he answered in English, and begged to carry on the conversation in that tongue. The machinery did not seem to me executed with the usual Chinese neatness, and the engine itself we thought too large for so small a vessel. Neither I nor my companions would have had the courage to make the first voyage with it.

The mandarin who had ordered its construction was gone to Pekin to receive his *button* as a reward,—as an order might be conferred amongst us ; the actual builder would probably have to content himself with the consciousness of merit.

From the dock-yard we went to the garden, which was very large, but ill kept. There were neither avenues nor dwarf trees, nor rock-work, nor figures of birds and beasts, but a wearisome succession of bridges, pagodas, pavilions, &c. The dwelling-house consisted of one great saloon and a multitude of lesser chambers. In the great saloon comedies and games were sometimes given for the diversion of the women, whose recreations are strictly confined to their houses and gardens. Chinese women of rank are much more confined than other eastern women : they are seldom allowed to visit one another, and then only in closed sedans or boats, and there are no public baths or gardens where they might meet. The best ornament of these gardens were several peacocks, silver pheasants, and mandarin ducks. In one corner a small gloomy bamboo grove concealed the family burying-place, and not far off we saw a little mound of earth, with a wooden tablet, on which was inscribed a long poetical epitaph to the memory of the mandarin's pet snake.

After inspecting all these various objects at our leisure, we returned home in safety, but another day I was not so fortunate. We went to see a tea-factory, and the proprietor himself conducted me into the large and lofty apartments in which the various operations were carried on, and where about 600 people, many of them old women and children, were employed. My entrance was the signal for a general insurrection. Old and young left their work; the grown people lifted the children in their arms to point at me, and altogether raised so fearful a howl that I was almost frightened. The master of the factory and the overseer had work enough to keep the pack from laying hands on me, and therefore begged me to look about me as quickly as possible, and be gone. In consequence I had a very superficial view of the operation; but I saw that the tea leaves were thrown into boiling water for a few minutes, and then put into flat iron pans fixed in an oblique direction, where they are lightly roasted at a moderate heat, and stirred by the hand all the time. As soon as the leaves begin to curl up they are thrown on large boards, and every leaf is rolled up singly. This operation is carried on with such rapidity that it really requires close watching to ascertain that only one leaf is taken up at a time. The whole quantity is then a second time put into the pans. The so-called black tea is roasted a longer time, and to the green a small quantity of Prussian blue is frequently added at the second roasting. Lastly, the tea is spread out again upon the boards, carefully examined, and every imperfectly closed leaf once more rolled up.

Before I left the house, the proprietor entertained me with tea in the manner in which it is drunk by the upper classes of Chinese. Some tea is put into a fine china cup, boiling water poured over, and the cup covered with a very closely-fitting lid. After the lapse of a few minutes the infusion is drunk from the leaves. The Chinese mingle with it neither sugar nor milk; they say that any addition whatever—nay, even stirring—destroys the aroma. Some sugar was, however, put into my cup.

The tea shrubs I saw in the neighbourhood of Canton were not more than six feet in height; if they exceed that measurement they are cut. The shrub is in use from three to eight years, when it is either cut down to the ground or rooted up. There are three harvests, in March, April, and May; the latter continues during May and the following month. The leaves of the first crop are so fine and tender that they may easily be mistaken for blossoms, and hence may have arisen the error that the so-called Bloom or Imperial tea * is not the leaves but the flower of the shrub; but the first harvest in March is so injurious to the shrub that it is often left ungathered.

I was told that the best tea comes from the provinces lying north of Canton; that growing in the neighbourhood of Canton itself being of very inferior quality. The tea manufacturers of Canton are accused of understanding too well how to give to the tea leaves injured by rain or that has been already made use of a fresh appearance by re-drying and colouring with Prussian blue and powdered *kurkumm*, and then rolling it tightly together. The price of the teas sent to Europe varies from fifteen to sixty dollars the *pikul* (100 lb. Austrian weight), but that at sixty dollars finds few purchasers, and those only in England. The so-called Blossom tea is never brought into the market.

I must not omit to mention a spectacle to which I was accidentally a witness on the Pearl river. It was, as I afterwards learned, a "thank feast," offered by the owners of two junks, which had made a tolerably long voyage without meeting either with pirates or with the hurricane called the typhoon.

Two of the largest flower-boats, splendidly illuminated,—the upper portions of the vessels so thickly set with lamps that they looked like galleries of fire,—were floating slowly down the stream ; every cabin was full of lamps and chandeliers, and on the deck burnt huge fires from which every now and then rockets ascended, with abundance of noise, but did not rise more than a few feet into the air. At the prow tall poles were reared, hung thickly with coloured lanterns in a pyramidal form. Boats, amply provided with torches and noisy music, preceded the larger vessels, and from

---

* These leaves are gathered with extraordinary care; each leaf is plucked singly by children and young people in gloves.

time to time a pause was made and fires blazed up from the little
boats fed by consecrated and perfumed paper. This paper, which
must be bought from the priests, is burnt on many occasions, sometimes before and after every prayer ; and the sale of it makes the
chief part of the priest's revenue.

Occasionally I took a walk with Mr. Von Carlovitz in the streets
near the factory. These streets were somewhat wider than those
round the walls of Canton, well paved, and protected from the
burning rays of the sun by boards or mats stretched as awnings
over head. The shops had doors and windows like our own ; and
we could enter them and thereby shelter ourselves from the
rudeness of the populace.

In the neighbourhood of the factory, in Fonsch-an, where are
the greatest number of manufactories, we can go to many places
by water, as the streets, like those of Venice, have canals cut
through them. This is not, however, the handsomest part of the
city, as the magazines lie along the canals, and the workmen in the
manufactories and day labourers are quartered here in miserable
barracks resting half on the land and half on rotten piles, and
projecting far into the water.

I once saw a disgusting spectacle as we came out of the canal
into the river. A negro had died on board one of the ships lying
there, and his naked body had been thrown overboard and was now
the sport of the current ; every boat thrust it as far off as possible
when it was tossed against them, but it approached ours much too
closely.

I had now passed five weeks in Canton, from the 13th July to
the 20th August. This was the hottest time of the year, and I
found it intolerably oppressive. In the house we had $27\frac{1}{2}°$ Reaumur,
in the open air 30° in the shade. People here have many con-
trivances to protect themselves from the heat, beside the punkahs.
A web of bamboo netting is stretched as an awning over the doors
and windows, over those parts of the roof beneath which the workshops are situated, and sometimes a kind of second wall is formed of
it eight or ten feet from the real wall, and provided with entrances
and passages, clothing the house as it were with a garment.

I returned to Hong Kong again in a Chinese junk — not quite so
fearlessly as I came, for the tragical fate of poor Vauchée was fresh
in my memory. I took care to pack up my small wardrobe in the
presence of the servants, that they might be aware how ill it would

reward the pirates to give themselves any trouble on my account.

On the 20th of August I bade my friends in Canton a hearty farewell, and at nine o'clock was floating down the renowned and mighty Pearl or Si Kiang river.

SINGAPORE.

The English Steamer from Hong Kong. — Singapore Plantations. — A Hunting Party in the Jungles.—A Chinese Funeral.—The Feast of Lanterns.—Climate and Temperature.

THE voyage from Hong Kong was somewhat tedious, owing to contrary winds, but without accident. The first night I was awakened by some shots fired ; but as we met with no further disturbance, they were probably not intended for us. My Chinese fellow voyagers were exceedingly polite and obliging ; and, had a look into the future been possible to me, I should have renounced my intention of pursuing my journey in an English steamer, and remained on board the junk ; as it was not, I took my passage in the " Pekin," Captain Fronson, which makes the voyage to Calcutta every month.

As the fares are extravagantly high (173 dollars the chief cabin, 117 the second), I was advised to take the third fare, and hire the cabin of one of the subaltern officers or engineers. I was quite pleased with the notion, and hastened to put it in practice : but what was my astonishment when I found it impossible to get a third fare ! I was told that the company would be very disagreeable, that the moon was exceedingly dangerous to passengers of the third class, who must sleep on deck, &c. In vain I urged that I knew perfectly well what I could and would do ; I was compelled, if I would not be left behind, to take a second place.

When I went on board I found no attendant for the second cabin, and was obliged to request a sailor to carry in my luggage. There was no appearance of the *comfort* so much talked of by the English ; the table and everything else was dirty and disorderly ; and there was but one sleeping-place for the passengers of both sexes. I was told, however, that if I applied to one of the authorities I should certainly obtain another berth. I did so, and got a neat little cabin, and the steward offered to let me eat with his wife. But this offer I would not accept;—I had not paid so much to receive every accommodation as a special favour. This was besides my first voyage in an English steamer, and I was curious to see how passengers of the second class were treated.

Our dinner party consisted not only of the passengers, of whom there were three besides myself, but of the cooks and waiters on the first-class passengers, of the butcher, and, in short, of the whole body of attendants, if they chose to favour us with their company. Not the slightest ceremony with regard to the toilette was observed; one would make his appearance without his jacket—the butcher generally forgot his shoes and stockings: truly a stout appetite was required to eat in such society!

The food was well suited to the ship's company and their style of dress, but not quite so agreeable to passengers who were to pay thirteen dollars a day. The tablecloth was covered with stains, and every guest had to use his pocket-handkerchief by way of table napkin. The knives and forks were partly white, partly black handled, the knives full of notches, the prongs of the forks broken. Spoons we had none the first day; on the second a solitary one was brought, and it remained solitary to the end of the journey. Two drinking glasses, of the commonest description, did duty for the whole party; but, as a woman, I obtained the distinction of a teacup with a broken handle, for my especial use. The head-cook, who did the honours, excused every irregularity by saying that " This time the servant was not at hand." This apology seemed rather too *naïve;* inasmuch as when I pay I expect to pay for what I get, not for what I do not.

As I have before said, the fare was bad; and the leavings of the chief cabin were what fell to our share. Two or three different kinds of food often lay sociably together in one dish, even when there was not the slightest harmony in their character; and no one seemed to care whether the meat was hot or cold.

Once when the cook was in a particularly good humour at tea-time, he said, " I do all I can to feed you well, and I hope there is nothing wanting." Two of the party (Englishmen) answered, " Oh yes, that is true." The third (a Portuguese) had not understood this astounding assertion. I, as a German, not possessing any English patriotism, could have given another answer if I had not been a woman, and if I had hoped to effect any improvement.

Our illumination consisted of one tallow candle, which was often burnt out by eight o'clock, after which we were obliged either to go to bed or sit in the dark.

In the morning our cabin served as a barber's shop, and in the afternoon as a sleeping-room, on the benches of which the worn out cooks and other servants stretched their weary limbs. To complete our *comfort,* one of the officers had quartered two young dogs upon us, who howled incessantly ; they would not have ventured to do this in the sailors' berths, as they would have pitched them out without ceremony.

This description of our style of living will perhaps be thought exaggerated, as every thing connected with the English is supposed to be in the highest degree comfortable and orderly ; I can only say, that I have spoken the strict truth, and I may add that although I have travelled much in steam-boats, and always in the second cabin, I never, before or since, paid so high a price for such miserable accommodation, never in my life have I been subject to a more infamous extortion. The only thing agreeable on board that ship was the behaviour of the officers, who were all very polite and obliging.

What most astonished me was the remarkable patience with which my fellow-voyagers bore this treatment. I should like to know what the English, who have so often the words "comfort" and "comfortable" in their mouths, would say, if they met with the like on board the steamers of any other nation.

The first few days we stood constantly out to sea, and it was not till the 28th that we saw the mountain coast of Cochin China. During the 29th we kept very close to the shore, and had a view of richly-wooded hills, but could perceive neither dwellings nor men, and but for some fires perceptible in the evenings that might be taken for beacon lights, we should have supposed the land quite uninhabited. The only object we saw in the course of the following day was a great isolated rock called the Shoe, but which more resembled in my opinion the head of a huge shepherd's dog. On the 2d of September we neared Malacca : along the coast ran a range of tolerably high wooded hills, in which, it is said, tigers lurk, rendering travelling in this peninsula extremely dangerous. On the evening of the 3d we ran into the harbour of Singapore, but so late that we could not land that night. On the following morning, I paid a visit to the firm of Behu and Meyer, to which I had letters; and in Madame Behu I met the first German woman since I had left Hamburg. I cannot describe my joy; I could talk to my heart's content once more in my native language: she would not allow me to go to an inn, but insisted on my remaining with her amiable family. My plan was to remain but a short time in Singapore, and then to proceed to Calcutta in the first sailing-vessel—I thought I had had too much of English steamers; and I was told that a week seldom passed without such an opportunity presenting itself. I waited however in vain for two or three weeks, and at last was obliged to betake myself to a steamer.

The Europeans in Singapore live much in the same manner as those resident in Canton, except that the family generally resides in the country, and the gentlemen only drive every morning into the town. They are obliged to keep a great retinue of servants; and the mistress of the family has little to do with its management, which is generally in the hands of an upper servant.

The servants are Chinese, with the exception of the Seis, coachmen or grooms, who are Bengalese. Every spring brings shiploads of Chinese boys, from the age of ten to fifteen, who are generally too poor to pay their passage; in which case the captain takes them at his own risk, and receives in return the first year's wages, which the master who engages these youths immediately pays in advance. These lads live with extreme economy, and return to their native land when they have saved a little money; many, however, settle here as artisans.

Singapore has a population of about 55,000, of whom 40,000 are Chinese, 10,000 Malays, that is natives, and 150 Europeans. The number of women is very small, as the immigrants are men and boys exclusively. The town of Singapore, with its immediate environs, reckons about 20,000 inhabitants. The streets are broad and airy, the houses not handsome; they are built on one story, and with the roof so close upon the windows that it looks as if it were squeezing them down. On account of the heat, wooden blinds are in use, instead of glass, for the windows. Here, as in Canton, every trade has its own place,—the side if not the whole of a street, and the market is handsome and lofty as a temple.

As the population of this island is so various, the number of temples is considerable; but the Chinese alone is worth looking at. The body has the form of an ordinary house, but the roof is perfectly Chinese in its decoration,—in its points and notches, wheels and arches, without end, in painted tiles, clay, and porcelain, all overloaded with ornament in the shape of flowers, arabesques, dragons, and other monsters. Over the chief entrance bas-reliefs are cut in the stone, and there is an abundance of gilded wood-carving, inside and out.

On the altar of the Goddess of Mercy fruits and pastry of all kinds were displayed, together with a small quantity of boiled rice. These refreshments are renewed every evening, and what the goddess does not eat naturally falls to the share of the bonzes. On the same altar lay two small oval-shaped and elegantly carved pieces of wood. These are flung up in the air by the Chinese, and as they fall, good or evil fortune is prophesied; but the good people have a knack of throwing them till they do fall in the desired direction. A second way of inquiring into the future consists in shaking a number of thin wooden sticks in a cup until one is shaken out. Each stick has a number indicating a passage in the Book of Moral Sentences. This temple seemed much more frequented than those of Canton, more, however, to try fortunes by means of the blocks and sticks than for the purpose of worship.

In the town itself there is nothing worth seeing but its environs; but the whole island is enchantingly beautiful, though the scenery cannot be called grand or sublime, as it wants the chief elements of grandeur and sublimity—high mountains. The highest hill, on which stands the governor's house and the telegraph, is scarcely more than 200 feet in altitude, but delightful is the fresh luxu-riant verdure, the beautiful gardens round the houses of the Europeans, the extensive plantations of costly spices, the elegant areka and feather palms, whose slender trunks attain a height of 100 feet, and terminate in a superb crown of feather-like leaves, differing from all other species of palms in the fresh green of their hue; and, lastly, the beautiful jungles in the back ground, and all these charms are yet more striking when the traveller comes, as I did, from the dungeon Canton, or from the desolate environs of the town of Victoria.

The whole island is traversed with fine roads, of which those that wind along the sea-shore are the most frequented. Here are seen a number of handsome equipages, horses from New Holland,

Java, and even from England*. Besides the beautiful European carriages, palanquins are much in use, covered and shut in on all sides with blinds. One horse only is harnessed to it; and the attendants run by the side of the vehicle. I could not conceal my dislike of this barbarous custom; but I was told that when the attempt was made to abolish it the servants themselves had objected, and preferred running beside the carriage to sitting or standing upon it. They sometimes cling to the horse or the vehicle, and are dragged along with them.

A day seldom passed on which we did not drive out. Twice a week a splendid military band played on the Esplanade close to the sea, and there rode or walked all the fashionable world: carriage followed carriage, and young men, on horseback and on foot, crowded round them, so that one might have fancied oneself in the midst of Europe. But I found more pleasure in visiting the plantations and other places than in viewing over again the old European life. I went frequently to the nutmeg and clove plantations, to enjoy their balsamic fragrance. The nutmeg-trees are enveloped from top to bottom in foliage, and attain the size of fine apricot-trees: they begin to spread from the lower part of the trunk; the leaves are bright and glittering, as if varnished, and the fruit resembles perfectly a yellowish brown-speckled apricot. When ripe it bursts of itself, and displays a round kernel about the size of a nut, covered with a kind of net-work of a beautiful deep red; this net-work is the so-called nutmeg bloom, or mace. It is carefully detached from the nut, and dried in the shade; during the process it is frequently sprinkled with sea water, as otherwise the fine crimson colour changes to yellow or black: in addition to this web the nutmeg is surrounded by a slight delicate shell. The nut itself is likewise dried, 'smoked, and then steeped in sea water, mingled with a slight solution of lime, to prevent its becoming rancid. Wild nutmeg-trees are found in Singapore.

The clove-tree is somewhat smaller, and the foliage is by no means so beautiful as that of the nutmeg-tree. The clove is the undeveloped flower-bud; when gathered they are first dried in smoke, and then for a short time laid in the sun.

The areka nut grows in clusters of from ten to twenty under the leafy crown of the palm of the same name. The fruit is somewhat

---

* Horses do not breed in Singapore, and must be constantly imported.

larger than the nutmeg, and the outward shell of so bright golden a hue that they look like the gilded nuts suspended to a Christmas tree. The kernel resembles the nutmeg, but without the net-like external covering : it is dried in the shade.

This nut, wrapped in betel-leaf, slightly smeared with lime obtained from burnt shells, is chewed both by natives and Chinese : when a little tobacco is added it produces a blood-red juice, and gives the mouth of the chewer a truly diabolical appearance ; especially when, as is frequently the case with the Chinese, the teeth are filed down and stained black. The first time I saw such a spectacle I was quite frightened : I thought the man had injured himself in some way, and had his mouth full of blood.

One day I visited a sago manufactory. The raw sago comes from the neighbouring island of Borromeo, and is the pith of a short thick-stemmed palm tree. The tree is cut down in its seventh year, split lengthways, and the pith, which is found in great abundance, is cleared of the fibres, pressed into masses, and dried in the sun or by the fire. In this condition its colour is yellowish; for some days it undergoes repeated waterings, when it becomes of a fine white; it is then dried again, crushed with a wooden roller, and passed through a hair sieve. The fine white flour is then put into a linen fan, which is previously watered in a very peculiar fashion, by the workman taking water in his mouth, and discharging it over the linen like a fine rain. In this fan the flour is well shaken by a couple of workmen, and watered from time to time in the same extraordinary manner, till it forms into grains ; it is then thrown into large flat kettles and dried slowly over the fire, being stirred constantly. Lastly, it is passed once more through a coarser sieve, in which the coarser grains are left. The factory was a large open shed, with a roof supported on trunks of trees.

I was indebted to the kindness of Messrs. Behu and Meyer for a very interesting excursion into the jungle. The gentlemen, four in number, were armed with their guns, as they purposed seeking for a tiger, and it was moreover necessary to be provided for the chance of meeting with bears, wild swine, or large serpents. We drove to the river Gallon, where two boats were in readiness for our party ; before embarking, however, we went to look at a sugar boiling near the river. The sugar was piled up in sheaves before the building : but only so much as can be boiled in one day is cut at once, as it turns sour by the heat. The cane is crushed in metal cylinders, whence the juice runs into great kettles, in which it is boiled and cooled, and afterwards dried in earthen vessels.

After we had seen the process, we entered our boat, and proceeded up the river. We soon found ourselves in the midst of a primeval forest, and the navigation became more difficult at every stroke of the rudder, on account of the many trees that had fallen into the water. Sometimes we were obliged to get out of the boat, and lift or push it over, and sometimes to lie down flat in it, in order to force a way under the prostrate trunks that spanned the stream like so many bridges. Shrubs thick set with thorns embarrassed us on all sides, and even some single leaves were of so gigantic a size as to form a hindrance; these leaves belong to a species of grass-palm, called Mungkuany; they are nearly five inches broad near the stem, and about twelve feet long, and as the river in that part scarcely exceeded ten in width, they reach from one bank to the other. The objects of natural beauty were, however, so many that such obstacles were easily borne with, if they did not perhaps actually enhance the enjoyment. The forest offered underwood, parasite plants, palms and ferns in the richest luxuriance; the latter, sometimes sixteen feet in height, formed as good a shelter from the burning sun as the palms and other trees. My satisfaction was not a little increased when I saw some monkeys springing from branch to branch in the tree-tops, and I heard the cries of others not far off: for this was the first time I had seen these creatures in a state of nature; and I rejoiced in my heart that none of the gentlemen succeeded in hitting the playful little creatures. They were more fortunate with some magnificent lorys (a species of parrot with the loveliest plumage), and squirrels. Our attention was, however, soon drawn to a more formidable object; we observed some dark body between the branches of a tree, which on nearer inspection proved to be a large serpent coiled up, and probably on the watch for prey. We ventured to approach pretty near; but it remained motionless with its glittering eye fixed upon us, and not suspecting its approaching fate; the first discharge hit the side of the creature; and quick as lightning the tail was coiled round the tree, while it darted forward, but a few more well directed shots put an end to it, when we steered directly under the tree to which it hung. One of our Malays made a noose of tough grass, and passing it over the creature's head, dragged it into the boat; he told us that we should be sure to meet with another, as this kind of serpent is always found in couples. The gentlemen in the second boat, had, in fact, found and killed another, which also had hung suspended from the bough of a large tree. These ser- pents were of a dark green colour, with beautiful yellow stripes, and about twelve feet long ; I was told they belonged to the boa species.

After a voyage of eight English miles in four hours we quitted the boat, and followed a narrow path which brought us to some cleared spaces in which pepper and gambic were grown.

The pepper-bush is a slender shrub-like plant, which, supported on props, attains a height of from fifteen to eighteen feet; the fruit grows in small grape-like clusters : these are at first red, then green, and lastly black. The shrub begins to bear in the second year ; but the white pepper is the production not of nature, but of art, and made by dipping the black pepper repeatedly in sea-water, by which process it becomes whitish. The gambic does not grow higher than eight feet ; the leaves are the only part made use of ; they are stripped off and boiled down in large kettles. The thick juice is then put into broad wooden vessels, dried in the sun and cut into pieces three inches long and packed. The gambic is of some importance to the dyers, for whose use it is sent to Europe. Gambic and pepper are always planted together, because the latter is manured with the gambic leaves after they have been boiled.

The plantations are managed and indeed almost all work in Singapore is done by freemen, whose labour I was assured was cheaper than that of slaves. Wages are excessively low; a common labourer receiving three dollars monthly without food or dwelling, yet on this he can subsist and even maintain a family. His house, or leaf-covered hut, he builds himself; his food consists of small fish, tuberous roots, and vegetables ; and his wardrobe causes him no great outlay, since out of the town he wears simply a cloth round his loins, and no other garment whatever : the children go quite naked, and the women alone can be said to be clothed.

The plantations, which we reached about ten o'clock, were cul- tivated by Chinese. Besides their huts we found here a little wooden temple which we made use of as an inn. The altar was quickly covered with the provisions furnished us by Madame Behr, but instead of offering them to the gods we devoured them our sinful selves and with an excellent appetite. When " the rage of hunger was appeased " we had the serpent we had caught skinned, and the carcass given to the Chinese labourers. They gave us to understand that they would not touch it, which surprised me not a little, as the Chinese eat anything; but subsequently I was convinced that this abstinence was only pretended, for when, after the lapse of some hours, we returned from a hunting expedition, and I entered one of their huts, I found them all collected round a huge dish in which lay certain round pieces of roasted flesh which had, beyond a doubt, made part of the serpent's body : the people would fain have hidden their banquet, but I came boldly up to them, offered some money, and requested to taste it : I found the flesh extraordinarily fine and delicate, more so, I think, than that of young chickens.

The creepers and orchideæ are by no means so numerous in the woods as in those of Brazil, nor were the trees so close together; but some of the latter were most magnificent specimens, reaching a height of above 100 feet. The trees I most admired were the ebony and *kolim* trees : the former yields two kinds of wood: a brownish yellow rind and the core of the trunk, which is much harder and black,—this is the true ebony.

The kolim tree has so strong an odour of garlic that it is perceptible at some distance: the fruit has the same flavour and is much used by the natives ; the Europeans find both smell and taste too powerful : I just touched a piece of the fresh bark and my fingers smelt of it the next morning.

Although Singapore is an island, and all possible pains have been taken to annihilate the race of tigers, the effort has been hitherto unsuccessful. The government gives a premium of 50 dollars for every tiger, and the club of Singapore merchants the same : the beautiful skin is also the property of the hunter, and even the flesh brings a profit, as it finds a ready market among the Chinese: but as tigers are numerous in Malacca, whence they swim over the narrow strait that separates that peninsula from Singapore, it would seem impossible quite to rid the island of them.

The fruits of Singapore are numerous and excellent : one of the best is the *mangustin,* which is said to thrive nowhere but in Singapore and Java. It is about the size of a middling apple ; the rind about a third of an inch thick, dark green within deep red, and contains a white pulp divided into four or five quarters : the flavour is exquisite, and it almost melts in the mouth. The pineapple is more juicy, sweeter, and much larger than that of Canton:

I saw some which weighed over 4 lbs. Whole fields are covered with them, and in the season they may be bought at from 300 to 400 for a dollar : they are generally eaten with salt. Another fruit is the sour-sop, which is also frequently found of some pounds weight : it is of a green colour externally, the flesh whitish or a very pale yellow, with a strong flavour of strawberries, and, like these, is eaten with wine and sugar. The *gumaloh* resembles a pale orange in appearance, but is five times as large : many people prefer it to the orange ; it is, however, neither so sweet nor so juicy. Of all these vegetable dainties, however, the custard-apple, in my opinion, deserves the prize ; the pulp, in which a black kernel is embedded, is extremely white, of delicious flavour, and about the consistence of butter : it is eaten with small spoons.

Some days before my departure from Singapore I had the opportunity of seeing the funeral of a wealthy Chinese. The procession passed our house, and in spite of the extreme heat I joined and accompanied it to the grave, a distance of some miles. The ceremonies at the grave lasted two hours, but I was too much interested to quit it till they were over.

The procession was opened by a priest, at whose side walked a Chinese bearing a lantern two feet high, over which was thrown a white cloth : then came two musicians, one armed with a drum on which he gave a roll from time to time, the other with a pair of cymbals : then came the coffin attended by a servant carrying a large umbrella over the head : by the side the eldest son or nearest male descendant walked with hair unplaited, and bearing a white flag. The relations were all in deep mourning, that is, entirely clothed in white ; the men had caps, also white, on their heads, and the women were muffled from head to foot in white cloths. The friends who attended observed no particular order in their march, but all wore a white cloth round their head, arm, or body. One of these persons when he observed me following the procession, offered me a strip of white stuff, which I wound round my arm.

The coffin itself was covered with a dark cloth ; some garlands of 'flowers hung about it, and rice tied up in a cloth lay upon it. Four-and-twenty men carried the coffin upon enormous poles, and a good deal of stir and bustle was made in changing the bearers, who were sometimes laughing and sometimes quarrelling. No appearance either of grief or devotion was observed in the general body ; some were smoking, some eating, and several men carrying pailsful of cold tea followed the train. The son kept apart from all, and walked beside the coffin with the air of one overwhelmed with grief.

When the train reached the street leading to the cemetery, the son threw himself on the ground, covered his face, and sobbed aloud. After a time he arose, and tottered after the corpse, supported by two men. He seemed to suffer greatly; but I was subsequently informed that his excessive affliction is mostly put on, in compliance with Chinese custom, which requires the chief mourner to be faint and sick with sorrow; and if he is not he must pretend to be so.

Arrived at the place of burial, which was on the side of a hill, the pall, flowers, and rice were laid aside, and a quantity of gold and silver paper scattered in the grave, which was dug about seven feet deep. The coffin, a tree trunk, handsomely carved and varnished, and hermetically closed, was now lowered; this operation occupying at least half an hour. The relations then flung themselves on the ground, veiled their faces, and howled lamentably; but finding the lowering of the coffin somewhat tedious apparently, they afterwards seated themselves in a circle, had their little baskets, containing betel, lime, and areka nuts brought to them, and began to comfort themselves with a chew.

After the coffin was lowered, one of the Chinese went to the upper end of the grave, opened the packet of rice, and took a kind of compass, while another person handed him a string, which he drew backwards and forwards over the middle of the compass, till it lay in the same direction with the needle. A second string, to which a lead was suspended, was then attached to the first, and dropped into the grave, and the coffin was pushed backwards and forwards, until its central point fell under the lead. At least another quarter of an hour was spent before this was accomplished: it was then covered with a number of large sheets of white paper; and the individual who had been so busy with the compass made a short discourse, during the delivery of which the children of the deceased prostrated themselves on the earth. At the end of his address the speaker scattered rice on the coffin, and threw some to children. The latter held up the corners of their robes to catch the grains; and as they caught but few, the speaker added some thimbles full, which they tied up carefully and carried away with them. The grave was at last filled with earth, upon which the mourners again raised a fearful outcry; but as far as I observed, not an eye was moistened.

After this ceremony, dressed fowls, ducks, pork, fruits, pastry, and a dozen cups and a pot full of tea were arranged in two rows on the grave, six painted wax candles were lighted and stuck in the earth by the food; and all this time some of the assistants were constantly burning gold and silver paper, of which there was a vast quantity consumed. The eldest son now again approached the grave, bowing repeatedly, till his forehead touched the earth. Six perfumed tapers of twisted paper were then handed to him, which he waved several times in the air, and then gave back to the assistants, who stuck them in the ground; and this rite was repeated by the other relations.

During the whole weary time the priest had kept at a distance from the grave, comfortably seated under the shade of a prodigious umbrella. He now advanced, repeated a short prayer, tinkling a bell from time to time,—and his part of the ceremony was over. The food was taken away, the tea poured over the grave, and the procession returned to the town in excellent spirits, to the acompaniment of music, which had been heard from time to time during the whole ceremony. The food, I was told, it was usual to distribute among the poor.

The day after I was a spectator of the celebrated Feast of Lanterns. On every house, on every projection of the roof, on lofty poles, &c., hung countless lanterns of coloured gauze and paper, tastefully decorated and painted with the figures of gods, warriors, and animals. In the courts and gardens, or where these were wanting, in the open street, before the houses, large tables were placed, on which were reared pyramids of food of various kinds and fruits, amid flowers and lamps innumerable. The inhabitants were roaming in crowds through the streets, courts, and gardens till past midnight, when the comestibles were vigorously attacked by the proprietors and their friends. This festival pleased me extremely, and in nothing more than the striking propriety of the demeanour of the crowd; every thing was looked at, admired, or criticised, but nothing was touched.

The climate of Singapore is very agreeable in comparison with that of other places near the line. During my stay there, from the 3rd of September to the 8th of October, the heat, within doors, rarely exceeded 23° (Reaumur) and 38° in the sun; and even this was not intolerable, as every morning brought a fresh sea breeze.

Singapore promises shortly to become the central point of India for steam navigation. Vessels from Hong Kong, Ceylon, Madras, Calcutta, and Europe, and Dutch ships of war from Batavia, touch here regularly every month ; and steam vessels from Manilla and Sydney will, no doubt, arrive as regularly at no distant time.

CEYLON.

Departure from Singapore.—The Island of Pinang.—Ceylon.—Pointe de Galle.—Excursion to the Interior.—Colombo.—Kandy.— The Temple Dagoha.—Capture of Elephants.—Return to Colombo and Pointe de Galle.—Departure.

ON the 7th of October I left Singapore for Ceylon, by the " Braganza," an English steam vessel of 350 horse power. The distance is about 1,500 leagues.

The accommodation on board this vessel differed in some respects from the former, but was very nearly as bad. I and my fellow-passengers,* four in number, dined alone, and had even a Mulatto to wait on us; but he was suffering under elephantiasis, and the sight was not calculated to improve the appetite.

We passed through the strait of Malacca, and did not, during the 7th and 8th, lose sight of land.

The foreground of Malacca is hilly ; and farther in the interior of the country, these hills rise to mountains. To the left lay several mountain islands, which entirely concealed Sumatra from our view.

Our crew consisted of seventy-nine persons, Chinese, Malays, Cingalese, Bengalese, Hindoos, and Europeans ; and at their meals, the different country people usually kept together. All had enormous vessels, containing rice, and small bowls of curry placed before them ; and pieces of dried fish served them for bread. The curry was poured over the rice, rolled by the hand into small

---

* One of these passengers had been turned out of the chief cabin, because he was not, it was said, quite in his right senses, and did not always know what he was about. The chief cabin passengers found this unpleasant, and the captain took upon him to order the poor man to the second, retaining, however, the fare for the first.

bowls, and thrust into their mouths with a piece of fish; but a full half of the portion usually fell back again into the dish.

The costume of the greater number of these men was simple in the highest degree, being merely a pair of linen drawers. The head was generally covered with a miserable, dirty turban, or in default of a turban, a coloured rag, or a sailor's old cap. The Malays wrap long cloths round their heads, of which a portion is thrown over the shoulder. The Chinese adhere closely to their national costume; and the coloured servants of the officers alone are well and tastefully dressed; they wear white trowsers and waist-coats, and white girdles, coloured silk jackets, and small embroidered caps, or handsome turbans.

The manner in which the coloured people were treated was anything but Christian-like: thrusts, cuffs, kicks, and brutal words were but too plentiful; and the meanest European permitted himself the coarsest freedoms with them. Poor creatures! how is it possible they should love or respect so-called Christians?

On the 9th of October we landed on the little island of Pinang. The town of the same name lies in a small plain; but not far off the town the ground rises into a chain of beautiful hills, which give great beauty to the prospect.

I obtained a furlough of five hours, which I made use of to traverse the town in a palanquin; and I even saw something of the country: but all I saw reminded me of Singapore. The town is not pretty, but the country houses, all standing in the midst of magnificent gardens, were beautiful. The island is crossed by many good roads.

I was told that one of the mountains afforded a lovely view over Pinang, a portion of Malacca, and the sea; and there was also a waterfall to be seen; but unfortunately, I had not time to visit them.

The population of Pinang is mostly Chinese, and all the small commerce and manual industry is in their hands.

On the 17th of October we approached the coast of Ceylon, and I gazed with eager curiosity on a country which had been described to me as a perfect Paradise, the chosen resting-place of our common father when he was driven out of Eden; as a proof of which fact the inhabitants point to the spots yet bearing his name—Adam's Peak, Adam's Bridge, &c. I was eager also to inhale the balsamic odours of which so many travellers have spoken. The island rose in wondrous beauty from the waves, and nobly did the many mountain chains that intersect it develope themselves; the highest summits were glittering in magic splendour in the setting sun, while beneath hill, and valley, and cocoa forest lay in purple gloom. The aromatic odours, however, I was not favoured with; for I smelt nothing but the usual ship's perfume—tar, coal, smoke, and oil.

Towards nine o'clock we neared Pointe de Galle; but as the entrance is extremely dangerous, we anchored for the night. On the following morning two pilots brought us safely into port.

We had scarcely landed before we were surrounded by scores of people offering for sale cut precious stones, pearls, and various articles in tortoiseshell and ivory. Those who understand these things might probably have made good bargains, but those who do not must beware how they allow themselves to be dazzled by the splendour and size of the gems, as the natives are said to have learnt from the cunning Europeans the art of profiting by the ignorance of their customers.

The position of Pointe de Galle is extremely beautiful: in the foreground noble masses of rock, in the back stately palm forests stretching to the fortifications of the town. The houses are neat, low, and generally shaded by trees; and trees on either side form in many of the clean-kept streets beautiful avenues.

Pointe de Galle is the meeting-place of the steamers from China, Bombay, Calcutta, and Suez: travellers from the three last places stop here twelve, or at most four-and-twenty hours, but those from China to Calcutta have to wait ten or fourteen days for the steamer that is to carry them to their journey's end: and I was not at all sorry for this delay, for I profited by it to visit Candy.

From Pointe de Galle to Colombo there are two conveyances: the mail daily, and a coach belonging to a private company three times a week; the distance is seventy-three English miles, and is traversed in ten hours: a place in the mail costs thirty shillings, in the private vehicle only twelve, but being pressed for time I was obliged to go by the mail. The road is magnificent—there is not a hill nor a stone to impede the horses, which besides are changed every eight miles; the greater part of it lies near the sea-shore, through thick woods of cocoa-trees: the roads are frequented and peopled as I have seldom before seen even in Europe: hamlet followed hamlet, and single dwellings lay so thick between that we passed one every minute: the small towns were numerous, of which Calturi, inhabited mostly by Europeans, pleased me most; near Calturi, on a rocky eminence by the coast, is a small fortress.

Along the roads, under little sheds roofed with palm leaves, large vessels filled with water were placed, and cocoa shells for drinking cups lay beside them; a not less kindly arrangement for the convenience of travellers were small open stalls, furnished with benches: many travellers pass the night under these places of shelter.

The constantly moving multitude of carriages and people made the way seem very short, and yielded abundant opportunity for studying the various component parts of the population of Ceylon: the majority, of course, are Cingalese, but here are also found the various races of India,—Mahomedans, Lascars, Malabars, Moors, Jews, and there are even some Hottentots. Among the three former races I saw many beautiful and agreeable countenances; indeed the Cingalese boys and young men are particularly handsome. They have delicate well-formed features, and such slender elegant forms that they might easily be mistaken for girls,—an error to which their manner of dressing the hair would not a little contribute, as they wear no kind of cap or turban, but comb the hair back and twist it up behind into a knot, secured by a broad tortoiseshell comb, four inches high. This style of *coiffure* is not particularly becoming to men. The Mahomedans and Jews have more strongly marked features,—the latter bear some resemblance to the Arabs, and like them have a noble cast of countenance; they are easily recognisable by their shorn heads, long beards, caps, and turbans. Many of the Indians wear turbans; the majority, however, prefer a simple cloth thrown over the head: the latter head-covering belongs also to the Malays, and men from the Malabar coast. The Hottentots allow their matted coal-black hair to fall in disorderly masses over the forehead and neck. None of these people, the Mahomedans and Jews excepted, trouble themselves much about dress. Some wear short drawers, and some kind of upper garment, but the majority are contented with a cloth about a hand's breath in width round the waist and drawn between the legs.

Of women I saw but few, and these only close to their dwellings, which they appear seldom to leave. Their costume was extremely simple,—consisting merely of an apron, a short jacket, which

rather exposed than covered the upper part of the person, and a
cloth thrown over the head : many wore only a large shawl thrown
in loose drapery round them.   The edges as well as the tips of the
ears were pierced and decorated with ear-rings; neck, arms, and
feet were adorned with chains and plates of silver and other metals,
and one of the toes was encircled with a large and very massive
ring.

One would have expected that in a country where the female
sex is kept so much secluded those persons would be closely
veiled : but this was so little the case in Ceylon that many seemed
to have forgotten both jacket and head-covering; and the old
ladies were more particularly oblivious in this respect, though their
appearance was not inviting.   There were many beautiful and
expressive faces among the younger women, but they should not
be seen without their upper covering, as their breasts descend
nearly to the loins.

The colour of the Cingalese varies between light and dark
brown, reddish brown, and copper-coloured : the Hottentots are
black, but not of the shining sable of the negroes.

The horror which these half-naked people have of rain and wet
places is singular.   During my excursion it began to rain a little,
and in a moment the natives sprang like rope-dancers over every
little puddle in their hurry to reach their huts, and hide themselves
from the dreaded shower : those who were too far off held the
leaves of the talipot tree (*corypha umbraculifera*) over their heads,
by way of umbrella.   These leaves are four feet in diameter, and
can be folded up like a fan, and such a giant leaf will shelter two
persons very completely.   They have no such terror of the sun's
rays, however powerful; but it is said that the thickness of their sculls
and the fat lying beneath render the heat innocuous to the natives.

The carriages in use here are of a very peculiar construction ;
they are wooden two-wheeled cars, with a roof of palm leaves,
projecting four feet before and behind ; and thus forming a protection against both sun and rain to the driver.   These cars are drawn
by two oxen, harnessed at such a distance from the carriage that
the driver can run between them with perfect safety.

I made use of the half hour allowed for breakfast to go down to
the sea-shore, where I saw a number of persons busily employed
upon some dangerous cliffs in the midst of a terrible surf : some
were loosening shell-fish from the rock by means of a long pole,

while others plunged into the sea to secure the booty. I thought that men would hardly expose themselves to such danger merely for the sake of oysters, and that there must be pearls in the shell. That was not the case, however, and I afterwards learnt, that although pearls were obtained in this manner, it was on the eastern coast only, and in the months of February and March. The boats made use of were of two kinds: the larger, which would hold forty persons, was made of planks, fastened together and bound with ropes of cocoa-nut fibre;—the smaller resembled those I had seen in Tahiti, but looked yet more dangerous. An excessively narrow, very shallow, hollowed trunk of a tree formed the body; the sides were raised a little by a plank with spars laid lengthways and obliquely. The vessel rose scarcely a foot and a half above the surface of the water, and the whole breadth at the upper part did not exceed a foot. A piece of plank lay across by way of seat, but the rower could find room only by crossing one leg over the other.

The greater part of the road lay, as I before said, through forests of cocoa-trees; the soil was sandy, and quite free from underwood and creeping plants; but in those parts where trees of more abundant foliage grew, the soil was rich, and both flourished in luxuriant profusion.

In the course of the journey we crossed four rivers,—the *Tindureh*, the *Bentock, Cattura*, and *Pandura*, two of which we passed in boats, the others over pretty wooden bridges. Two English miles from Colombo the cinnamon plantations begin. On this side of Colombo all the country houses of the Europeans are situated: they are extremely simple in construction, surrounded by walls and shaded by cocoa-trees. At three o'clock in the afternoon our carriage rolled over two draw-bridges, and through two fortified gates into the town. The site of Colombo is far more beautiful than that of Pointe de Galle, as it is much nearer the mountains. I stopped the night here, and set off on the following morning with the post for the town of Candy, seventy-two English miles distant.

Colombo is built over a great extent of ground. We drove through broad streets of endless length, between rows of beautiful houses, with verandahs and colonnades; and a strange ghastly effect was produced by a number of human forms lying stretched out under white cloths in these verandahs and arcades: at first I took them for corpses, but the number was too great, and I found at length that they were only sleepers; for they began to move, and throw off their winding sheets. The inhabitants of Colombo, I heard, think it more agreeable to sleep in the verandahs than inside the houses.

A long bridge of boats crosses the important river Calanyganga, and when the road quits the sea-coast the character of the landscape begins to change considerably. Fine rice plantations stretch over vast plains, whose tender green reminded me of our wheat-fields in spring. The foliage of the woods becomes thicker, and the palms fewer; only here and there they steal, as it were, among the stronger growth of the forest, rearing their tall heads over all. Nothing is more beautiful than one of these vegetable Titans clothed to the very summit with the luxuriant climbing plants.

After we had advanced about sixteen English miles the ground began to rise, and we were soon shut in on all sides by high mountains, at the foot of which we found relays of horses ready. The seventy-two miles, although we ascended to a height of above 2,000 feet, were traversed in eleven hours.

The nearer we approached Candy, the more varied became the mountain scenery. Now we were completely enclosed, now height was piled on height, and each mountain top seemed to surpass the other in beauty and in altitude; for the height of some thousand feet their sides were luxuriantly wooded, beyond, their aspect became more rocky. Not less interesting than the face of the country were the singular teams we encountered. Ceylon, it is well known, is rich in elephants, of whom many are captured and made use of for various kinds of labour; and we saw huge waggons filled with stones to mend the roads drawn by two and sometimes three elephants.

Four miles from Candy we crossed the river Mahavilagunga, which is spanned by a magnificent bridge of satin-wood in a single arch; to this bridge the following tradition is annexed.

After the Cingalese were subdued by the English, they still cherished hopes of regaining their freedom, because an oracle had announced that it would be as impossible for an enemy to maintain a lasting dominion over them as to unite the two banks of the Mahavilagunga by a single road. When the bridge was begun they laughed, thinking it an impossible undertaking; but now that it is accomplished I was assured that all hopes of shaking off the yoke were given up.

Near this bridge a botanic garden is laid out, which I visited the following day. I was astonished at the beautiful order in which it is kept, as well as at its wealth of flowers, plants, and trees. Opposite this garden lies one of the largest sugar plantations, and in the neighbourhood are several of coffee.

The situation of Candy is in my opinion exquisite; some people assert that the mountains are too near, and that the town lies in a basin. If so, the basin is most beautiful, and full of the richest vegetation. The town itself is little and ugly, nothing but a heap of small shops; the few houses inhabited by Europeans, places of business, and the barracks lie without the town on small eminences. A part of the valley is filled by vast reservoirs of water, surrounded by richly wrought open masonry, and shaded by avenues of the mighty tulip-tree. Near one of these reservoirs stands the celebrated Buddha temple Dagoha, built in the Moorish-Hindostan style, and richly decorated.

When I left the coach, one of the passengers recommended me to a good hotel, and was also so obliging as to call a native to show me the house; but when I reached the hotel, I found that not a room was to be had, I requested the people of the house to name another to my guide, which they did. The fellow led me out of the town, pointed to a neighbouring hill, and gave me to understand that the house indicated was situated behind it. As I saw that all the buildings lay considerably apart from each other I believed him, but when we came near the hill I saw instead of a house, a solitary looking spot and a wood. I would have turned back but my guide paying no attention to my signs made straight for the wood, whereupon I snatched my portmanteau from his shoulder and stood still. He would have taken it again by force, when luckily I espied at a little distance two English soldiers, to whom I called for assistance, on which the fellow instantly made off. I related my adventure to the soldiers, who congratulated me on my escape, and took me with them to the barracks, where one of the officers was so kind as to send a person with me to an hotel.

My first visit was to the temple Dagoha, which contains a precious relic of Buddha,—one of the god's teeth. The temple with its supernumerary buildings is surrounded by walls; the circumference is inconsiderable, and the tabernacle which contains the sacred tooth is a small chamber scarcely twenty feet in diameter: within reigns

the deepest darkness, as there are no windows, and a curtain is
suspended before the door to keep out the external light: the walls
and ceiling are overlaid with silk coverings, which, however, have
no merit but that of age. They were, it is true, wrought with
gold threads, but not very richly, and I could not believe that the
effect produced was ever so dazzling as some travellers have asserted.
A sort of altar plated with silver and with hangings, of which the
edges are set with precious stones, takes up one half of the space:
on this altar stands a clock-shaped cover, at least three feet in
diameter at the lower end and about as much in height, and made
of silver, thickly gilt, and adorned with a number of gems. A pea-
cock in the centre is wholly composed of precious stones, but no
great effect is produced after all, as they are very ill-placed and
clumsily set.

Under this large cover there are six smaller ones, said to be of
pure gold,—the last of which conceals the precious tooth of the
divinity. The outer cover is secured by three locks, two of the keys
belonging to which were deposited with the English governor,
the third is in the keeping of the chief priest of the temple, but
a short time ago the government restored the two keys with great
solemnity, and they are now in the custody of one of the Radschas
(princes) of the island.

This relic is only shown to princes or other great ones of the
earth ; meaner persons must content themselves with the word of
the priest, who is so good as to describe its glories for a consideration. Its dazzling whiteness shames the purest ivory, its form
surpasses all excellence hitherto beheld, and its size that of the
largest ox-tooth. Countless multitudes flock hither yearly to
adore this sacred object. Faith makes blessed, and there are
many among Christian sects who believe in things demanding
quite as strong a dose of credulity to accept. I remember in
my youth to have been present at a yearly celebration at
Calvaria, a place of pilgrimage in Galicia. A great number
of pilgrims flock hither yearly to fetch splinters of the true
cross. The priests make little crosses of wax, which they
assure the credulous people contains each a morsel of the real
cross of Christ: these waxen crosses are wrapped in paper and
stand by basketsfull for distribution, that is, for sale. Every
peasant takes at least three, one for the dwelling, a second for the

stable, and a third for the barn. The most extraordinary part of the story was, that this purchase had to be repeated every year, as the crosses lose their healing virtue in that space of time.

But to return to Candy. In a second temple adjoining the sanctuary are two gigantic statues of the god Buddha in a sitting posture, said to be of pure gold (they are hollow). Before these colossal Buddhas stand whole rows of little Buddhas in crystal, glass, silver, copper, and other materials. In the vestibule there are a number of divinities hewn in stone, and fragments of others, all very rude and stiff in workmanship : in the midst stands a small monument resembling a reversed bell in shape, said to mark the grave of a Brahmin. On the external walls of the temple there are some awful frescoes representing the eternal punishment of the wicked: human figures half or whole roasted, torn with red hot pincers, or swallowing fire, crushed between rocks, having the flesh cut piece-meal from the bodies, &c.; but fire plays the principal part in the Buddhist hell.

The gates of the chief temple are of metal ; the posts ivory. On the former are some magnificent arabesques in high relief; on the latter similar decorations are inlaid. Before the chief entrance four of the largest elephants' tusks I ever saw are placed as ornaments.

Ranged round the court are the tents of the priests : they go constantly with their closely-shorn heads uncovered, and wear long light yellow robes tolerably sufficient as coverings. Formerly 500 priests were employed in the service of this temple alone ; at present the divinity must put up with a few dozen.

The devotional service of the Buddhists seems to consist princi-pally in making offerings of flowers and money. Morning and evening an ear-splitting music called *Tam-tam* is performed before the gates of the temple, accompanied by a frightful drumming and fifing within. Shortly after the commencement of this concert, people come thronging from all sides, carrying baskets full of the most beautiful flowers, with which the priests decorate the altars with a taste and elegance that can scarcely be exceeded.

There are many other temples in Candy, but only one at all worthy of note. It lies at the foot of a rocky hill, out of which a statue of Buddha, six and thirty feet high, is cut, and protected by an elegant little vaulted temple. The divinity is painted in the most glaring colours. The walls of the temple are overlaid with a fine red-coloured cement, divided into compartments, in which the image of Buddha is repeated in fresco. Vishnu, another of their divinities, is also here represented ; I was particularly struck by the beauty and freshness of the colours on the southern wall of this temple.

There also is a monumental stone, similar to that in the temple Dagoha, not however within the walls, but under God's free heaven, and shaded by some venerable trees.

Schools taught by the priests are frequently found in the vicinity of the temples. Near this one we saw about a dozen boys (the girls are not allowed to attend schools) busied in writing. The copies were very beautifully written with a style on narrow palm leaves, and the same material served the boys as copy-books. The valley traversed by the *Mahavilaganga* well rewards the trouble of the walk to view it. A range of wavy hills runs through it, whose sides form regular terraces planted with rice or coffee. Nature is here young and vigorous, and yields a rich harvest to the diligence of the cultivator. Thick dusky groves of palms and other trees of more abundant foliage form the shade of the picture, and mountains clothed in verdure of velvet softness, and wild romantic dark grey rocks, the back-ground.

I saw many of the highest mountains in Ceylon, but not, unfortunately, the most celebrated, Adam's Peak. This mountain, 6,500 feet in height, is said to be so steep on the last peak, that it has been necessary to hew out steps in the rock, through which an iron chain is drawn. The labour of the bold climber is however richly repaid. On the highest level a faint impression of a foot, five feet in length, is to be traced, by the Mahomedans said to be the foot-print of our common father ; by the Buddhists, that of their large-toothed divinity. Many thousands of both sects make it the object of a yearly pilgrimage.

In Candy, the palace of the former king or emperor of Ceylon is still to be seen, a handsome walled building, but offering little that is peculiar ; I should have taken it for a European work. It consists of a somewhat elevated ground floor with large windows, and handsome porticoes resting on pillars. The only thing remarkable in this palace is a spacious hall, the walls of which are adorned with some coarse and stiff reliefs representing animals. Since the native monarch of Ceylon has been dismissed from office by the English, the resident or governor of that nation inhabits this palace.

If I had timed my visit to Candy fourteen days earlier, I might have witnessed an elephant hunt, or rather an elephant capture. For this object the banks of a river frequented by these animals is sought, and a great space enclosed within piles, to which various narrow paths strongly enclosed lead. A decoy elephant led within this space allures his thirsty fellows by his cry, who, once entangled within the passages, can no longer escape, and they are driven by the yells and outcries of the hunters into the greater space. The finest animals are taken alive and guarded, till hunger renders them so tame as to submit to receive a noose round them, and to follow the tame elephants unresistingly; the animals inferior in size and beauty are killed or set at liberty again, according as they possess tusks more or less valuable.

The preparations for such a capture, the seeking out the creatures to drive them towards the watering place, enclosing the space, &c., are often the work of several weeks. The elephant is sometimes hunted simply by armed men; but this is dangerous. It has, as is well known, only one very vulnerable point, the middle of the forehead: if this is hit, the huge animal may be destroyed by the first shot; but if it miss, woe to the hunter,—the infuriated beast will trample him to death in a few minutes. The elephant is, however, by nature a peaceable animal, and does not readily attack men.

The Europeans make use of the animal for draught and for carrying burdens, but the natives chiefly for riding and for state.

After a stay of three days I returned to Colombo, where I had to remain another day, as it was Sunday, when no mail is despatched. I went to the Catholic church, which was full of Irish soldiers and Portuguese; the latter were very richly dressed in silk stuffs and pearl ear-rings, precious stones round their necks and arms, and gold and silver chains on their ancles.

In the afternoon I visited the cinnamon plantations, of which there are many in the vicinity of Colombo. The cinnamon-trees or shrubs are planted in rows; their height does not at the utmost exceed nine feet; the blossoms are white and scentless. From the fruit, which is smaller than an acorn, oil is obtained; when the fruit is crushed and boiled the oil swims at the top: it is used for lighting, mingled with cocoa-nut oil. The cinnamon harvest takes place twice in the year: the first, called the great harvest, from April to July; the second, the little harvest, from November till

January. The bark is pulled off the slender branches with a knife, and dried in the sun, by which process it acquires a yellowish or brown colour. The finest cinnamon is light yellow, and about the thickness of card-board. The fine cinnamon-oil used in medicine is obtained from the cinnamon itself : it is shaken in a vessel full of water, in which it is steeped for eight or ten days; the whole is then thrown into a still, and distilled over a slow fire ; on the surface of the water thus obtained the oil after a short time collects, and is removed with the greatest care.

Among the animals of Ceylon, after the elephants, I was most interested by the ravens. Their numbers and their tameness are remarkable. In every little town and village they are to be seen in multitudes round the doors and at the windows, picking up whatever is to be found ; and they perform here the same service as the dogs do among the Turks, that is, they act as scavengers. The horned cattle are small and provided with fleshy humps between the shoulder-blades, which are considered an especial dainty.

In Colombo and Pointe de Galle there are many white buffaloes of a large race belonging to the English government, and which were brought hither from Bengal. They are used for heavy draught.

Among the fruits the pine-apple is admirable for size and flavour.

The temperature I found pretty moderate, especially in Candy, which lies high, and where after much rain it was almost cold.

In the mornings and evenings the thermometer fell to 13° (Reaumur) ; at noon in the sun it did not rise above 21°. In Colombo and Pointe de Galle the weather was beautiful, and 7 degrees warmer than in Candy.

On the 26th of October I left Colombo for the peninsula of India, by an English steamer.

BENGAL.

Calcutta.—Mode of Life of Europeans.—The Hindoos.—Things to be seen in the Town. — Visit to a Baboo. — Religious Festival. — Dying Houses, and Places for Burning the Dead.—Mahomedan and European Weddings.

THE first land which you catch a glimpse of on approaching Calcutta is flat and sandy, and without the slightest pretensions to natural beauty.

We made it on the 2nd of November, and saw at the same time ten or twelve ships, among them some of the great East Indiamen, which, like ourselves, were bound for the wealthy city. Towards evening we had neared the mouth of the giant river, which pours such a flood into the ocean that several miles from its mouth the water tastes quite fresh; and I filled a glass from the sacred tide of the Ganges, and drank it to the health of my dear ones in my native land.

As you enter the Hoogly, one of its seven branches, you see boundless plains extending along both shores,—fields of rice, with sugar plantations, and palms, bamboos, and trees with various kinds of foliage scattered about them, and the richest vegetation clothing the ground quite to the water's edge. As we proceeded up the river we saw boats of a very singular construction; the fore-part almost level with the water, and the stern about seven feet high. Half-naked men, too, began to make their appearance, and here and there a very poor-looking village, with huts made of clay or palm branches, and covered with rice straw thatch or tiles.

About fifteen miles below Calcutta a palace-like building made its appearance, with a pleasant dwelling-house beside it; this was a cotton factory, and from this point many most elegant mansions in the Greek-Italian style, and richly ornamented with columns, terraces, &c., presented themselves on both sides of the river; but we flew too quickly past to catch more than a glimpse of them. Many ships of the largest size sailed by,—steamers dashed up and down, taking them in tow, and the strange and animating bustle constantly increased, and made it easy for us to see that we were approaching the metropolis of Asia. We anchored at Garderich, some miles below Calcutta, and our engineer took compassion on the difficulty I found in making the natives understand where they were to take me, as signs would not always answer the purpose, and took me ashore, engaged a palanquin for me, and gave the bearers proper instructions.

The palanquins are about five feet long and three high, and well furnished with mattrasses and cushions, on which you lie as on a bed; but it was very unpleasant to me the first time I made use of this mode of conveyance: it seems to be degrading men to employ them as animals of burthen. Four bearers are enough for the town, but for further excursions you require eight, who constantly relieve one another, going about four or five miles in an hour.

The palanquins are painted black outside, so that they always looked to me as if they were carrying sick people to the hospital, or the dead to the churchyard.

The first object that struck me as I passed along was the magnificence of the ghauts, or broad flights of steps leading down to the river, and where boats lie for ferries or pleasure parties. The splendid palaces of the city are in great gardens, and into one of these my bearers soon turned, and placed me under a beautiful portal.

This was the residence of the family of Heiligers, to whom I had letters. The amiable young mistress of the house received me in the most cordial manner, saluting me in our common language (she was from the north and I from the south of Germany); and here I was quartered with true Indian luxury—having a bed-chamber, a reception-room, a bath-room, and a dressing-room placed at my disposal.

My arrival at Calcutta occurred at one of the most unfortunate periods that the city had ever experienced. Three successive bad harvests over almost the whole of Europe had brought on a commercial crisis, which threatened the ruin of Calcutta. Every post from Europe brought accounts of important failures of houses, which drew after them in their fall that of some of the wealthiest firms in this city. No merchant could venture to say, " I am worth so much;" for the next newspaper might show him that he was a beggar. A feeling of trembling expectation—of terror, even—took possession of every family. The losses here and in England were reckoned at thirty millions sterling, and still there was no check to the calamity.

Such misfortunes fall more heavily on those who, like the people of Calcutta, are accustomed to every indulgence and luxury. We Germans have no conception of what the housekeeping of Europeans in India is. Every family inhabits a palace, and keeps from twenty-five to thirty servants;—two cooks, a dish-washer, two water-carriers, four to wait at table, four room-cleaners, a lamp-lighter, half-a-dozen stable men (for there are at least six horses, and every horse must have his own attendant), a pair of coachmen, ditto of gardeners, a waiting maid for the lady, a nurse for every child, and a maid to wait upon the nurses; two tailors, two punkah pullers, and a porter. I have visited families that kept as many as sixty or seventy servants. Their wages run from four to eleven rupees a month, but they receive no food, and only a few sleep in the house ; board and lodging are reckoned in the wages. Most of them are married, and go home daily to eat and sleep ; they also buy their own clothing, except turbans and girdles, and provide for their own washing. The linen of the family is put out to wash, notwithstanding the crowd of servants ; and a common rate for this is three rupees for a hundred pieces ; but the quantity of linen required is extraordinary, for everything is worn white, and the entire dress is usually changed twice a day.

Provisions are not dear, but horses, carriages, furniture, and clothes excessively so ; the three last come from Europe, the horses frequently from Australia or Java, though sometimes from Europe ; and I have known people keep twenty of them.

In my opinion, all this inordinate expenditure is, in a great measure, the fault of the Europeans themselves. They see the rajahs and great people of the country with these swarms of idle attendants, and they will not be outdone by them ; by degrees the custom becomes established, and now, I believe, it would be difficult to break through it ; I was told that it could not be otherwise, as long as the Hindoos were divided into castes. The Hindoo who cleans the rooms would, on no account, wait at table ; the child's nurse would scorn to clean the basin that the little one is washed in ; yet, nevertheless, even allowing for this, the number of attendants is needlessly great. Even in China and Singapore I was struck by the same circumstance, but here the number is double or treble what it is there.

The population of Calcutta is about 600,000, without the English troops, of which not much more than 2,000 are English or American. The city is divided into several portions,—the Business town, the Black town, and the European quarter. The two former are very ugly, filled with narrow crooked streets and wretched dilapidated houses, and huts of baked clay, between which lie shops, and a few large houses of wealthy natives. Narrow canals lined with stone run through all the streets, for the Hindoos require much water for their many daily ablutions. The streets in the Black and Business quarters are so thronged, that when a European equipage drives through it the servants have to get down, and run and shout constantly to get people out of the way. The district inhabited by Europeans is sometimes called the City of Palaces,—and it deserves the name.

The notorious "Black Hole," in which, in the year 1756, the Rajah Suraja Dowla, when he took Calcutta, shut up and suffocated 150 of the most distinguished prisoners,—is now turned into a warehouse ; but before the entrance stands an obelisk about fifty feet high, on which the names of the unfortunate men are inscribed.

The Botanical Garden which I went to see is more like a park, as there are few flowers and rare plants, but an immense number of trees and shrubs, which lie scattered over spacious lawns with pleasing irregularity. The most remarkable things in it are the two bananas, which with their family of descendants now occupy a space of more than 600 feet, and the principal trunk measures 50 feet in circumference. It is well known that when this tree reaches a height of about forty feet, it flings out horizontal branches in all directions, from which shoot forth fibrous roots that sink into the ground. These in their turn send forth other branches which again take root, so that a single tree will at length form an entire grove in which thousands of men may find shelter. Next to the Botanic Garden lies the Episcopal College, in which natives are educated for missionaries, and which, after the Palace of the Governor, is the most splendid edifice in Calcutta ; the Library, a magnificent apartment, is rich in the best authors, and is at the disposition of the students, but I fear their zeal for learning does not quite keep pace with the imposing character of the building. I happened to take down a large book from a shelf, but I immediately let it fall, and fled to the other end of the room, for a swarm of bees rushed out upon me from behind the books.

The dining halls, sitting rooms, and so forth, are richly and commodiously fitted up, so that altogether one might take this for an institution for the sons of the richest English families, but scarcely for the training of "labourers in the vineyard of the Lord." I contemplated that grand establishment with melancholy feelings, and so much the more as it was intended for natives. Here they have to put off their own more simple modes of life, and study themselves into superfluity and self-indulgence, and then they are to be sent out into woods and deserts to fulfil their office and become the teachers of the heathen !

I paid a visit during my stay in Calcutta to a wealthy native, whose property, with that of his brother, is estimated at 150,000l. sterling. He received me himself at the door, dressed in an immense piece of white muslin, over which was thrown in picturesque fashion a costly Indian shawl that covered much of the body, and was, fortunately for decorum, not so transparent as the muslin. The reception-room, into which he conducted me, was arranged in the European manner ; in one corner stood a chamber-organ, in another a book-case with the works of the most renowned English poets and philosophers—but I could not help suspecting these were more for show than use, as some of the volumes of Byron's works were turned upside down, and Young's Night Thoughts were stuck in the middle of them. Some pictures and engravings, which the good Baboo doubtless thought decorated his walls, were certainly of much less value than the frames that contained them. The great man sent for his two sons, handsome boys of four and seven years of age, to present to me, and I inquired after his wife and daughters, though aware that I was a little out of order in so doing. Our poor sex stands so low in the opinion of a Hindoo, that even a question about them is half an insult; he forgave me for it however, as I was a European, and ordered his girls also to be summoned : the youngest was a lovely baby of six months old, tolerably white and with splendid eyes; the eldest a rather common-looking little girl of *nine*, whom her father presented to me as a bride, and invited me to the wedding, which was to take place in six weeks ; I was so surprised that I said I supposed of course he meant not wedding but betrothal, but he assured me that the child was to be really married and given over to her husband.

When I asked whether she liked the bridegroom, I was told that they were to see each other for the first time on the wedding day ; and he assured me further, that among his people a father must make all possible haste to provide husbands for his girls, as an unmarried daughter would be the disgrace of the father, who would be regarded as wanting in natural affection. When he has found a son-in-law whom he approves, he describes to his wife his qualities, person, property, and so forth, and with his description she must be content, for neither as bridegroom nor husband does she ever see the man to whom her daughter is given. He is never considered as belonging to the family of the bride—but the young wife goes over entirely into the family of her husband.

She on her side must never see the male relations of her husband, nor appear unveiled before a servant, and if she go to visit her mother it must be in a closed palanquin.

I was introduced to the wife of the Baboo, and to one of his sisters-in-law. The former, about twenty-five, and somewhat corpulent, the latter only fifteen, and quite slender. The cause of this difference was explained to me. The girls, although married at so preposterously early an age, are seldom mothers before fourteen or fifteen, and till then they retain the slenderness of their forms. But after the first lying-in, they are shut up for seven or eight weeks in their rooms, fed with all the daintiest dishes that can be procured, and not allowed to take the slightest exercise: the consequence of this feeding-up is that they grow very corpulent, but the Hindoos as well as the Mahomedans admire this style of figure, and perhaps the more because it is seldom seen among the common people.

The two ladies were not very decorously attired. Abundant draperies of blue and white muslin embroidered with gold, and trimmed with broad gold lace, rather veiled than covered their figures—for through the ethereal fineness of its web every outline could be seen; and as it was merely twined about them, every time they moved, an arm or a part of the breast or of the body would become visible. They seemed, however, to be only disturbed when the muslin fell off their heads, which they always hastily replaced. In addition to the muslin, they are covered with gold, pearls, and jewels so richly that they were really almost like animals of burthen; immense pearls and precious stones covered neck and breast, and between them hung heavy gold chains, with gold coins attached to them. Their ears were pierced with so many holes, (I counted twelve upon one), every hole being filled with an ornament, that one could scarcely see a morsel of the ear itself,— nothing was visible but gold, pearls, and gems : on each arm were eight or ten costly heavy bracelets—amongst which the principal piece was four inches broad of massive gold, and with six rows of brilliants—a heavy gold chain was twined three times round the waist— and ankles and feet were loaded with chains, bands, and rings.

Notwithstanding this display, the ladies, when they brought their jewelled caskets, showed me that they had by no means exhausted their contents. The Hindoos must spend enormous sums in these things, for every rich woman seeks to outdo the other.

On the present occasion, of course, the ladies were in grand state, and fully intended to dazzle me with their Indian magnificence.

The Baboo afterwards led me into a room, the windows of which looked towards the court; and among other European articles I noticed a glass case containing dolls, little horses, coaches, &c., with which not only the children but the women are accustomed to play. Poor things ! they are not allowed even the amusement of looking through a window into the street, for fear a man should happen to look at them ; and the only recreation permitted them by their severe husbands is that of going in a strictly closed palanquin to visit their female relations : so that it is no wonder if they have recourse to childish playthings. I was told also that they were passionate lovers of cards.

Before I left the house I went to see an apartment in the lower story, in which, once a year, a domestic religious service is performed, called the *Natsch*. This festival — the greatest of the Hindoos—falls at the beginning of October, and lasts fourteen days, and during that time both rich and poor carefully refrain from every kind of work. The merchant closes his shops and warehouses, the servant procures himself a deputy to do his work, and master and man pass their time, if not in praying and fasting, at least in doing nothing else. The Baboo related to me, that during the festival his saloon was richly ornamented, and the ten-armed goddess Durga set up in the middle of it. She is made of clay or wood, painted in the gaudiest colours, and decorated with flowers, ribbons, gold and silver spangles, and often real jewels. The saloon, the courtyard, and the outside of the house glitter with hundreds of lamps and lights intermixed with vases and garlands of flowers. Many animals are sacrificed, though they are killed not in the sight of the goddess, but in some remote corner of the house. Priests come to wait upon the divinity, and dancing-girls display their art to the sound of loud music : there are among these women, I was told, Indian Elslers and Taglionis who, like them, obtain large sums for their performances ; at the time I was there, there was a Persian dancer, who never came for an evening under 500 rupees.

During the Natsch, crowds of visitors, amongst whom are many Europeans, go from temple to temple, and the more distinguished guests are entertained with sweetmeats and fruit.

On the last day of the festival, the goddess is carried with music and pomp to the Hoogly, placed on a boat, and carried down the middle of the river, and amidst the shouts and joyous cries of the multitudes assembled on the shores, thrown into the water.

In former days the real jewels were thrown in with her, though carefully fished up again in the night by the priests; but now the giver of the festival manages to withdraw them during the progress down the river; but he must do it cautiously, so as not to be seen by the people.

A Natsch often costs thousands of rupees, and is one of the principal expenses of the wealthy.

Weddings also cost great sums, and amongst other expenses, the Brahmins have to be paid for making observations on the stars, to find out the fortunate day and hour for the celebration. Sometimes, even at the last moment, they discover that there is another hour more fortunate still; and then the marriage is put off for some hours, and the Brahmin has to be paid again.

Festivals in honour of the four-armed goddess Kally take place several times a year, and there were two while I was in Calcutta. Before every hut I saw a crowd of little idols, formed of clay, and gaily painted, but representing the most horrible figures. The goddess Kally is of the size of life, and stretches her tongue as far as possible out of widely opened jaws, but she is adorned with garlands of flowers. Her temple is a wretched building, or rather a dark hole, with a few turrets at the top of it: the statues in it are distinguished by most enormous heads and long tongues; their faces are painted red, yellow, and sky-blue.

This I saw through the door; for as I belonged to the feminine gender I was not deemed worthy to enter so great a sanctuary as the temple of Kally;—but I was quite resigned to the prohibition.

One remarkable but most painful spectacle that I witnessed in Calcutta was that of the dying-houses on the banks of the Hoogly. The one I saw was small and contained only one chamber with four empty bedsteads, and hither the dying are brought by their relations to pass their last moments, and placed on the bedsteads, or, if these are full, upon the ground, or even outside the huts in the burning sun. The places for burning the dead are in the immediate neighbourhood. I found five dying persons inside the house, and two outside: the latter were so completely enveloped in straw and coverings that I thought they must be dead already, but when I inquired, the attendants threw back the covering and I saw the poor creatures move : I think they must have been almost stifled. Inside the hut a very old woman lay on the floor journeying heavily and painfully through her last hour ; and the four bedsteads were similarly occupied, while the relations sat quietly round and awaited in the utmost tranquillity the last breath of the sufferer. To my question as to whether nothing was given to them, it was answered that if they did not die immediately they had from time to time a spoonful of the Ganges water, but less and less and at greater intervals, for when they were once brought there *they must die.* As soon as ever they are dead, almost before they are cold, they are carried out to the burning-place, which is enclosed by a wall.

In this place I saw one dead and one *dying* man, and on six funeral piles six corpses, which the high darting flames were rapidly consuming. Birds of the stork kind larger than turkeys, small vultures, and ravens were sitting round in great numbers on the neighbouring roofs and trees, and eagerly waiting for the half-burnt bodies. I hastened shuddering from the spot, and could for a long time not banish its painful image from my memory.

To the rich the burning of their dead often costs as much as 1,000 rupees, as they use sandal-wood, rose-wood, and other expensive kinds, and employ a Brahmin, musicians, and mourning women. The nearest relation must kindle the pile, and after the burning the bones are collected, put into a vase, and either buried or sunk in the Ganges.

With poor people, of course, there is not so much ceremony : they burn their dead simply upon wood or cow-dung, and when they are too poor to afford even these, they tie a stone to the body and throw it into the river. Before leaving this subject I must mention a little anecdote related to me by a person on whom I have the greatest reliance, and which may serve to show to what cruelty mistaken notions of religion will often lead.

Mr. N—— was one day on a journey through a district not far from the Ganges, and had with him a few servants and a dog : all of a sudden the animal disappeared, and at length he was found on the river's bank by the side of a human body, which he kept constantly licking. Mr. N—— went up to the spot and found that it was that of a man who had been exposed and left to die, but in whom a spark of life still lingered. He called his servants, made them wash the mud and dirt from the poor creature's face, and then wrap him well in a blanket and take care of him.   In a few days he was perfectly well, but when Mr. N—— was about to dismiss him he implored him most earnestly not to abandon him, saying that he had now lost caste, that he would not be acknowledged by any of his relations, and that, in short, he had been struck out of the list of the living.   Mr. N—— therefore retained the man in his service, and he is still in perfect health, though the circumstance took place several years ago.

The Hindoos themselves acknowledge that their manner of disposing of the dead leads to many a murder; for it is a precept of religion with them that when the physician declares there is no hope, the sick person must die.

BENARES.

Departure from Calcutta.—The Ganges.—Rajmahal.—Monghyr.—Patna.— Benares.—Description of the City.—Palaces and Temples.—The Sacred Apes.—The Ruins of Sarnath.—An Indigo Plantation.—Visit to the Rajah of Benares.—Martyrs and Faquirs.—Indian Peasants.—The Missionary Establishment.

On the 10th of December, after a stay of five weeks, I left Calcutta for Benares.   The journey may be made either by land or water, that is, by the Ganges: by land the distance is 470 miles; by water, in the rainy season, 685, but in the dry time of year 400 miles more, on account of the enormous circuit that must be made to get from the Hoogly to the main river.

The land journey is made in a post palanquin, with bearers who are changed like horses, but at every five or six miles, and people travel day and night: as their coming has always been announced beforehand, they find at every station fresh bearers ready; but at night a torch-bearer also has to be taken in order to frighten the wild beasts by the glare of the flame; by this mode the journey costs about 200 rupees for each person, with something additional for luggage.   The water way is by a steamer, which goes almost every week as far as Allahabad, more than a hundred miles beyond Benares, but it is very slow, as, on account of the numerous sandbanks, it only goes on with daylight, and notwithstanding this precaution, frequently runs aground when the water is low; but the prices are nevertheless high—275 rupees for the first place and

216 for the second, besides three rupees a day for board without wine: but I had heard so much of the beautiful banks of the
Ganges, and of the renowned cities upon them, that I decided on
adopting this plan.

According to announcement, the steamer "General Macleod,"
140 horse power, was to leave Calcutta on the 8th, but as soon as I
got on board I had the pleasure of hearing that our departure was
to be put off for four-and-twenty hours, and this ultimately proved
to be eight-and-forty, so that we did not really get away till the
10th. The first day we got down the river as far as Katscherie,
and on the following one turned into the Sunderbunds at Mud
Point, and then entered the Gurie, a considerable tributary of the
Ganges.

The first part of the journey was tedious enough, there were
neither towns nor villages to be seen ; the shores are perfectly flat,
and the country far and wide was nothing but a high close thicket,
which the English call a jungle: in the night we heard the growl-
ing of tigers, which are quite at home in this district, and the river
was full of crocodiles ; I have seen as many as six, from five to
fifteen feet in length, lying sunning themselves on the sand-banks
or the muddy shores of the Ganges ; at the approach of our noisy
steamer, however, they slipped away into the dirty yellow flood.

The channel in the Sunderbunds and the Gurie is often so
narrow that two vessels can hardly pass, but sometimes many
miles wide, so as to form an immense basin: in one of the narrow
places our vessel had to be detained to let another sail by, and in
effecting this one of two ships that we had got in tow struck so
violently on ours that the wall of one of the cabins was broken in,
though fortunately no one was hurt : in another, two vessels full
of natives were lying at anchor, and as their crews did not perceive our approach until too late, they were still engaged in getting
up their anchor when we came rushing on ; our captain, however,
would not stop, but turned rather too much aside, and in so doing
ran the boat fairly into the jungle, so that some of the blinds of our
cabin windows remained hanging on the branches as trophies ;
provoked at this accident, he actually got out a boat and sent it
back *to cut the cable of the native vessel*, by which, of course, their
anchor was lost.

We entered the main stream of the Ganges at Gulna, about six
days after leaving Calcutta, and having once run aground by the

way : we stopped for the evening at a village called Commercally ; the inhabitants brought provisions of all kinds, and we had now an opportunity of learning their prices : a fine sheep cost three rupees (6s. 1½d.)—a fish, weighing several pounds, three halfpence— eighteen young fowls, two shillings English—eight eggs, five far- things—twenty oranges, three halfpence, and so on,—and with these prices the captain charged his passengers three rupees a day for their board, and was, moreover, not ashamed to let the passengers buy eggs, fresh bread, and oranges for themselves, and to see these articles make their appearance at his dearly-paid table.

The jungle had now disappeared from the shores, and given place to beautiful rice and other plantations ; villages were not wanting, though they mostly consisted of straw or palm-leaf huts, and looked very poor ; our steamer appeared to be an attractive sight to the inhabitants, for they left house and field and ran shouting after us along the banks.

At a place called Bealeah which we passed, there is a depôt for criminals, who are brought hither from great distances. Apparently they are not so anxious to run away as our prisoners in Europe, for they were very slightly fettered, and allowed to go about with- out any guard ; they are well taken care of, and employed at light work : a paper manufactory, for instance, is almost wholly wrought by them.

The inhabitants of this town appear very fanatical, for when I went to take a walk with one of the passengers, and we wished to turn into a bye-street, where there was a Hindoo temple, the people, the moment they perceived our intention, set up such a dismal howl, that we thought it best to turn back and leave our curiosity unsatisfied.

December 19th.—To-day for the first time we saw hills, though not high ones, and towards evening we were for the second time fast upon a sand-bank. We passed the night quietly enough, but in the morning we made every effort to get off again, the vessels we were towing were cast off, the machines heated to their utmost, the sailors laboured most perseveringly, yet at noon we were still as firmly fixed as ever. A steamer passed us from Allahabad, but our captain was so angry at being seen by a comrade in this position, that he would not put up a flag. The captain of the other vessel offered his assistance nevertheless, but it was abruptly declined, and it was not till after many hours severe toil that the steamer was again got afloat.

In the course of the day we touched at Rajmahal, an extensive village, but which is said to be very unhealthy, from the thick woods and morasses by which it is surrounded. Here once stood the great city of Gur, one of the largest in India, which is said to have occupied twenty square miles, and contained nearly two millions of inhabitants, and travellers still find numerous and stately ruins.

Since this was fortunately a coal station, we were allowed some hours on shore, which the young men employed in the chase, for which the fine woods, the grandest I have as yet seen in India, offered tempting opportunities : they are said, indeed, to be full of tigers, but no one stopped for that, I myself went hunting, *videlicet* for ruins, which I sought far and wide in the forest and the morass. But though I sought, I did not find, or at least only what was very insignificant : the best things I saw were two simple gates of sandstone covered with sculptures, and a small temple; but all the ruins together that I saw certainly did not occupy a space of two English square miles. Some hundred paces within the forest lay many native huts to which led the prettiest possible paths under leafy arcades.

Towards the end of my ramble, I was joined by one of the passengers, but the moment the men of the village perceived that my companion was of the male sex, they roared to the women to escape into their huts ; and they obeyed indeed, but I noticed that they remained standing at the doors, and moreover that they forgot to cover their faces.

In this region there are whole woods of cocoa-palms, of which India is the native land, and here they reach a height of eighty feet; and bear fruit in six years: whilst in other countries they are seldom more than fifty feet high, and do not bear for fifteen years. It is, perhaps, the most useful tree in the world, giving a large nourishing fruit, a delicious milk, large leaves for covering huts, the strongest ropes, the purest oil, besides mats, woven stuffs, dye stuffs, and a spirit called palm-brandy, which is obtained by making incisions in the crown of the tree. During a whole month the Hindoos climb up every morning and evening, to take the juice that has dribbled into pots placed ready to receive it.

December 22d.—This day brought us to a most singular group of rocks, which rise like a fairy island out of the majestic Ganges.

In former times this place was honoured as the most sacred in the whole river, and thousands of boats and ships were found furrowing this part of it. Faquirs carried on a flourishing trade, edifying poor pilgrims with their pious speeches, and receiving from them gifts in return; but the place has now lost its reputation for sanctity, the thankful offerings come but slowly in, and two or three faquirs at most pick up upon it a poor living.

In the evening we stopped at Monghyr, a tolerably large town with ancient fortifications; but one of the first objects that strikes the eye is a European cemetery, extremely full, and which I should, certainly, from the style of the monuments, never have supposed to belong to any Christian sect; for they were all pyramids, temples, kiosks, and so forth. That it should be crowded is not surprising; for this is considered one of the unhealthiest places in all India, and whoever is ordered here for a few years may generally take a final farewell of his friends.

Patna is one of the largest and oldest cities in India, and consists of a single broad street—eight English miles long, and many small short ones that turn out of it. The houses are, with very few exceptions, small and wretched-looking, and the temples, the ghauts, and the Mahomedan mosques, as seen from the river, promise much more than on a nearer approach they fulfil.

Patna is a very important place for the opium trade, by which many of the inhabitants have become wealthy; but they do not display their wealth either in clothes, or in any thing else that appears in public. I saw but two costumes; and that of the poor is nothing more than a cloth round the loins; the better-off classes wear one much resembling the European.

The principal street is very animated with carriages as well as with pedestrians; for the Hindoo is such a sworn enemy to the exertion of walking, that he will never go on foot if he can get the worst place on the most wretched conveyance. The one commonly in use consists of a narrow wooden car, on two wheels, with four stakes, sticking up, connected with cross-poles, on which are hung long coloured curtains, and it is protected at the top by a canopy: there is really room in them for only two persons, but three or four often get into them; so that these bailis, as they are called, put me in mind of the Italian carriages, with as many people clinging round about them as can find standing room.

In the evening, when we returned to the steamer, we found it in a bustle, like a camp. All sorts of articles for sale had been brought and spread out upon the deck by the natives ; and the shoemakers, especially, had some excellent and durable specimens of their art, which, besides, were extraordinarily cheap. A pair of men's boots, for instance, cost two rupees, though it is true double the price was asked. I saw on this occasion some specimens of the way in which the European sailors sometimes deal with the natives. One of the engine-men wanted a pair of shoes, but offered for them only the fourth of the price asked ; the shoemaker would not agree to this, and took them back again ; but the engine-man snatched them out of his hand, flung him a trifle over what he had first offered, and ran with the shoes into his cabin : the shoemaker ran after him, and asked again to have them back ; but instead of the shoes he got a few hard cuffs, with the addition of sundry threats if he did not keep himself quiet ; and the poor fellow returned to his goods almost crying. Another case happened the same evening : a Hindoo boy having brought a box on board for one of the passengers, begged a trifle for his trouble, but it was refused ; the boy remained standing, and from time to time renewed his request, but they drove him away, and struck him when he would not go. The boy told his story, sobbing, to the captain, but he only shrugged his shoulders ; and the poor boy was at last turned out of the ship. How many similar instances have I seen, and how little is it to be wondered at, if these barbarous and heathen nations often hate us ! Wherever the European comes he will reign supreme ; and his rule is often more oppressive than that of the natives.

December 26th.— The practice of exposing the dying on the banks of the Ganges does not appear to be here so common as I had been led to expect by the accounts of travellers ; for, in fourteen days I have seen but one instance of it. The dying man lay quite close to the water's edge, and some people, probably the relatives, sat round him, waiting for his last breath. Sometimes one of them took some water or mud from the river in his hand, and touched the nose and mouth of the sufferer with it ; for it is an article of belief that if any one dies with his mouth full of holy water from the Ganges he will go immediately to heaven. The relations and friends remain by the dying man till sunset, and then they depart and leave him to his fate, which is very frequently to become the prey of a crocodile. Of floating corpses I saw but two, as the greater number are burnt.

Ghazipoor is a considerable place, remarkable at a distance for its beautiful ghauts. As you approach you see enormous fields of roses, for its most important manufacture is that of attar of roses, which is made in the following manner :—on forty pounds of roses are poured sixty pounds of water, and they are then distilled over a slow fire, and thirty pounds of rose-water obtained. This rose-water is then poured over forty pounds of fresh roses, and from that is distilled at most twenty pounds of rose-water ; this is then exposed to the cold night air, and in the morning a small quantity of oil is found on the surface. From eighty pounds of roses, about 200,000, at the utmost an ounce and a half of oil is obtained ; and even at Ghazipoor it costs forty rupees an ounce.

December 28th.—At ten o'clock this morning we reached at length the holy city of Benares, and cast anchor at Radschgal, where coolies and camels stood ready to receive us ; and as I left the Ganges I could not but remark, that on this whole long journey of a thousand miles I had not seen a single spot distinguished for natural beauty. The shores are flat, or, perhaps, from ten to twenty feet high, and more inland, sandy spots alternate with plantations or jungle ; towns and villages there are plenty, but, with the exception of the ghauts, there is little to admire in them ; and in many parts the river is so broad that it looks more like the sea, and you can scarcely perceive the distant shore.

Whoever visits Calcutta only, can have very little idea of India, for Calcutta is almost a European city : the palaces, the equipages are European ; there are parties, balls, concerts, promenades, as in Paris or London ; and if it were not for the yellow brown faces in the streets, and the crowds of Hindoo servants in the houses, you might really forget that you were in so distant a part of the world.

But at Benares it is quite different—there the European feels himself a stranger ; out of the 300,000 inhabitants the Europeans are scarcely 150, and they are reminded every moment, by the foreign manners and customs surrounding them, that they are only tolerated intruders.

Benares is to the Hindoo what Mecca is to the Mahomedan, or Rome to the Catholic—the sacred city ; and any one, even without distinction of religion, may secure eternal felicity merely by spending four-and-twenty hours in it. It is not surprising, therefore, that it is constantly visited by great crowds of pilgrims, not fewer than three or four hundred thousand every year, by whose gifts and offerings, as well as the traffic they bring with them, the city is much enriched.

It is a handsome town, especially when seen from the water, whence its defects are not visible; and its magnificent flight] of steps, made of enormous blocks of stone, leading up to the houses and palaces, and elaborate city gates, have a grand effect. In the handsome part of the town they extend uninterruptedly for a distance of two English miles along the river. These steps have of course cost immense sums, and there are stones enough used in them to have built a great town. The palaces are antique, but many in the Moorish and Gothic, as well as the Hindostanee style.

They are sometimes six stories high, with superb gates, and have their fronts ornamented in a masterly manner with arabesques, reliefs, and sculptures, as well as with colonnades, verandahs, balconies, and friezes : the windows only displeased me—they are low, narrow, and seldom regularly placed.

The countless temples afford a proof at the same time of the riches and of the religious temper of the inhabitants of this town : every opulent Hindoo has near his house a temple of his own ; that is to say, a small tower of often not more than twenty feet high, and which, like other Hindoo temples, has no windows, and only a small entrance. The other temples are from thirty to sixty feet high, and look very well from a distance, covered as they are with elaborate decorations: unfortunately, however, many of these handsome buildings are in ruins; and as the Ganges is in many places undermining the city, palaces and temples will, sooner or later, sink into the loose earth, or totter to their fall.

Already poor little huts have been built over the ruins of many stately piles, and disfigure the city far more than the ruins themselves, which, even in that state, are often beautiful.

At sunset the river at Benares presents a spectacle that can be seen nowhere else in the world. The religious Hindoo comes here to perform his devotions, and descending into the water turns towards the sun, pours water three times over his head, and murmurs at the same time his prayers. With the large population of

Benares, even without the pilgrims, there are never less on an average than 50,000 devotees in the river at once—besides the Brahmins, who sit on the steps or on little kiosks, to receive the gifts of the pilgrims and others, and present them, in return, with absolution for their sins.   Every Hindoo must bathe at least once a day,—and if he can, twice—though the women need only pour water over themselves at home.   At the time of the festival called Mela, when the throng of pilgrims is greatest, the broad river is all covered with black spots—namely, the heads of bathers ; and the steps are so thronged that you can scarcely come to them.

The interior of the city is by no means so handsome as the part along the Ganges ;—the streets are, for the most part, dirty, ugly, and so narrow that you cannot pass through them with a palanquin; and in all corners, and almost at every house, stands the symbol of the god Shiva.

The handsomest of the temples in the town is the *Visvishas,* which consists of two towers connected by rows of columns, and having their peaks covered with plates of gold.   The temple is surrounded by a wall, but we were allowed to enter the court and look into it.   We saw symbols of Vishnu and Shiva, crowned with flowers, and sprinkled about with grains of corn and rice : in the outer hall stood images of bulls in metal or stone, and living white bulls (I counted eight) were wandering freely about. These are considered sacred, and are allowed to go anywhere they like, and even to satisfy their appetite on the flowers and corn offered in sacrifice ; you meet these sacred animals in the streets, and the people respectfully make way for them, and often bring them food,—but they do not now, as I am told they once did, allow them to eat the corn, &c. put out for sale.   When one of them dies, he is treated exactly as the Hindoo himself is, that is, he is burnt or thrown into the river.

When I looked into the temple I saw men and women occupied in wreathing and adorning the images with flowers, under which many put a piece of money ; they then sprinkled them with Ganges water, and scattered corn and rice about.

Near the temple is a holy well, of which I heard the following account :—When the English had conquered Benares, they planted a cannon opposite the temple to destroy the god Mahadeo.   The Brahmins, incensed at this outrage, sought to excite the people to insurrection ; but the English, in order to prevent hostilities, proposed a mode of settling the dispute. " If," said they, "your god is stronger than the God of the Christians, our ball will do him no harm ; but in the other case he will be shattered to pieces." The Brahmins, however, were not to be beaten in this way, and when the cannon was fired, and the poor god Mahadeo fell in fragments, they declared that it was because he had left that form,—they themselves had seen him leave it and plunge into the neighbouring well, and from this time the well has been regarded as holy. Another holy place, also close to the temple, is the *Mancarnika*, a deep basin, of perhaps sixty feet long, and an equal breadth, and lined with stone; broad steps lead down from the four sides into the water, to which there is a similar story attached ; but in this case it is the god Shiva who plays the part assigned in the other to Mahadeo. Both deities reside at present in the waters, and every pilgrim who visits Benares must bathe here, and leave a small gift, for the reception of which there are always some Brahmins ready. They are not distinguished by their costume from the more opulent classes, but their complexion is fairer, and their features often noble. The place for burning the dead is near these holy ponds ; and when I came in they were *roasting* some bodies,—I cannot call it by any other name, the fires were so small, and the bodies stuck out so far over them.

Not more than fifty paces from the pond on the shore of the Ganges stands an uncommonly beautiful temple consisting of three towers, but the ground has given way under them ; one is lean_ ing to the right, the other to the left, and the third has almost sunk in the Ganges.

One very remarkable building of Benares is the Observatory, built under the renowned Emperor Akbar, more than 200 years ago. There are no telescopes or instruments of the ordinary kind—but all that there are, are constructed of massive freestone. On a raised terrace, which you reach by a flight of stone steps, stand tables of an exactly circular form, and others of half and quarter circles, full of lines, characters, and writing. With these instruments the Brahmins have long made, and still make, their calculations. We found several of them busily engaged in writing when we entered. Many of the Brahmins, as is known, give instruction in astronomy, Sanscrit, and other scientific subjects.

Another of the sights of Benares is the abode of the Sacred Apes —some enormous mango-trees in the suburb of Durgakund. As we approached the trees, the animals perhaps perceived that we were coming to pay them a visit, for they came without any shyness quite close to us; but when the servant, whom we had sent for something to feed them with, came back, it was amusing to see the merry little race hurrying to us from all quarters—the streets, the roofs of the houses, and the tops of the trees—leaping and running with the most comic agility. In a few moments we were enclosed in a circle of some hundreds of them, mostly about two feet high, and of a dirty yellow colour, fighting and wrestling in the drollest way with each other for the fruit and corn thrown to them. The oldest, or largest among them, played the commander, and wherever he saw a dispute going on, sprang towards the contending parties, grinned, muttered, and distributed cuffs to one and the other till they jumped away. It was the largest and most amusing company of apes that I had ever seen.

Among the thousands of temples to be found in Benares, few are worth seeing, much less describing—but among the things that interested me I may mention an indigo plantation, which was the first I had seen—and an Indian prince, namely the Rajah of Benares, to whom I had the honour of being introduced. The indigo is a shrub-like plant two or three feet high, with delicate blue green leaves, which at the harvest time, about the month of August, are cut off close to the stem, tied into bundles and laid in great wooden tubs. Planks are then laid on them, and great stones to cause a pressure, and then water is poured over them, and after a day or two the liquor begins to ferment. In this process of fermentation lies the principal difficulty, and every thing depends on allowing it to continue just the proper time. When the water has acquired a dark green colour it is poured off into other tubs, mixed with lime, and stirred with wooden shovels, till a blue deposit separates itself from the water, which is then allowed to run off. The remaining substance, the indigo, is then put into linen bags, through which the moisture filters, and as soon as the indigo is dry and hard, it is broken into pieces and packed up.

For my visit to the rajah I was indebted to a travelling companion, Mr. Law. On the day when it was to take place, I found a splendidly adorned boat waiting for us near the bank of the river, and on the opposite side was a palanquin, which was to carry us to the residence of the prince, the citadel Ramnaghur, which lies on the left bank of the Ganges above the town. We were soon before the entrance of the palace, a lofty and majestic-looking gate—and I hoped, therefore, that in the interior I should find an edifice of corresponding grandeur ; but in this I was disappointed, for I saw only irregular courts, and small unsymmetrical buildings, without any pretension to either taste or luxury. In one of the courts on the ground floor was a simple hall supported on columns ; and full, overfull indeed, of European furniture, with some wretched daubs of pictures hanging on the walls. The court, however, was crowded with attendants, who contemplated us with great attention.

The rajah now made his appearance, accompanied by his brother, and some other great men, and followed by a crowd of attendants, whom from their appearance I could hardly distinguish from them.

The two princes were very richly dressed in gold-embroidered satin, with their caps set with diamonds, silk shoes thickly worked in gold, and large brilliant rings on their fingers. The brother, a lad of nineteen, whom the rajah had adopted as his son, wore a white turban, with a costly agraffe of diamonds and pearls, large pearls in his ears, and large heavy bracelets rich with gems. The elder prince was a handsome man with a good-natured and intellectual expression ; the younger did not please me so well.

We had scarcely taken our places before large silver bowls were brought with elegantly wrought nargilehs, which we were invited to smoke. We returned thanks for the honour, but declined it, and the prince smoked alone—but never more than a few puffs out of one nargileh ; he would then lay it aside, and another and handsomer one was presented to him. The deportment of the rajah was both decorous and lively, and I regretted my inability to converse with him otherwise than through an interpreter.

He inquired whether I had ever seen a natsch or festive dance, and on my replying in the negative, ordered one to be exhibited immediately.

In about half an hour two dancing-girls and three musicians made their appearance ; the dancers were dressed in gold-embroidered muslin and wide trowsers, which descended to the ground, quite covering the shoeless feet, and they made animated movements with their arms, hands, and fingers, and sometimes with the feet, on which they wore silver bells, while the musicians stood behind them playing, two of them on four-stringed instruments, something like our violins, and the other on small drums. Sometimes the dancers formed pretty graceful figures and draperies with their upper garments, and when the performance had lasted about half an hour they accompanied it with a song, but the two sylphs made so lamentable a screeching that my ears and my nervous system could hardly endure it, even with the help of the refreshments that were handed to us the while.

When the dance was over, the prince asked me through the interpreter if I would like to visit his garden, which lay about a mile from the palace, and I was so indiscreet as to accept the proposal.

We then betook ourselves to the fore-court of the palace, where some richly-adorned elephants stood ready, and the rajah's own elephant, an animal of uncommon size and beauty, was assigned to me and Mr. Law ; a scarlet covering with gold fringe borders and tassels was thrown quite over him, and on his broad back was placed a convenient seat, like a phaeton without wheels, and he was then made to kneel down, and a step-ladder being placed against him we mounted and took our places on the huge monster, and a servant placed himself behind us, holding an enormous umbrella over our heads, while the driver sat on the neck, and from time to time pricked the elephant slightly between the ears ; the young prince with his companions and servants were distributed amongst the other elephants, some officers on horseback rode at our sides, two soldiers with drawn sabres led the way, and the procession was closed by a dozen soldiers on foot and some on horseback.

I was quite pleased with the genuine Indian style of this party, although the motion of the elephant is like that of the camel, very jolting and disagreeable.

When we arrived at the garden, the proud glance of the young prince seemed to ask whether we were not enraptured with its magnificence, and we pretended to be accordingly, but, I must own, somewhat hypocritically,—for there was really nothing to admire in it.

As we left it, the gardeners, according to Indian custom, brought us some fruits and flowers tied into nosegays ; and on the following morning the rajah sent to inquire politely how the excursion had agreed with us, and to present us again with pastry, sweetmeats, and choice fruits, amongst which were grapes and pomegranates, which at this time of year were great rarities, and were brought 700 miles from Cabul.

The rajah of Benares receives from the English government a pension of a lak (100,000) of rupees, and draws an equal revenue from his territories, yet he is, notwithstanding, deeply in debt, from the enormous expenses of his living,—the luxury of dress and decoration, his numerous wives, his countless servants, the throng of horses, camels, and elephants which he has to maintain.

Concerning the palace of his highness we heard a wonderful story—that for many years no one had ever died in it ; but for this fact we discovered the following explanation. One of the former rulers one day inquired of a Brahmin what would become of the soul of a man who should die in his palace ; and the Brahmin, as in politeness bound, replied it would go to heaven : but the rajah, it is to be presumed, was troubled with some doubts on the subject, and thought proper to repeat the question ninety-nine times, and then again for the hundredth, when the Brahmin lost all patience, and replied it would go into an ass ; and thenceforward every one, from the prince to his meanest servant, when they find themselves in the least indisposed, hastens from the palace in order to avoid having to repeat after death a part which they have already perhaps played to perfection during life.

I had twice during my stay in Benares an opportunity of seeing the martyr faquirs, who torture themselves by running iron hooks through their flesh, standing for years upon one leg, holding weights in painful positions, and so forth ; indeed, they sometimes carry their self-inflicted torments so far as to kill themselves ; but they are now much fewer than in former days : one of the two whom I saw was holding a heavy hatchet over his head, and at the same time stooping in the position of a man splitting wood ; I observed him in this position for a quarter of an hour, and he remained as firm and still as if he had been turned to stone, and he had already continued this useful occupation for several years. The other was holding up his toe to his nose. Some impose on themselves the penance of eating only disgusting food, putrid meat, half-decayed vegetables, mud, earth, and filth of every kind, maintaining that it is quite a matter of indifference with what the stomach is filled ; they all go almost entirely naked, and smear their bodies with cow-dung, and then strew them with ashes; their breasts and forehead are painted with symbols of Shiva and Vishnu, and their tangled hair is coloured of a dark brownish-red; they run about the streets preaching whatever comes into their heads; but this class is not regarded with the same veneration as the martyrs.

One of the gentlemen whom I knew in Benares was so good as to communicate to me some intelligence concerning the relation of the peasants to the government. All the land belongs either to the English government or the native princes, and they let it in large estates to the chief farmers, who then sub-let it to the peasants, and the fate of the latter depends wholly on their will and pleasure. Very frequently the head farmer will demand the rent when the harvest has not yet been gathered in, and the poor peasant is obliged to sell the standing crops for whatever they will fetch, and can scarcely get enough out of the fields to keep life in himself and his family. He seldom makes any appeal to the law for redress, for though the law is not severe nor usually the judges unjust, the districts are so large that he would often have to make a journey of seventy or eighty miles to obtain redress; and then it would be of little use to attempt to obtain a hearing without bringing a gift with him; and where could he obtain it, when almost his last farthing has been wrung from him by the head farmer? On the whole I could not but come to the melancholy conviction, that the position of the slaves in Brazil is preferable to that of the peasantry here. The slave has no care in providing for his wants, and he is not overburdened with work, as the interest of the master would suffer by it; for a slave costs 700 or 800 gilders; and though there are cases in which the slave is tyrannically treated, these are very few.

In the environs of Benares live several German and English missionaries, who go regularly to preach in the city, and at one of these institutions there is even a Christian village inhabited by some twenty Hindoo families; but notwithstanding this, Christianity makes little or no progress. I used to inquire of the missionaries, whenever I had an opportunity, how many Hindoos or Mahomedans they had converted during the time of their mission, and in general the answer was *none*, or sometimes *one*. The history of the twenty baptized families is this: in 1831, when all India was desolated by the cholera, the nervous fever, and the succeeding famine, many children were made orphans, and left to wander about without home or shelter: some of these the missionaries took charge of and brought up in the Christian religion. They were instructed in various kinds of work, placed in cottages, provided with employment, and afterwards married ; and their descendants are still kept under close care and superintendence ; but the number of converts has never increased. I attended some of the examinations of these children and found that both boys and girls were well instructed in reading, writing, geography, and arithmetic, as well as in religion ; the girls also embroider, knit, and do all kinds of white sewing work ; the boys and men make carpets, do printing, bookbinding, carpentering work, and so forth, and every department seems to be managed in an orderly and intelligent manner by Mr. and Mrs. Luitprand, who appear to treat their pupils with true Christian kindness. But what are such instances as these but drops in the immeasurable ocean?

ALLAHABAD, AGRA, AND DELHI.

Allahabad.—Cannipoor.—Agra.—The Mausoleum of Sultan Akbar, Taj-Mahal.—The Ruined Town of Fatipoor.—Sikri Delhi.—The Main Street.—Public Processions.—The Emperor's Palace.—Palaces and Mosques.—Old Delhi.—Remarkable Ruins.—The English Military Station.

I LEFT Benares for Allahabad in company with Mr. Law, in a *Post Dock,* a convenient palanquin for two persons, placed on wheels and drawn by two horses. It was about six o'clock in the evening, on the 7th of January 1848, and early on the following morning we were crossing the long bridge of boats that leads across the Ganges to the city of Allahabad. As soon as we arrived in the town, we exchanged our palanquin for another, which was carried by men to the hotel, situated about a mile from it. On reaching it we found it quite filled by the officers of a regiment on the march; my companion was only admitted on condition of contenting himself with a place in the public dining-room, and nothing remained for me but to avail myself of a letter of introduction to Dr. Angus. My arrival threw the good old gentleman into some embarrassment, for his house was already overfilled with travellers, but his sister, Mrs. Spencer, got over the difficulty by kindly offering me the half of her sleeping apartment.

Allahabad lies partly on the Jumna and partly on the Ganges, and is a large handsome town with 25,000 inhabitants. It is one of the sacred cities too, and is visited by many pilgrims. The Europeans live outside the town in pretty houses in gardens.

One of the most remarkable objects in it is the Fort and Palace built under Sultan Akbar, which lies at the confluence of the Jumna with the Ganges. The fortress has been much strengthened by the English, and is now one of the strongest places in British India.

The palace is an ordinary building enough; but the arrangement of the interior is curious. Some of the halls are intersected by three rows of columns, which form three arcades, crossing each other, and in others flights of steps lead up into small chambers contained in the large ones, like boxes in a theatre. The palace is now used as an armoury, and 40,000 men can be completely armed there, and provided with heavy artillery. In one of the courts is a metal column, six and thirty feet high, covered with inscriptions, and having a lion on the top. Another remarkable thing is a small insignificant temple, in a rather decayed state, now enclosed within the limits of the fort, which is regarded by the Hindoos as of such extraordinary sanctity, that a wealthy native, who had made a pilgrimage hither, lately offered the commandant 20,000 rupees to allow him to perform his devotions in it; but this, it seems, could not be allowed. The tradition concerning the fort is, that when Sultan Akbar began to build it, no wall could be made to stand, but fell in immediately, and at length an oracle declared that the building would never be completed till a man should devote himself to a voluntary death; such a one really presented himself, merely making the condition that the fortress and town should bear his name. The man bore the not very poetical name of "Brog," and by this name accordingly the town is more frequently mentioned by the Hindoos than by the more euphonious one of Allahabad. A little subterranean temple near the fortress is consecrated to the memory of the hero who lies buried in it, and many pilgrims visit it every year; you always have to carry torches or candles into it, as it is quite dark, and indeed it is like nothing but a large handsome vaulted cellar. The ceiling is supported by simple columns, the walls are full of niches, all occupied by images or symbols of gods; but the greatest curiosity in it is a leafless tree, which has sprung up in the temple and forced its way through the roof.

In a large beautiful garden stand four Mahomedan mausolea, with sarcophagi of white marble, and the walls painted with stiff flowers and wretched attempts at trees, between which are inscriptions. One place on the wall was covered with a curtain, which the guide put back very reverentially, and showed me the impression of a colossal hand, which he assured me was made by a great-great-grandson of Mahomed, who, when he stood up after finishing his prayer, supported himself against this wall, and left on it the impression of his sacred hand.

In the garden I saw the most enormous tamarind-trees perhaps in the world. I thought I had seen the largest in Brazil, but here the soil or climate appears to be still more favourable to this species of tree; not only is the garden full of magnificent specimens, but superb avenues of them extend round the city. I find, indeed, that the tamarinds of Allahabad are quite celebrated.

On one side of the wall surrounding the garden are two serais, whose internal arrangements do not disgrace the stately portals that form their entrance. They were animated by the presence of a great number of guests in all costumes, besides horses, oxen, camels, and elephants, and a great quantity of goods in chests, bales, and sacks.

We travelled to Cannipoor, an important military station, distant 150 miles, by the same conveyance by which we had come to Allahabad. The way showed little variety of scenery, as it lay entirely through a richly cultivated plain; and we met no travellers, except some English troops on the march.

A military march in India resembles the migration of a small nation; and it is easy, after seeing one of them, to form a very clear idea of the movements of the enormous Persian and other Asiatic armies of antiquity. The greater part of the native soldiers, as well as the European officers, are married; and when a regiment sets out on a march there are almost as many women and children as soldiers. They ride by twos or threes upon horses and oxen, or in carts, or trudge along on foot, with bundles upon their backs; having their household goods packed in cars, and driving their cows and goats before them. The officers and their families follow at short intervals in European carriages, palanquins, or on horseback; their household goods are packed on camels and elephants, and these commonly close the procession. The camp is pitched on both sides of the way, and the men are on one side, and the animals on the other.

Towards noon we reached the small village of Beara, where we found a bongolo; that is, a small house with four rooms, scarcely provided with the simplest and most necessary furniture. These bongolos are erected by the government; they lie on the high roads, and serve in some measure as inns. For the use of a room in them a single person pays a rupee, and a family two, and in most bongolos the same payment is required for the shortest stay as for a night. There is always a native appointed to wait on and cook for travellers, over whom control is exercised by means of a book, in which every one writes an account of the way in which he has been treated. When there are no other guests you may remain in them as long as you please, but, in the opposite case, only four-and-twenty hours.

It took us three nights and two and a half days of travelling to reach Agra, the former residence of the Great Moguls of India. The suburbs have the appearance of wretched villages : nothing was to be seen but high walls of mud or clay, and within these lay little dilapidated huts. But the scene changed when we passed through a stately gate, and found ourselves in a spacious square enclosed by walls, whence four other gates led to the town, the fortress, and two other suburbs. Like most towns in India, Agra possesses no inn; but a German missionary received me kindly, and afterwards continued his friendly attentions so far as to take me to visit all that was worth seeing in the city and its environs.

Our first visit was to the magnificent mausoleum of Sultan Akbar, at Secundra, four English miles off. The entrance is a masterpiece, and I remained long standing in admiration before it. The vast building lies on a stone terrace, to which you ascend by broad steps; the doors are lofty, and an imposing dome rises above all; at the four corners stand minarets of white marble, three stories high, but unfortunately a little fallen in. There are also the remains of a stone wall in open fretwork in front.

The mausoleum stands in the middle of the garden, and forms a quadrangle of four stories high. The lower story is surrounded by beautiful arcades ; the apartments are simple ; the walls covered with a polished cement, intended to supply the place of marble ; some sarcophagi stand in it; and the second story is surrounded with beautiful arabesques. It consists of a great terrace, which covers all the lower buildings, and from the midst of which rises an open airy apartment, supported upon pillars and covered with a light roof. A great number of little kiosks in the corners and sides of the terrace give to the whole a whimsical but elegant appearance. The small cupolas of the kiosks must once have been very splendid, and you still see in them remains of glazed and coloured clay, and white marble. The third story resembles the second ; the fourth, and uppermost, is most beautiful, being entirely of white marble, while the three lower are of red sand-stone. Broad covered arcades, whose outer marble trellis-work is inimitably beautiful, form an open quadrangle, above which lies no covering but the bright blue sky ; and here stands the sarcophagus in which the bones of the sultan rest ; over the arches of the arcades are sentences from the Koran in black marble letters.   This is, I believe, the only Mahomedan monument in which the sarcophagus is placed at the top of a building, and in the open air.

In the citadel is a fine specimen of Mogul architecture in the palace of the Mogul sultans.   Many of the more modern Indian towns originate from the Moguls, or have been so altered by them that they have quite lost their original character.   The fortifications here form a circuit of two English miles, and consist of two and threefold walls, of which the outermost is seventy-five feet high.   The interior of the fortress is divided into three courts : in the first reside the guards, in the second, the officers and civil dignitaries, and in the third, which comprises the side towards the Jumna, lie the palaces, baths, harems, and gardens.   In this court every thing is of white marble ; the walls of the rooms in the palaces are covered with semi-precious stones,—agates, onyxes, jasper, cornelian, lapis-lazuli, inlaid in mosaic work, and forming vases of flowers, birds, arabesques, and various figures.   Two of the apartments have no windows, and are calculated exclusively for the effect of illumination.   The walls and vaulted ceilings are covered with mica, in narrow silver frames : waterfalls rush over glass walls, behind which lights can be placed, and sparkling fountains rise in the midst of the apartment ; even without being lit up it glittered and sparkled in a wonderful manner ; and when the radiance of countless lamps is reflected from these thousand dazzling points, the effect must be like that of an enchanted palace in the Arabian Nights.   By way of contrast to this scene of gay and fairy splendour, we were conducted, before we left the fortress, to the theatre of many a stern and dismal tragedy of real life—the subterranean dungeons, where the secret executions used to take place.

Outside the fortress, and near the river, lies the Jumna mosque, which is often considered to excel the celebrated one of Soliman in Constantinople.   It is placed on a lofty terrace of red sandstone, and has three magnificent cupolas, in the vaulted ceilings of which appear remains of costly paintings in blue and gold, unfortunately in rather a decayed state ; but the English government has begun some repairs in it.

From the mosque we returned to the town, which is surrounded by ruins. The principal street, " Sander," is broad and cleanly, and paved in the middle with flag-stones, and on the sides with bricks. The houses, from one to four stories high, are almost all of red sandstone, mostly small, but many of them surrounded by columns and galleries, and ornamented with beautiful portals. The bye-streets are crooked and ugly; the bazaars insignificant—for in India, and generally in the East, the really costly articles must be sought for in the interior of the houses.

The population of Agra once, it is said, amounted to 800,000; but at present it is scarcely 60,000. The whole neighbourhood is full of ruins, and whoever wishes to build need only to pick up the materials from the ground: many Europeans inhabit half decayed edifices, which with a little trouble and expense might be changed into palaces.

Agra is the chief seat of two missionary societies, one Catholic, and one Protestant; and here, as at Benares, the chief pupils are the foundlings of 1831. They showed me a little girl too, who had been lately bought of a poor mother for two rupees.

At the head of the Catholic mission is a bishop, Mr. Porgi, who has built a tasteful church and a handsome dwelling-house; and in no similar establishment have I ever seen so much order, or the natives so well managed as here. On Sundays, after prayers, they amuse themselves with cheerful decorous games, whilst in the Protestant establishment, after having been at work all the week, they have to pray the whole day on Sunday ; or at most, by way of recreation, sit at their doors quite still, and with serious faces. One would really suppose from their manner of passing the blessed day of rest, that the All-Merciful God grudged His creatures the most innocent enjoyment.

It is unfortunate, too, for the cause of Christianity in this country, that the Catholics and Protestant societies spend much of their energies in watching and criticizing each other, and present there-by no very edifying spectacle to the natives.

The last sight I went to see in Agra was the admired and world renowned Taj-Mahal, a monument erected by the sultan Jehan to the memory of his favourite lady, Narr-Mahal: but the sultan's own memory has been more indebted to it : for every one who sees it naturally asks after the name of the monarch whose word of power called such a structure into being. The names of the architect and builder have unfortunately been lost : many have ascribed it to Italian masters ; but when we see so many magnificent works of Mahomedan artists, we should either deny them all or be willing to acknowledge this.

On an open terrace of red sandstone twelve feet high, standing in the middle of a garden, is reared an octangular mosque of white marble, with high arcades and minarets at the four corners. The principal cupola rises to a height of 260 feet, and is surrounded by smaller ones. All round the outside of the mosque are sentences from the Koran in letters of black marble, inlaid. In the principal apartment stand two sarcophagi, in one of which repose the remains of the sultan, and in the other those of his favourite, and they, as well as the lower half of the walls, are of the richest mosaic inlaid with semi-precious stones. One of the most beautiful things about it is the trellis-work of marble by which the sarcophagi are surrounded, and which is so delicately and exquisitely wrought that it looks like carved ivory : it is also enriched at top and bottom with semi-precious stones, and among them one was pointed out to me called the "gold stone," and which has perfectly the fine colour of that metal : it is very costly, more so than lapis-lazuli.

Two other mosques stand at a short distance from the *Taj Mahal*, which, anywhere else, would be much admired, but they are little noticed in the presence of a structure, of which a traveller says, not without reason, that " it seems too pure—too holy to be the work of human hands. Angels," he adds, " must have brought it from Heaven ;" and a glass case should be thrown over it to preserve it even from every breath of air ; yet this mausoleum has already stood 250 years, but it is as perfect as if it were just finished. Many travellers have asserted that its effect is peculiarly enchanting by moonlight, and accordingly I paid it a visit when the moon was shining gloriously, but I did not at all agree with them that the effect was improved, and almost regretted to have weakened thus my first impression. Amidst ancient ruins or Gothic buildings moonlight exercises a magic power, but not so on a monument of polished white marble, for that only falls into vague undefined masses like heaps of snow. I cannot but suspect that the first traveller who visited it by moonlight, did so in company that made everything charming, and that the subsequent ones have only repeated after him.

The ruined city of *Fattipoor-Sikri* lies about eighteen English miles from Agra, and as we had relays of horses we made the excursion in a day.

The road lay across extensive heaths, on one of which we saw a herd of small antelopes, which crossed the road before us without much fear, making great leaps of twenty feet, and seeming as light and graceful in their motions as if they were dancing on air. But what especially pleased me was a pair of wild peacocks; for accustomed as we are in Europe to regard them as exotic rarities to be kept in narrow limits, I was glad to see them here in the wild freedom of nature, and the colours of their plumage seemed to me more splendid than in any I had ever seen : these birds are regarded in India with almost the same veneration as the cow, and you often see them reposing on the roofs of cottages, or walking through the villages like tame poultry. In many districts a European who should presume to shoot one would expose himself to great danger; and only four months before this two English soldiers had fallen victims to their disregard of Indian feelings and customs with respect to these birds; they had killed some peacocks, and the people fell upon them with such fury that they died shortly after of the wounds they received.

Fattipoor-Sikri comes into sight at a considerable distance, as it lies on a hill. The ruins begin before you reach the walls, and on both sides lie the remains of handsome houses, the fragments of fine pillars, &c., which I saw with great regret the inhabitants of the country were breaking up for building materials. Over rolling stones and ruins we passed through three once handsome gates into the fortress and the city, and then the solemn and touching prospect lay before us—a vast space filled with magnificent buildings, with mosques and kiosks, with palaces and pillared halls, and arcades and all the creations of art, and not a single piece but is wasting rapidly away, and falling to dust and rubbish. It looks like the scene of some tremendous earthquake, and is a more melancholy sight than Herculaneum or Pompeii, for there, at least, everything looks as clean and orderly as if the streets and houses had been deserted but yesterday ; but this city, instead of being covered up carefully in ashes, is exposed to every storm that blows. Sorrow and astonishment increased with every step I took—sorrow for the destruction, astonishment at the magnificence yet visible, at the grand style of the buildings, at their fine sculptures, and rich decorations.

I saw buildings covered inside and outside with sculptures so thickly, that not the smallest space remained empty. The Great mosque exceeds in size and elaborate art the Jumna mosque, at Agra. The entrance gate into the fore-court is 72 feet high, and the height of the whole building 140 feet; the fore-court of the mosque also is among the largest in the world, as it is nearly 440 feet long, and 400 broad, and surrounded by beautiful arcades and small cells. This court is considered almost as holy as the interior of the mosque, because on a certain spot in it the Sultan Akbar was accustomed to perform his devotions, and after his death this spot was marked by an altar of white marble. The interior of the mosque, which, like that of the Jumna, has three mighty domes, is full of sarcophagi, in which lie either relations or favourite ministers of the sultan, and a neighbouring court is full of similar memorials.

In the Hall of Justice Sultan Akbar used to sit for several hours daily, giving audience to the meanest as well as to the most distinguished of his subjects. A broad low pillar, that stands isolated in the middle of the hall, used to serve as his divan; it spreads out towards the top ; the capital is beautifully carved, and it is surrounded by a richly wrought stone gallery ; from this divan four broad stone bridges led to the neighbouring apartments of the palace. These are richly, perhaps too richly decorated, but I found less to admire in the renowned Elephant gate ; it is lofty, but scarcely as much so as those at the entrance to the mosque, and the two stone elephants are so much decayed that one can hardly see what they are intended for. In better preservation is the Elephant's tower, of which some descriptions say that it is made entirely of elephants' teeth, and, moreover of the teeth only of those elephants which were taken by Akbar in war, or slain in the chase ; but this is not really the case, the tower, which is sixty feet high, is built of stone, and the teeth are only fastened upon it, so that they stick out like porcupines' quills. All these buildings, even the immense wall, is built of red sandstone, and not, as is sometimes asserted, of red marble, and in the numerous clefts and holes, hundreds of little green parrots have made their nests.

On the 19th of January I left the renowned city of Agra to visit the still more renowned city of Delhi, 122 miles off, and to which a fine post-road leads. The country continued much the same,—cultivated tracts, alternating with sand and heath; and far and wide not the smallest hill to be seen. The villages we occasionallly passed looked so very uninviting that they did not tempt us to delay our journey an instant.

We entered Delhi at about four o'clock in the afternoon, and I was there met by a kind friend and countryman, Dr. Sprenger, whose talents and learning have gained him a high reputation, not only among the English, but throughout the whole learned world: he is here the director of the Students' College, and lately received from the English Government the commission to go to Lucknow to examine and arrange the King's Library there, and draw up a report concerning the most valuable works. He is well acquainted with the Sanscrit, old and new Persian, Turkish, Arabic, and Hindostanee languages; and he has made some extremely difficult translations from them into the German and English; besides which he has enriched our literature with some very clever and valuable essays. He was just about to set off for Lucknow when I arrived, but he had the great kindness to delay his journey in order to act as my *cicerone*.

To the great imperial city of Delhi the eyes of all India—almost of all Asia—were once directed: it was in its time what Athens was to Greece, and Rome to Europe; and a similar fate has befallen it, for of all its greatness only the name is left. The present town is called New Delhi,—although it is 200 years old, and is a continuation of the old towns, of which there have been seven,—for as often as the palaces, mosques, &c., became dilapidated, they were left to fall to ruin, and new ones erected by the side of them; so that at last, ruins included, the town extended eighteen miles in length, and more than six in breadth: indeed, if many of them were not covered with a thin stratum of earth, it would appear the most extensive city in the world.

New Delhi has a population of about 100,000, of which not more than 100 are Europeans. The streets are broader and finer than

I have seen in any other Indian town ; and the principal one, the *Chandui Chauk,* would do honour to any European city ; it is three quarters of an English mile long, and 100 feet broad, but it is intersected along its entire length by a narrow ill-supplied canal, half filled with rubbish. The houses are not fine, and the goods exhibited in the shops appeared of little worth : of the "costly magazines—the jewels—the countless lamps by which they are exhibited at night," I saw nothing. I afterwards discovered that the best houses and the richest shops were to be found in the side streets : there I saw the productions of Indian art—gold and silver stuffs and shawls, as elegant and tasteful as one could find in Paris. The gold and silver embroideries on the stuffs and cash-mere shawls are perfect ; but the best shawls cost here, on the spot, 4,000 rupees (about £400). The skill of the mechanics, too, is admirable, when it is considered with what rude tools and simple means they have to work.

It is extremely interesting to take a ramble at night about the streets of Delhi, and observe the movements of the Indian great men,—princes and others, who abound here more than in any other city. Besides the pensioned emperor and his relations, whose number is said to amount to thousands, there live at Delhi many other pensioned and deposed sovereigns and ministers, who bring much bustle into the town, as they are fond of showing themselves in public, of giving large and small parties, and riding on elephants in the gardens, or up and down the streets. The elephants are decked in the most costly manner with rich carpets and hangings, trimmed with gold lace, and festooned with gold cords and tassels. The howdah (or seat) is draperied sometimes even with Cashmere shawls ; and in the day-time gorgeous canopies, or servants holding enormous umbrellas, protect them from the sun. The princes and grandees sit three or four together in the howdah, superbly dressed in the showy Eastern style ; and in a single procession you will sometimes see a dozen or more of these elephants, attended by fifty or sixty ser-vants, and as many soldiers on horseback and on foot. In the evening these gentlemen care less for pomp ; they content them-selves with one elephant and a few servants, and ride up and down the streets coquetting with girls of a certain class, who stand at the windows or on the galleries in full dress, and with unveiled faces. Other Indian beaux prance about on fine Arab horses, whose naturally proud appearance is rendered still more stately by gold-embroidered housings, and bridles inlaid with gold and silver. Among these come, thoughtfully stepping, laden camels from distant regions ; and bailis drawn by splendid white buffaloes, bailis and buffaloes alike covered with scarlet trappings, and the animals with their horns and feet painted, and a handsome collar round the neck to which bells are attached. The prettiest girlish faces peep modestly out of these curtained bailis, and did not one know that in India an unveiled face is never an innocent one, the fact certainly could not be divined from their looks or behaviour. Unhappily there is no country in the world where there are more of this class than in India ; and in a great measure on account of an absurd and unnatural law : the girls of every family are betrothed when they are only a few months old; and should the bridegroom die even immediately after, the child is considered as a widow, and cannot marry again. The estate of widowhood is regarded as a great misfortune, for it is supposed that only those women are placed in it who have, in some preceding life, deserved such a punishment. Most of the young women so situated become dancing-girls.

In addition to the other sights of the streets are snake charmers' and conjurors, who move about surrounded by admiring crowds. Some of their tricks really appeared to be incomprehensible. They spirt fire out of their mouths—fire from which real smoke proceeds ; they mix together white, red, blue, and yellow powder, and swallow it, and then spit it out again quite dry, and each colour separate ; they cast down their eyes, and when they raise them again the pupils are gold : they then bow the head, and when they lift it up, the eyes are of their natural colour again, but the teeth have turned to gold. Others will make a small incision in the skin, and out of the aperture draw ell after ell of silk thread and narrow ribbon. Then come the snake-charmers, with their well known exploits, and sometimes a fight between an ichneumon and a great serpent ; which generally terminates in favour of the ichneumon— as he knows how to seize his enemy very skilfully by the neck.

At the end of the main street lies the imperial palace, which is reckoned one of the handsomest edifices in Asia : taken with its subordinate buildings, it extends two English miles, and it is surrounded by a wall forty feet high. At the entrance the perspective through many successive gates to a distant hall of white marble, inlaid with semi-precious stones, is very beautiful. Here the ex-monarch of Delhi is accustomed to show himself to the people, who still from habitual reverence or curiosity visit the palace; and here also he receives the visits of Europeans.

The finest parts of the palace are the mosque and the magnificent Hall of Audience. This stands in the midde of an open court, forming a long quadrangle. Its ceiling or canopy is supported by thirty columns, and some steps lead up to the divan, which is open on all sides, and encircled by a prettily wrought marble gallery.

The present Grand Mogul has, however, so little taste for the beautiful, that he has had the divan divided into two by a miserable wooden partition, and the same wooden wall carried along to both sides of the hall, so that he literally sits there "in boards." The largest crystal in the world is in this divan, and served the Mogul formerly as a throne : it is a piece four feet long, two feet and a half broad, and a foot thick, and very transparent; at present it is hidden behind the boards, and had I not from books known of its existence, and asked to see it, they would not have shown it me. The mosque is small, but, like the judgment-hall, of white marble, with beautiful columns and sculptures. Adjoining it is a fine but neglected garden. In the courts lay much mud and filth, and many of the buildings were falling to decay so rapidly that it seemed to me it would soon be necessary, for the Mogul's sake, to build another New Delhi.

As we entered, I had noticed in one of the courts a circle of people sitting, whose attention seemed entirely occupied ; and when we came back, an hour after, they were still sitting in the same position ; I was curious to see what engaged them so much, and I found it was some dozens of tame birds sitting upon poles, and feeding out of the hands of the attendants; the spectators were almost all princes, who were amusing themselves in this lively manner with their attendants behind them. There was little distinction in their dress between them and their servants, and perhaps still less in knowledge and education.

The Mogul has some other playthings : he has a company of little soldiers, boys of from eight to fourteen, who wear wretched little uniforms, like those of the English soldiers. I pitied the young warriors from my heart, for I could see it was as much as they could do to carry the heavy muskets and colours. The monarch sits daily in his Hall of Audience and amuses himself with seeing them go through their exercises ; and this is the time when it is easiest to obtain a presentation to his Majesty ; but the old gentleman (who is eighty-five) was unwell when I was at Delhi, so that I did not enjoy this honour.

The Mogul receives from the English government a yearly pension of 1,400,000 rupees, and he draws from his landed property a revenue of about an equal sum ; yet he, like the Rajah of Benares, is a gentleman in difficulties, or, at all events, his exchequer is constantly empty ; but it must be recollected that he has an enormous crowd of people to maintain : the immediate royal family amounting to 300 persons, without counting his complement of 100 wives, besides 1,000 servants.

His pension is paid on the 1st of every month, and is brought to his treasury under a strong escort of English troops, otherwise it would certainly be plundered by his loving subjects.

His Majesty is, it is said, very anxious to neglect no means of increasing his revenues : he distributes, for instance, offices and places of honour, for which he receives considerable sums of money ; and the wonder certainly is not so much that he should be willing to sell, as that any one should be inclined to buy : parents even are found who will purchase this valuable property for their children, especially the rank of officers in his Majesty's forces ; and the present commander-in-chief is a gentleman of ten years old. What appeared to me the most singular arrangement was, that the Vizier, who is charged with all the Mogul's receipts and expenditure, not only receives no salary, but pays 10,000 rupees for his place : one would like to know what the profits may be.

The Mogul publishes in his palace a newspaper, or Court Circular, with which I was much amused. It does not, as may be supposed, contain any political information, but is exclusively occupied with domestic occurrences of the august household. For instance, in the number I saw, it was mentioned that one of the sultan's wives owed her washerwoman three rupees, and that the said washerwoman, having come to the palace to dun the sultana, she had sent to request the sum from her illustrious consort ; he, however, had referred the applicant to the treasurer, who had assured his Majesty that there did not remain a farthing at his disposal; and that, consequently, the washerwoman had been under the necessity of extending the sultana's credit to the following month.   Besides this piquant piece of intelligence, there were other paragraphs of as an important and interesting character as we often see in European journals : that the Prince C——visited, at this or that hour, the Prince D—— or F—— ; that he was received in such or such a room, and stayed so long; and the conversation turned on such or such subjects.   This last item, however, is something of an improvement upon the European originals.

The palace occupied for the college—of which Dr. Sprenger is the Director—is one of the handsomest in Delhi.   It is a majestic building in the Italian style, with immense and lofty apartments, and lies in a beautiful garden encircled by a high wall.   The residence of Dr. Sprenger within its precincts is really in princely style.   Of the mosques I only visited two— the *Roshun-ud-dawla*, and the Jumna mosque.   The first lies in the main street, and has its cupolas and minarets richly gilt ; and it was in one of these that Shah Nadir, when he conquered Delhi in the year 1739, took his seat to witness the execution of the orders he had given for the slaughter of 100,000 of the inhabitants, and the subsequent plundering and burning of the city.

The Jumna mosque, built by Shah Jehan, is regarded as a masterpiece of Mahomedan architecture.   It rises from an enormous platform, to which you ascend by forty steps, and look majestically down on the surrounding mass of houses.   The three domes and the small cupolas are of white marble ; and even the large flags with which the court is paved are of red sandstone.

We devoted two days to an excursion to the more distant monuments of Old Delhi, and spent the night in a palace belonging to the king of Lucknow, which is kept in tolerable repair, and provided with necessary furniture by some of the Europeans settled at Delhi—and, thanks to the kind care of Madame Sprenger, we found every thing provided for our convenience and comfort.   One should be doubly grateful for such attention, when one recollects what trouble they must occasion—for not only provisions and a cook are needed, but kitchen utensils, crockery, bed clothes, necessaries for servants and so forth, which have all to be sent forward, so that it is quite a little migration.

One of the most remarkable monuments I saw was what is called the *Kotab-Minar*, in which is the "grand pillar," a polygon of seven and twenty hills, and five stories or galleries. The diameter at the base is fifty-four feet, its height 226. It is of red sandstone, and the upper part white marble—but it is chiefly admirable for the marvellously wrought sculptures and decorations whith wind round it in broad stripes, and which are so delicately and exquisitely chiselled that they resemble the finest lace. Every description of the effect of the wonderful work must be far excelled by the reality, — and fortunately the column is in as good preservation as if it had not been standing 100 years, though it dates from the thirteenth century. The upper division leans a little forward, it is not known whether intentionally (like the tower at Pisa) or otherwise, and it terminates in a flat terrace, which does not seem to harmonise well with the rest of the structure. Possibly something may have formerly stood upon it, although this is not known. It was in its present state when Delhi was taken by the English.

We ascended to the summit and obtained a magnificent prospect over the world of ruins,—New Delhi, the Jumna, and the wide country round.

Here in the various heaps, piled one upon another, you might study the history of the various races that have ruled over Hindostan. Over many spots, where once stately palaces arose, the corn is now waving ; and every where when the earth is turned you come upon fragments and rubbish. Opposite to the Kotab-Minar is a similar structure, quite unfinished, but exceeding the complete one in diameter. It is conjectured that the two belonged to a magnificent mosque, of which some gates, columns, wells, &c., are extant, and are remarkable for their beautiful sculptures : in the fore-court stands a metal column like that of Allahabad, but only thirty-six feet high ; there are some slight injuries on it, which proceeded from the Monguls, who when they took Delhi, endeavoured in their rage for mischief to destroy this column. They tried to overthrow it, but it stood too firm ; and with all their efforts they could not stir it ; nay, they could not even succeed in effacing the inscription.

This column is called the *Feroze-Schah-Lath,* and from the inscription it appears it existed 100 years before the birth of Christ, and was brought from Lahore at the time when the palace of Feroze-Shah was built.

These and other monuments originated with the Patans or Affghans, and though they lie scattered among the other ruins, they may easily be distinguished from the Hindostanee or Mahomedan buildings. The ruins of Totluhabad are scarcely worth a drive of seven miles to see them, and the countless others that lie around are mostly repetitions of those already described.

Not far from Kotab-Minar the traveller is agreeably surprised by finding three rooms of a dilapidated edifice fitted up comfortably, and provided with some furniture for the benefit of wayfarers. Near New Delhi, in the midst of ruins and mighty blocks of red stone, the memorial of times gone by, there lies a modern English military station.

JOURNEY FROM DELHI TO BOMBAY.

Thugs.—Departure.—The Cattle Market.—Kind Disposition of the Indians.
—Kottah.—Description of the Town.—The Royal Castle.—Entertain·
ments and Dances.—The Holy Town of Kesho Rae.—Patun.

In order to reach Bombay I had two roads before me; the one
led by Simla to the promontories of the Himmalaya; the other to
the renowned rock temples of Adjunta and Elora. I would willingly have chosen the first, and penetrated to Lahore and the
Indus ; but my friends dissuaded me from it, on the simple ground
that the mountains were at this time covered with deep snow, and
I should therefore have to delay my journey at least three months.
I could not do this, and therefore decided for the other route. In
Calcutta I had been strongly advised not to extend my journey
further than Delhi. The countries beyond, they said, were not
under the English rule, and the population was in a very demo-
ralised condition. Especially they endeavoured to awaken my
apprehensions by terrible accounts of the Thugs. These Thugs,
as is well known, form a regularly organised society for robbery
and murder, which they scarcely regard as at all blameable, and
easily expiate by a trifling gift to their priests. They must, however, take the greatest care not to shed the blood of their victims,
as that would involve them in disgrace with their companions,
and occasion their expulsion. They therefore invariably adopt the
method of strangulation. Many travellers have maintained that
the Thugs belong to a particular religious sect, and do not commit
their crimes either for the sake of robbery or revenge, but with a
fanatical idea of performing a meritorious action. I inquired,
however, very closely into this point, and the result of my inquiry
was, that no distorted view of religion, but mere hatred, or more
frequently the love of gain, had been the impelling motive of their
actions. These miscreants have acquired extraordinary skill in
their dreadful trade, and manifest the utmost endurance and perse-
verance in watching their opportunities. They will follow a marked
victim for months.

In Delhi I found, however, that the danger of being attacked by them was by no means so great as it had been represented to me ; that the number of Thugs had greatly declined, and that, besides, they never ventured on the murder of a European, as the English government would in such a case institute the strictest search after the perpetrators.   As to any possible danger, therefore, I felt tolerably calm ; but I had to make up my mind to a good deal of hardship and privation.

The first station on my journey was to Kottah, a distance of 290 English miles, and to reach this there were three methods ; by palanquin, by camels, or waggon or *baili* drawn by oxen.   All three are, of course, slow enough.   There are no post roads, and no regularly established methods of communication.   You must keep the same people and the same animals to the end of the journey, and you cannot go more than about twenty miles a-day.   For the palanquin one has to hire eight bearers, as well as some for the luggage ; and although each one costs only eight rupees a month, and feeds himself, the expense is considerable, especially as they must be paid for their back journey.   Travelling with camels is also expensive, and very inconvenient.   I therefore decided for the most modest conveyance, the oxen waggon ; and my friend Dr. Sprenger was so kind as to make all the arrangements for me. He drew up in the Hindostanee language a written contract with the driver, according to which I was to pay him the half of the fare, namely, fifteen rupees, immediately, the other when we should arrive at Kottah, to which he was to bring me in fifteen days. For every day longer that the journey lasted I had the right to subtract three rupees.

For further security, Dr. Sprenger gave me, by way of escort, one of his most trustworthy *cheprasses,*—servants of the English government,—who wear an official red scarf, and a brass plate on the shoulder, on which is engraved the name of the town to which they belong.   One or more of these is appointed to every government officer, and they hold a much higher rank than ordinary servants.   Besides this, my kind country people furnished me with such ample stores of provisions and warm covering that my waggon could hardly contain them.   God grant that I may one day see them again.   I could not but part from them with melancholy feelings.

I left Delhi early in the morning on the 30th of January 1848 and the first day we made only eighteen miles, as the heavy animals required to be accustomed to the pace; but I found much interesting occupation in seeing again the numerous ruins that lay on both sides of the road, which I had visited a few days before with my friends. This night, and all the following ones, I passed in a *Serai;* for I had no tent, no palanquin, and bongolos are not to be found on the road. The Serais in the little villages are, unfortunately, not to be compared with those in the larger towns, being merely cells built of clay, scarcely seven feet square, with a narrow entrance of not more than five feet high. To my surprise, however, I found them always swept quite clean, and there was brought to me a sort of low wooden bedstead made with plaited cords, on which I threw my coverings, and which made me a magnificent couch. The cheprass lay down like Napoleon's Mameluke, at the door of my cell, and I had the satisfaction to think he enjoyed a sound sleep, as he heard nothing of a rather brisk engagement which I had with a very large dog that had been attracted by the smell of my well-filled provision basket.

January 31*st.*—Towards the afternoon we came to the little town of Balamgalam, in which there is an English military station, a mosque, and a quite new Hindoo temple. The night was passed in the little town of Palwal. In that district the peacocks are so numerous and so tame that I used to see every morning dozens of these beautiful creatures on the trees and in the villages, where they come for the food given them by the good-natured inhabitants.

February 1*st.*—This day's station was the little town of Cossi, and during the last few miles, before reaching it, we had been continually overtaken by natives, who were hurrying busily towards it on account of a cattle market held there. This market presented a picture of the greatest confusion. The animals were standing all about, amidst heaps of hay and straw, the sellers screaming without intermission in praise of their goods, and half persuading, half dragging, purchasers about by force, whilst they, on their parts, bawled no less loudly, so that altogether the uproar was stunning. What most struck me was the appearance of the shoemakers or cobblers, who, with the simple materials of their trade,—a little table, with thread, leather, and wire, stuck in somewhere among the bundles of hay,—were, in the midst of the tumult, quietly following their occupation of the cure of soles! On this and on many other occasions it appeared to me that the natives of Hindostan are by no means so idle as they are generally considered, but, on the contrary, that they are ready to take every favourable opportunity of earning a little money.

As all the Serais at the entrance of the town were overflowing with guests, we had to pass through it to the opposite side ; and it was curious to enter beneath the high vaulted stately looking archway that formed the gate into the miserable collection of mud huts, ranged along streets so narrow that the people had to get under their doorways to let my waggon pass.   The country round had consisted for a long time of boundless plains, where spots of cultivation alternated with dry burnt-up-looking heaths. The corn stood already a foot high, but was so full of yellow flowers that one could not really tell by looking at it whether the corn or the weeds had been sown.   The culture of cotton is, however, very considerable here.   The plant does not, indeed, attain the height or size of the Egyptian, but the quality of the cotton is not at all dependent upon the size of the plant, and that produced here is of the finest and whitest kind.   On these plains I saw here and there small houses built on artificially raised perpendicular mounds of clay, from six to eight feet in height.   There were no steps, but the inhabitants ascend to the platform by ladders, which are drawn up at night.   As well as I could make out from the account of my servant, which I only half understood, they were built thus for protection against tigers, which are here very frequently seen.

February 3rd. Baratpoor.—We passed this day over a wide tract of dwarfed crippled-looking trees, which reminded me of nothing so much as of some parts of Ireland ; and at the end of the wooded region we came to a place where the ground was rent into chasms and thrown up as if by an earthquake.   Some of the people whom we met, too, had so wild an appearance, that I felt half inclined to be afraid of them.   They behaved perfectly well to me, however, and morning and evening made me a very hearty salam, carrying their hands from the forehead to the breast.   In many more civilised-looking countries I should not have met with the same courtesy.

February 6th.—This morning, as I was about to leave the Serai, three armed men planted themselves before my *baili*, and stopped me, in spite of the vociferations of my people.   I understood at length that the matter in dispute was only a few pence which they claimed for having, as they said, watched before my sleeping apartment.

The cheprass, it is to be observed, had an idea that the Serai was haunted, and he had therefore requested from the *Serdar* the favour of an additional watch. Possibly these men may have lain and slept in some corner of the court. Certainly, though I have repeatedly looked out, I had seen nothing of them ; but what can one expect for a few pence ? I made them happy with the trifle they demanded, whereupon they made a regular military wheel to the right about, and with many salams left me to pursue my way in peace. Had I been at all inclined to fear, I must for some days past have been in constant apprehension, for the appearance of the people was by no means calculated to inspire confidence. They all carried swords, bows, and arrows, strong cudgels covered with iron, iron shields, and even muskets. The very shepherds in the fields were armed to the teeth. Nothing, however, could disturb the tranquillity of my mind. I seemed to feel a perfect conviction that my last hour had not yet struck ; yet for all that I must own I was not sorry that we should pass the deep caverns and awful looking ravines, through which this day's journey lay, in bright daylight. From these ravines we entered a deep valley, at the beginning of which, on a solitary hill, stood a fort ; four miles further we came to a group of trees, in the midst of which, on a pedestal about five feet high, stood a figure of a horse in stone, and near it was a well made with great blocks of red sandstone, with three steps leading down to the water. Similar and much larger wells and cisterns, shaded by the most magnificent mango and tamarind trees, are frequently found in India, especially in districts where, as here, good springs are wanting. It is a beautiful faith of Hindoos and Mahomedans, that by the erection of such works for the public good they improve their own prospects of future felicity. Near many of the wells is placed a man whose business it is to spare the weary wanderer even the trouble of fetching the water.

Pleasant as it is, on many accounts, to meet with these wells, it is, however, very disagreeable to see the men going down into the water, washing themselves, and pouring it over them, and to con-sider that this is the water one has to drink. But the necessities of thirst "have no law," and so I went and filled my pitcher with the rest.

February 7th. Dungerkamalama, a little village at the foot of a pretty hill. A short distance from the station lay a bit of genuine

Arabian sandy desert, which, however, fortunately, did not extend far. The sandy plains of India are mostly capable of cultivation, for you need only dig a few feet to find water enough to overflow the fields. Even in the midst of this little desert, too, there lay some fields of fine-looking wheat.

This afternoon I thought I should have had to make use of my pistols, in order to settle a quarrel. My driver always required everybody to give way to him, and when this was not done he began to wrangle. To-day we met with half-a-dozen armed drivers, who paid no attention to his screams, whereupon in a great fury he seized his whip, and threatened to lash them with it. Had it come to a fight, we must certainly have had the worst of it, but fortunately our antagonists contented themselves with abuse, and at last gave way. I had before remarked that the Hindoo screams and threatens a great deal, but seldom or never comes to blows. I have lived much among the people, and seen many a quarrel, but never a fight. Indeed, when the quarrel lasted too long, they generally sat down to it. Even the boys do not struggle and fight, either in play or in earnest. Once only I saw two boys engaged in what seemed a serious dispute, and at length one gave the other a box on the ear, but he did it as cautiously as if he had been hitting himself. The one who had received the considerate blow just passed his sleeve over his cheek, and there was an end of the matter. Other boys had been looking on from a distance, but took no part in the quarrel. This mildness of disposition may proceed in part from their vegetable diet, and in part from the precepts of their religion, which are so merciful towards animals ; but I cannot help thinking that cowardice has something to do with it. I have been told that it is scarcely possible to induce a Hindoo to enter a dark room without a light, and if a horse or an ox makes the slightest spring, great and small scream, and fly in all directions. On the other hand, I heard from English officers that the Sepoys are quite brave soldiers. Does, then, the valour come with the coat, or is it from the example of the English ? Of the tenderness of the Hindoo towards animals, I saw a pretty instance in a little town I passed through. There was a donkey that either by accident or nature was a perfect cripple, and was dragging itself with great effort along the street, at an extremely slow pace. Some people with laden beasts of burthen were behind him, and stopped by the slowness of his movements, but they waited in patient resignation, without uttering a syllable of displeasure, much less lifting a hand to urge the poor beast to greater speed. Many of the inhabitants came out of their houses and gave it food, and every passer-by went carefully out of its way.

February 11*th.*—To-day, the thirteenth from Delhi, I arrived at Kottah, and I had been on the whole journey very well satisfied with my servant and my driver. The owners of the serais had not asked more from me than they would have done from a native, and had shown me all the civilities consistent with the austere precepts of their religion. I had passed the nights indeed in open cells, and even under God's free sky; but, though surrounded by the poorest and lowest of the people, I was never insulted by deed, word, or even look. Never was I robbed of the smallest article; and if I gave a trifle to a child, the parent always endeavoured to acknowledge the gift in some way or other. Oh, if Europeans only knew how easily these unsophisticated people are to be won by kindness and indulgence! But, unfortunately, they try to rule over them by force, and treat them almost always with contempt and harshness.

Kottah is the capital of the kingdom of Rajpootan, and here, as in all the other provinces which the English Government has still left under the rule of the native princes, is an English officer, who bears the title of the Resident, though he might rather be called the king, or the king's governor, for the poor king can do nothing without his consent. These shadows of sovereigns cannot even cross the frontiers of their states without the permission of the Resident. Their most important fortresses have English garrisons, and smaller English military stations are scattered about. For the people this superintendence is in some measure injurious—in some measure useful. The burning of widows, and the cruel punishments formerly practised, such as the being trampled to death by elephants, or dragged along at their tails, are abolished; but, on the other hand, the taxes are become heavier, since the king has to pay, for the right of governing according to the will of the Resident, a considerable tribute, which of course he gets out of the pockets of his people.

Captain Burdon, the Resident of Kottah, was an intimate friend of my kind countryman of Delhi, Dr. Sprenger, who had announced to him beforehand my arrival. Unluckily he was at the time absent on a journey of inspection to the several military stations; but before his departure he had made every preparation for my reception, and commissioned his physician, Dr. Rolland, to see his commands executed. He had even carried his attention so far as to send forward to the last night station books, newspapers, and servants for my use, though they happened to miss me, from my driver having taken, for the two last days, what he considered a short cut, away from the main road.

I alighted at the beautiful bongolo of the Resident. The house was empty, for Mrs. Burdon and her children had accompanied her husband, as it is very common to do in India, where Europeans require frequent change of air, but the house, the servants, the Sepoys, the Captain's palanquin and carriage,—all stood at my disposal; and, to complete my good fortune, Dr. Rolland was so good as to offer himself as the companion of my excursions.

February 12th.—This morning the king, Ram Singh, who had been informed of my arrival, sent me some large baskets of fruit and sweetmeats, and at the same time, what pleased me still more, his beautifully decorated elephant, as well as an officer on horseback and some soldiers. I was soon seated with Dr. Rolland on the lofty howdah, and moved off pretty quickly towards the town.

Kottah lies on the river Chumbal, in an extensive and partly rocky plain, 1,300 feet above the level of the sea. It is advantageously situated, and surrounded with strong fortifications. The interior of the town is divided, by three gates, into three different districts. The first, which is inhabited by the poorest class of people, looks deplorable enough; the two others, where the merchants and richer people live, look much better, and the principal street, though rugged and stony, is at least broad enough to enable a carriage to pass without inconvenience to the passengers.

The style of building in the houses is quite original. In Benares I had been struck with the smallness of the windows, but here they are so low and narrow that people can hardly put their heads out of them. Many houses have large balconies ; others, on the first floor, spacious halls, resting on columns, sometimes taking up the whole front of the house — sometimes divided into two or three apartments, but open to the streets. At the two corners of the large halls are pretty pavilions, at the back of which are doors leading into the interior of the house.

These halls mostly serve for shops and places of business, but they are, at the same time, lounging places for idle people, who sit upon mats and smoke their hookahs, while they amuse themselves by looking on at what is passing in the street. In other houses, again, the front walls were painted in fresco, with terrible giants, tigers, and lions, twice or thrice as large as life, with their tongues hanging out in the most alarming manner, or sometimes with deities, flowers, arabesques, &c., thrown together without taste or meaning, but daubed over with the most frightful colours. The numerous Hindoo temples are a handsome decoration to the town ; they stand on high terraces, and are every way more spacious and beautiful than those of Benares, with the exception only of the Visvishas. The royal palace lies at the end of the third quarter, and forms a town within a town, or rather a fortress within a fortress, since it is surrounded not only on the outer side, but also towards the town with enormous walls.

From the city we took our way toward Armornevas, one of the pleasure palaces of the monarch (had the Resident been in Kottah, I should have had the honour of a presentation, but as he was not, etiquette did not allow it). The road was most immoderately bad, and covered with great stones, so that I could not sufficiently admire the skill of our elephant in placing his clumsy feet so as to avoid them, and yet trotting along as briskly as if he were on the finest road.

I expressed to Dr. Rolland my surprise that as his Majesty frequently visited this palace he did not improve the road a little, but he replied that it was a maxim with Indian monarchs never to make any roads, because they say it would, in case of a war, be such a great convenience to the enemy.

The gardens of the palace are so thickly set with orange, lemon, and other trees, that there is not room for the smallest flower-bed or lawn. The few flowers to be found, as in most Indian gardens, were at the entrance. The walks are raised two feet high, as the ground, from the frequent irrigations, is almost always damp and dirty. At this palace the monarch enjoys the diversion of tiger hunting, or rather tiger shooting. Small towers are erected a little way further down the river, to which the tigers are gradually driven up, and then the king and company sit securely within, and fire away valiantly on the wild monsters below.

We afterwards visited some beautiful groves of tamarind and mango trees, beneath whose shade repose the ashes of many royal princes. The evening was closed by all kinds of entertainments. The good doctor wished to make me acquainted with the various performances of the Hindoos, most of which, however, were not new to me. He brought before me a man who had got together a company of monkies which performed divers feats very cleverly; then a snake charmer, who let the largest and most poisonous snake twist round his arms and legs ; lastly appeared four elegant dancing girls, dressed in gold and silver muslin, and loaded with ornaments on forehead, throat, bosom, hands, arms, feet, and even toes, besides a large jewel that hung down from their noses. I recollect to have read in books that the performances of these Indian dancers was more graceful than those of Europeans, that their songs were melodious, their pantomime tender and impassioned, &c. I should like much to know whether those who gave this description have ever been in India at all. Not less untrue is, as far as I have seen, the statement of the extreme indelicacy of these dances. Those who say this must have forgotten the Sammaqueeca and Refolosa in Valparaiso, or the dances of the women of Otaheiti, or, indeed, those of our own opera ballet dancers with their silk fleshings.

The dress of the women in Rajpootan is very different from that of other parts of India. They wear long, full-coloured petticoats and close boddices, scarcely high enough to cover the bosom. Over this they have a blue or white shawl or veil, in which they envelope the head, face, and shoulders, leaving a piece hanging down in front like an apron. When they have not this veil on, they look a good deal like our own peasant girls. They are, however, like the dancers, usually laden with ornaments of gold or silver, or, if they cannot afford this, of some other metal, or even horn or bone. They have also little bells to their ankles, so that one can hear them coming sixty paces off ; their toes are covered with heavy rings, and, what is worse, they have them hanging from the nose to the chin. I could not help pitying the poor creatures when I saw them taking their meals. They must suffer grievously for their finery.

Among the other ornaments I noticed that many of the people wore amulets or images hung round their necks, so that I took them at first for Catholics, and rejoiced at this evidence of the success of the missionaries; but, alas! when I came nearer, I saw that, instead of a saint or heavenly Madonna, it was the head of an ox, or the long-tongued goddess Kalli, or the light-armed god Shiva, who was grinning at me.

February 13*th.*—To day Dr. Rolland took me to a little town considered one of the holiest in the country, which lies on the opposite side of the river, about six miles from Kottah. Beautiful stone steps lead down to the sacred water, where many pilgrims come to bathe themselves, and in some elegant kiosks Brahmins were sitting receiving the money of the faithful for the honour of the gods. On one of the steps lay a large turtle sunning himself, and no one seemed to dream of interfering with his comfort.

The temple, which is very large and handsome, though the town is small and wretched-looking, is open on all sides, and of an octagonal form. In the upper part are galleries, destined for women and musicians. The sanctuary stands in the back ground, and before it hang five bells, which are rung whenever a woman enters the temple, as they were when I came in. Thereupon the closed and draperied doors were opened, and a full sight of the interior permitted us. We saw there a small party of gods cut in stone, and a Brahmin engaged in driving with a large flapper the flies from their *spirituel* [countenances. The chapels contained red painted images or stones. In the fore court was seated the figure of a saint dressed quite decorously, and even with a cap upon his head. On the opposite side of the river is a hill denominated the Holy Hill, on which stands the figure of an ox coarsely cut in stone. Near this hill Captain Burdon has built himself an elegant house, and here he keeps a fine collection of stuffed birds, which he has brought himself from the Himmalaya.

CONTINUATION OF THE JOURNEY.

*Meeting with the Burdon Family.—Women of the Lower Class in India.—
Captain Hamilton.—Indor.—Presentation at Court.—Manufacture of Ice.
—Industry of Women and Children.—The Rocky Temple at Adjunta.—A
Tiger Hunt.—The Rock Temple of Elora.—The Fortress of Dowlutabad.*

IN the countries under the rule of the native princes there are
neither post-offices nor roads, but in all the towns and villages
there are people appointed to show the way to travellers and carry
their luggage.   Those who travel with a guard or cheprass pay
them nothing, others give them a trifle for their services, more or
less, according to the distance.   On my leaving Kottah the king
had had the complaisance to offer me camels for the journey, as
well as Sepoys for my escort; and when I arrived at the end of
my first stage every one came forward to serve me, as well as,
perhaps, to see a European woman,—here a great rarity.   They
brought me milk, eggs, and wood.   My style of living was very
simple and frugal ; my best meals were of rice boiled in milk, or
eggs, but usually I had only rice, with water and salt.   A leathern
bottle for water, a small pan for cooking, a handful of salt, and
some bread and rice, constituted my whole preparation for wants
of this kind.

Late in the evening I arrived at Nurankura, a hamlet surrounded
by low hills.   Here I found some tents belonging to Captain Burdon, and a male and female servant waiting for me.   I was excessively fatigued, for the movement of the camel is very disagreeable,
and I immediately retired into one of the tents to try and get some
sleep ; but I was followed by the maid, who began, almost whether
I would or not, to knead me all over with great energy, assuring
me that it was extremely good for me, and would take away my
fatigue ; and it was true that, after I had gone through this disci-
pline for a quarter of an hour, I felt greatly refreshed.   She then
explained to me, half in words half by signs, that the family had
expected me to dinner, that a palanquin was in readiness, and that
I could sleep in it as well as in a tent.   I thought this was very
likely, so at eleven o'clock I continued my journey.   The country
was indeed, I was informed, very much infested by tigers, but
since I had several torch-bearers with me—and tigers are sworn
enemies of light—I had no reason to fear that my sleep would be
disturbed by them.   At three o'clock in the morning I was again

deposited in a tent that stood ready for my reception, and furnished with all conveniences, and the next morning I had the pleasure of becoming acquainted with the amiable family of Captain Burdon, who leads the most happy domestic life with his wife and seven children, whom the parents instruct almost entirely themselves.

They seem perfectly gay and contented, although they are confined wholly to their own society and that of Dr. Rolland, who is the only European besides themselves in Kottah. Now and then they receive a visit from some officer who is travelling through the country, and I was myself the first European woman whom Mrs. Burdon had seen for four years. I passed the whole day most agreeably in the family circle, and was not a little astonished to find in this wild country all the comforts and conveniences of a well-arranged house. I will take this opportunity of giving some idea of how English officers, civil and military, travel in India.

In the first place, they possess tents so large as to contain three or four rooms, and they carry with them all the proper furniture, including carpets, elegant divans, and all manner of household and kitchen utensils, as well as a great number of servants. After having passed the night comfortably in their beds, they get into convenient palanquins, or on horseback, about three in the morning, and travelling four or five hours alight at their tent, which is again in readiness for them, and take a capital hot breakfast. They never go more than about eight miles in the day, and they have about them all the articles to which they are accustomed, and take all their usual meals. The cooks continue their journey always in the night, and the moment the masters are gone the tents are broken up and carried forward as quickly as possible: there is, of course, no lack of human hands to labour, or of beasts of burden. In the most civilised countries of Europe people do not travel as conveniently and luxuriously as they do in India. Captain Burdon wished to give me the use of his palanquin, and the bearers belonging to it, as far as Indor, my next stopping place ; but I really could not help pitying the fatigue of these poor people so much, that I pretended I did not mind travelling on a camel, nay, even preferred it to the palanquin on account of the prospect. At Runcha I had to take up my quarters in the midst of the Bazaar, under an open veranda, whilst half the population of the town gathered round me to watch every look and motion. They had, at all events, a good opportunity of observing what a European woman looks like when she is angry, for I gave my people a famous scolding, on account of the sleepy pace they had allowed the camels to keep : we had been from early in the morning till late at night upon the march, and had not made more than twenty or twenty-two miles, the pace of an ox waggon.

During the following days we passed over low hills, where the uncultivated land was already burnt up by the sun, and although we were not yet out of February, the thermometer rose during the day to 28 or 30 deg. of Reaumur, and the plantations of poppy, flax, corn, and cotton were flourishing luxuriously. Every where runlets of water were conducted through the fields, and peasants with teams of oxen were occupied in drawing water out of the wells and rivers. I did not see any women engaged in the work, and in general it appeared to me that the lot of the poorer classes of women in India and the East is not so hard as is commonly supposed. All the hard labour is performed by men, and they take part even in the work properly belonging to women ; as for instance, in the cities inhabited by Europeans, men do the washing and ironing. On the fields at harvest time you may see women, but they perform only the lightest of the work, and when there are no animals of burden the men carry both the burdens and the children. I never once saw a man ill treat either his wife or child ; and I wish from my heart that the poor women in our countries were only half as well treated as in many which are considered in a very rude state. During the journey I was one day witness of a mournful scene, originating in the mistaken notions of religion prevalent among the Hindoos. Not far from the veranda where I had taken shelter for the night,—for there were now no more Serais,—an old man was lying stretched out on the ground without giving any sign of life; the passers by stopped, looked at him for a moment, and then went on their way. No one offered to help him, or asked a question about him. The poor fellow had sunk down in such a state of exhaustion that he could not say to what caste he belonged. At length I took courage, approached him, and lifted up the head cloth which had fallen down partly over his face ; but two glazed eyes met mine—the body was stiff and cold —my help had come too late. The next morning the body still lay in the same place. I was told it was left to see whether any relations would take it away ;—if not, the Pariahs would.

On reaching Indor, I found, as I approached the town, that Mr. Hamilton, the resident, to whom I had letters, was out taking an airing, and soon after I met his equipage, which was very magnificent; an open landau, with four fine horses, and four servants in Oriental costume running beside it. The gentlemen had scarcely perceived my approach when they stopped, and sent one of their servants towards me. Probably they were curious to know what accident had thrown a solitary European woman into this remote region. My servant, who had the letters for Mr. Hamilton already in his hand, hastened to him, and delivered them. He read them hastily through, and then immediately got out of his carriage, came to me, and gave me a most cordial reception, without taking any offence at my shabby clothing or scanty attendance. He led me himself into the bongolo destined to the reception of strangers, placed several rooms at my service, and did not leave me till he had seen that the servants had punctually fulfilled his orders. He then went away, promising to send for me in an hour to dinner.

The palace of the resident, distant scarcely a hundred yards from the bongolo, is a splendid edifice in the true Italian style; broad steps lead up to halls, which, for space and beautiful proportions, excel any of the kind I had ever seen, and all the internal arrangements correspond with expectations excited by the exterior.

It was Sunday, and I had therefore the pleasure of meeting assembled at Indor the whole European world; videlicet, three families; and my surprise at the magnificence surrounding me, and at the luxurious banquet, was completed by hearing an excellent, well-practised band strike up some of the well-remembered melodies of my father-land. After dinner, Mr. Hamilton presented to me the leader, a Tyrolese of the name of Näher, who in the course of three years had drilled a corps of young natives into this excellent orchestra. He is married, and I went afterwards to see his wife, who was moved even to tears at the sound of her native German language, which she had not heard for fifteen years.

The town of Indor contains about 25,000 inhabitants. The royal palace stands in the midst of it, and forms a quadrangle; the front rises in a pyramidal form six stories high, and the entrance gate, with a tower on each side, is very handsome. The outside is covered with frescoes, mostly of elephants and horses; the interior is divided into several courts, and on the first floor is a large open hall, which serves as the residence of several holy oxen. Opposite to this hall is the reception room, but to reach the royal apartments you have to go through passages so dark that lights are necessary in the brightest sunny day. This is the case in most of the palaces of Hindostan, and it is said they are made so with a view of concealing their occupants from the enemy, or at least of rendering the access to them difficult.

We found the queen, an aged, childless widow, with her adopted son, Prince *Hury-Rao-Holcar*, a lad of fourteen, with a good-natured expressive face. They were both dressed in white muslin, and the latter had jewels on his turban, his breast, and his arms. All the apartments and passages were crowded with servants, who thrust themselves into the reception room without the smallest ceremony, in order to look at us a little closer, so that we sat in a perfect mob. Sweetmeats and fruits were brought, rose-water sprinkled over us, and some attar of roses poured upon our handkerchiefs. After a time they brought us some areca nut and betel leaf on a silver cup, which the queen herself presented to us. This is the signal for the termination of the audience, and until it is given one must not go. Before we got up, large garlands of jessamine were hung round our necks, and I had them also placed round my wrist, and when we got home fruits and sweetmeats were sent after us. The queen, who had remained unveiled, though Mr. Hamilton was present, gave orders that we should have the palace shown to us, and we were led round it by the *Mundsch*, or tutor of the young prince; but with the exception of the hall of audience, the rooms are all extremely simple, and with scarcely any furniture but cushions, covered with white muslin, which lie on the ground. When we came out upon the terrace, we found the prince riding out, with a numerous train, mounted, some on horses, some on elephants. The soldiers were well dressed in white trousers and blue caftans, and a sort of murmur, which I was told expressed approbation, arose on the appearance of the prince. His highness can speak broken English, and he put some questions to me implying that he was not ignorant of geography, so that I could compliment the mundsch on the success of his education.

This Mundsch had the complaisance also to show me over the ice manufactory. The ice is usually made in the months of December and January, but even in February the nights, and still more the early morning hours before sunrise, are so cool, that shallow water is easily covered with a coat of thin ice. For this purpose, where the ground is impregnated with saltpetre, flat pits are dug, in which are laid thin flat pans of porous clay filled with water, or, where there is no saltpetre in the ground, the highest terraces of the houses are covered with straw, and the dishes placed upon them. The thin coat of ice thus gained is then broken into pieces, poured over with water, and placed in the ice pits, which are also kept covered with straw.

Besides his attentions to me at Indor, Mr. Hamilton was so good as to provide for my further journey, for which I might again have had the use of the royal camels ; but to avoid fatigue I preferred the ox waggon. He made himself the agreement with the driver, arranged my stations for me from here to Aurunjabad (230 miles), gave me an excellent servant and a sepoy to accompany me, furnished me with letters, and even asked whether I had money enough, and all that with a manner so kind and friendly, that it was of as much value as the services themselves. Not merely in Indor, but everywhere, I heard the name of this gentleman mentioned with the highest respect.

The road on leaving Indor led through palm groves and a richly cultivated country to a village called Simarola, where I found ready for me a pretty tent, which Mr. Hamilton had sent forward in order to surprise me with one more good night, and I thanked him most fervently in my heart for the attention. From Simarola the country becomes picturesque. A narrow mountain ridge, in many places scarcely broad enough for the road, leads across small valleys at whose sides the most beautiful lightly-wooded mountains are piled up. Among the trees I particularly noticed two species, one with red, the other with yellow flowers, but both strangely wanting in leaves. Ever since leaving Kottah, on account of the increasing stonyness of the road, the camels had been getting scarcer, and they were replaced by trains of oxen. I have met herds, which must have consisted of several thousands, laden with corn, wood, salt, &c. It is inconceivable to me where food for all these animals can be found, for no meadows are to be seen, and, except the plantations, the ground is burnt up or covered with fine withered grass called jungle grass, which I never saw any animal taste. The activity of the women and children in the villages through which these trains pass is most striking. They furnish themselves with baskets, and follow the trains to an immense distance, collecting the dung of the animals, which they make into flat cakes and dry in the sun for fuel. Late in the evening we entered, amidst thunder and lightning, the village of *Burwai,* where there was said to be an open bongolo, but as we could not find it in the dark I had to content myself with the shelter of a projecting roof.

February 29th.—This day's stage was one of the longest we had, and our road led through dreary wildernesses and jungles. We had been jogging for some time quietly along, when all on a sudden our animals made a stop, and stood as if they were rooted to the ground, trembling at the same time all over. Their fear communicated itself to the men, who began in a tone of horror to scream, " Tiger! tiger!" I ordered them to go on shouting as loud as they could, and also to tear up some jungle grass and set fire to it, in hopes of terrifying any beasts that might be near us, though I saw nothing of them, but I learnt afterwards that scarcely a night passed in which a horse or an ox did not become the prey of a tiger, and only a few days before a poor woman who had lingered late in the jungle was torn to pieces. All the villages were surrounded by high walls of earth or stone, whether from fear of beasts or from any other cause I could not with certainty learn. These fortress-villages extend as far as Aurunjabad, a distance of 150 miles.

March 3d.—*Adjunta.*—Before arriving at this place we passed through a tremendous, but easily defended, mountain pass, closed at the top by an immense fortified gate, which now, however, in time of peace, was left open. The heights on each side were defended by high strong walls. At every step the scenery became more wildly romantic; picturesque masses of rock and mighty walls lay on either side, and valley receded behind valley far into the mountains, while in front the eye ranged freely over a far extending plain.

At Adjunta I found the resident, Captain Gill, to whom I had letters from Mr. Hamilton, and after the first salutations I expressed a wish to see the renowned rocky temple of Adjunta. I then learned, to my vexation, that I could have reached it by a much shorter route from my last night's station, Furdapoor, to which it really lay much nearer. What was to be done? The temple I would see; but I had little time to lose, so I resolved at once to go back again, and taking with me a little provision and mounting the best horse in Captain Gill's stud, I was through the mountain pass again in little more than an hour, and on my way to the temple.

The road lies through some wild desolate valleys, whose death-like stillness is disturbed by no song of bird, no sound of life, and which are perfectly well adapted to excite expectation of the wonders here to be beheld. The temples are twenty-seven in number, cut in lofty perpendicular rocks of a semi-circular form. On some of these rocky walls there are two stories of temples, one above another, with paths leading to the top, but so narrow and broken that you scarcely know where to set your foot. Below, you look into tremendous abysses, in which a mountain torrent loses itself, while above, to the height of several hundred feet, rises the face of the smooth perpendicular rock. Most of the temples form quadrangles, into which you enter through verandahs and beautiful portals, which, supported upon columns, seem to bear up the massive pile of rock. I counted in the larger twenty-eight, in the smallest eight columns. At the sides of the temples are little perfectly dark cells, in which, probably, the priests used to live. In the back ground, in a larger chamber, was the sanctuary, and here are gigantic figures in all positions, some measuring above eighteen feet, and reaching nearly the ceiling of the temple, which is four-and-twenty feet high. The walls of the temple and verandahs are full of gods and statues of good and evil spirits. In one of the temples is represented a whole giant war, and all the figures, columns, verandahs, and portals are cut out of the living rock. Their immense numbers and the great beauty of the sculptures and reliefs, on the columns, capitals, friezes, doors, and even on the ceilings of the temples,—the inexhaustible variety in the drawings and patterns,—is truly admirable. It seems as if it were scarcely possible that these masterly and at the same time gigantic works could be executed by human hands. The Brahmins ascribe them to supernatural agency, and maintain that the epoch of their creation cannot be discovered. Besides the sculptures, there are in many places paintings, with colours brighter and fresher than those of many modern works.

The temples of the second kind have an oval form, and majestic lofty portals, which lead immediately into the interior. The largest of these has on each side a colonnade of nineteen columns, the smallest of eight ; but in these are no priests' cells and no sanctuary. Instead of the latter, there stands at the end of each temple a high monument of a cupola form, and on one of these is hewn out a statue of Buddha in a standing position. On the walls of the larger temple are gigantic figures cut out of the living rock, beneath which is a sleeping Buddha, twenty-one feet long. After I had spent some hours in climbing and creeping about, and had closely viewed each individual temple, I was led back into one that I had already seen, and behold there stood a little table, most richly furnished with refreshments, and inviting me to a welcome meal. It was Captain Gill who had been so kind as to send after me into this desert all that was required for an elegant tiffin, including a table and chairs. Thus strengthened and refreshed, I found the way home by no means fatiguing.

The house which Captain Gill inhabits in Adjunta is singularly situated. A pleasant garden, with flowers and foliage, surrounds the front, whence you look over a beautiful plain, whilst the back is on the brink of a really terrible precipice, where the head grows giddy at the sight of precipitous crags and awful chasms and abysses.

When Captain Gill understood that I wished to visit the renowned fortress of Dowlutabad, he told me that no one was admitted to it without an order from the commandant of Aurunjabad ; but he added, that he would immediately send a messenger thither for one, and he could at the same time bring me a card of admission for Elora. There and back the messenger would have a distance of 140 miles to go, and all this courtesy was shown by Englishmen to me, a German woman, without rank or distinction of any kind.

At four o'clock in the morning the captain favoured me with his company at the coffee table, and half an hour afterwards I was sitting in my baili pursuing my journey.

March 6.—Early in the morning I mounted my horse, to visit the rocky temple of Elora ; but, as it often happens in life, I was reminded of the proverbial saying, " Man proposes and God disposes," and instead of the temple I saw a tiger hunt.

I had scarcely turned my back on the town where I had passed the night, when I saw advancing towards me from the bongolo several Europeans, sitting upon elephants. We stopped on coming up with each other, and began a conversation, from which it appeared that the gentlemen were out on a tiger hunt, as they had had information of some being in the neighbourhood, and they invited me, if such sport did not terrify me too much, to join them. I was very glad of the invitation, and soon found myself in company with two of the gentlemen and one native, seated in a box about two feet high, which was placed on the back of a very large elephant. The native was to load the guns; and they gave me a large knife to defend myself with in case the tiger should spring up to the edge of the box.

Thus prepared, we set off for the hills, and after the lapse of some hours thought we had come, probably, pretty close to the tiger's den, when suddenly one of our servants exclaimed, " *Back, back !* that is Tiger !" Glaring eyes were seen through the bushes, and at the same moment several shots were fired. The animal was soon pierced by several bullets, and now dashed at us full of fury. He made such tremendous springs that I thought he must infallibly soon reach our box, and choose himself a victim out of our party. This spectacle was terrible enough to me, and my fear was presently increased by the sight of a second tiger. I behaved myself, however, so valiantly that no one of the gentlemen suspected what a coward I was. Shot followed shot. The elephants defended themselves very cleverly with their trunks, and after a hot fight of half an hour's duration we remained victors, and the dead animals were in triumph robbed of their beautiful skins. The gentlemen were so courteous as to offer me one of them, but I declined accepting it, as I could not have delayed my journey long enough to have it dried and put into a proper state.

I got a good deal of praise for my courageous behaviour, and I was told tiger hunting was really extremely dangerous where the elephants were not very well trained. If they were afraid of the tigers, and ran away, one would be very likely to be dashed off by the branches of the trees, or perhaps left hanging upon them, and then would infallibly become the prey of the enraged animal. It was of course too late for my visit to the temples this day, so I had to put it off till the following morning.

The temples of Elora lie on one of the table lands which are so peculiarly Indian. The principal one, that of Kylas, which is the most remarkable, exceeds in size and completeness the best architectural works of India ; indeed it may well vie with the astonishing works of the ancient Egyptians. It is of a circular form, 120 feet high and 600 feet in circumference. For the execution of this masterpiece, a colossal block has been separated from the living rock by a passage of 100 feet wide and 240 long. The interior consists of a principal hall and some subordinate ones, all filled with sculptures and gigantic statues of gods. Its greatest magnificence, however, appears in the rich sculptures and elaborate arabesques which decorate the towers.

The temple rests on the backs of countless elephants and tigers, which are lying near each other in peaceful attitudes. All, as I have said, are cut out of the solid rock, and it surrounds them on three sides, at the distance of a hundred feet, like a colossal perpendicular wall. Further on, in another rock, is another group of temples similar in many respects, but simpler and less ornamented. Had these rocks consisted of granite or any equally hard stone, these works would have been, not difficult, but impossible.

The fortress of *Dowlatabad* is one of the oldest and strongest in India, and is regarded as the greatest curiosity of its kind, not only in the Deccan, but in all India. It has a most imposing aspect, lying on a rock 600 feet high, which by some convulsion of nature has been rent from the mountains to which it belongs. It is cut perpendicularly to a height of 130 feet, and also 30 feet below the moat by which it is surrounded, and it appears entirely inaccessible. No path leads up to it, and I could not help feeling very curious as to the means by which we were to get in, when a very low iron door in the face of the rock opened, and gave us admittance. This door is only visible in peaceful times, as during war, the moat can be filled to a foot above it, so as entirely to conceal it. Torches were kindled, and we were cautiously conducted through low, narrow, winding passages, cut through the heart of the rock, and leading gradually upwards. Even these passages were closed in many places by massive iron gates. We emerged again into daylight a considerable height above the rocky wall, and thence narrow paths and steps, also protected by strong fortifications, lead to the highest point. At the foot of the hill lie the ruins evidently of a considerable town, though now there is nothing left of it but the three or four lines of fortification which you must pass to reach the existing fortress.

The numerous fortresses and fortified villages found in this part of the country, date, I was told, from the time when Hindostan was parcelled out into many states which were engaged in incessant war with each other. In consequence of these perpetual wars also, there were gradually formed bands of mounted robbers, ten or twelve thousand strong, which laid siege to the smaller towns, and sometimes entirely destroyed the harvests ; and they were obliged, in consequence, to make treaties with these hordes— and buy their peace with a yearly tribute.

Since the English have conquered India, peace has been every where established ; the fortifications are falling to decay and are not repaired, and though the people still go armed, it is more from habit than necessity.

Aurunjabad.—On the 7th of March late in the evening I arrived at Aurunjabad, and Captain Stewart, who lived outside the town, received me in just as friendly a manner as the other residents had done. In the morning I accompanied him and Mrs. Stewart into the city to see the lions, which consisted merely in a monument and a holy well or pond.

Aurunjabad is the capital of Deccan and has 60,000 inhabitants, but it lies partly in ruins. The monument, which is outside the town, is one built 200 years ago by a certain sultan to the memory of his daughter : it is of white marble, in which elegant arabesques and flowers are carved with great skill, and the doors are ornamented with plates of metal, in which also are flowers and ornaments. Near the mosque is a handsome marble hall, and round it a neglected garden.

The present reigning king wished to take away some of the marble in order to employ it for a building in which his own remains are one day to repose, and he endeavoured to obtain permission to do so from the English government. The answer came, that he could do so if he pleased, but that he had better consider, that if he showed so little respect for his ancestors his own monument would probably be treated with no more ; and this answer seems to have induced him to renounce his intention. The holy pond (regarded as such by the Mahomedans) is a large basin lined with freestone. It is full of large pike, of which however not one is allowed to be caught, and there is even a guardian appointed, who provides them with food. The pike are therefore so tame and friendly that they will eat bread, turnips, and so forth out of your hand, and, but that the rainy season kills many of them, the pond would long since have had more fish than water in it. Since the arrival of the English however the guards are no longer so conscientious as they used to be, and many of the fish are "for a consideration" smuggled into the English kitchens.

As I came nearer to Bombay I again met vast herds of laden oxen, and most of the drivers had their families with them. The women were to the last degree ragged and dirty, but overladen at the same time with finery. Worsted tassels were dangling all over their bodies and also their ears ; their arms were loaded with bands of metal, bone, and glass beads, and their feet with heavy rings and chains, and, thus burdened or decorated, the ladies sat upon the backs of the oxen, or trotted after them.

March 17.—Since the attack of the negro in Brazil I have not had such a fright as I had to-day. My driver had from the beginning of the journey appeared to me very strange, indeed insane, in his behaviour. Sometimes he was wrangling with his oxen, sometimes caressing them, sometimes he would scream to the passers by, and then he would turn and stare at me for several minutes together. As long however as I had a servant with me, who always kept near the baili, I cared little about him; this morning however, my servant went on without permission to the next station, and I found myself left alone with the mad driver, on a very solitary road. After a time he got down from his seat and walked close behind the waggon. These bailis are covered with straw mats at the sides, but open before and behind, so that I could have seen very well what he was doing, but I would not turn round, in order not to put it into his head that I thought his intentions evil. I only turned my head partly to one side that I might be able to observe a little what he was about. Presently he returned again and pulled to my horror a hatchet, which every driver carries with him, out of the waggon, and taking it with him again went behind me. I now thought he certainly meant mischief, but I could not escape from him, and my best chance was therefore to show no fear. Quite softly, and so as not to be noticed I drew round me my mantle and rolled it together in order at least to protect my head, should he strike at me with the hatchet. For a considerable time I remained in this painful situation, but at last he came back to his place, and resumed his staring; my torment was not yet over however, for after remaining quiet awhile he got up and repeated the very same manœuvre, and this he did several times. That hour seemed to me an eternity; but in two hours we reached the station, and I found my servant, whom I now took care not again to lose sight of.

The villages through which we passed after this have a very wretched appearance. The houses are merely reed or cane huts, covered with palm leaves, many of them even without front walls. They are mostly inhabited by Mahrattas, a race once very powerful in India, and especially on this side of the Ganges; but in the eighteenth century they were driven out of the peninsula of Hindostan into the mountains which extend from Surat to Goa, and in the nineteenth century they were subjected by the British. One Mahratta chief only, it is said, still maintains his independence; the rest have submitted to receive pensions.

The Mahrattas live only on rice and water, but in opposition to a theory sometimes maintained, they are ferocious as well as artful and cowardly. When they are going into battle they intoxicate themselves with opium, and with smoking wild hemp. They profess the religion of Brahma.

In the afternoon of this day I reached the hamlet of Pannwell, on the river of the same name, and towards evening embarked in a boat upon it, and after going a short distance out to sea landed towards morning in Bombay, having completed the long and difficult journey from Delhi in seven weeks.

For reaching it in safety through so many difficulties, I am especially indebted to the English authorities, who with word and deed came to the assistance of the solitary German woman; their humanity, their cordial kindness will never be forgotten by me. Once more I return them my deepest, warmest thanks.

BOMBAY.

Bombay, the principal place of Western India, lies on a pretty little island, separated from the main land by quite a narrow arm of the sea. It contains 250,000 people; and you may hear in it all the languages of the civilized world. The most beautiful prospect over the island and city, as well as of the neighbouring islands of Salsette, Elephanta, &c., may be obtained from Malabar

Point. The town itself lies on a flat along the sea-shore, but the
environs at a short distance consist of low hills covered with
beautiful groves of cocoa and date trees.   The natives generally
seek the shade of large trees for their houses, but the Europeans
seek for light and air.

The bustle of the rich inland and European trade, and the
handsome shops and warehouses, are to be found in the fortified
part of the city, which forms a large quadrangle, and here the
streets are handsome, and the great square called the Green magnificent.   The Open Town and the Black Town adjoin this : in
the former the streets are more regular and broad than I have
seen in any Indian town ; and here is the Bazar, which is worth
visiting on account of the great variety of different nations you
meet with in it.   Three-fourths of the inhabitants of this quarter
indeed are Hindoos, but the other fourth is made up of Persians,
Fire-worshippers, Mahrattas, Jews, Arabs, Bedouins, Negroes,
descendants of Portuguese, some hundreds of Europeans, and
even Chinese and Hottentots.   It is, however, long before one
can distinguish these different races from their features and
costume.   Of all these the Fire-worshippers are the richest.
These people were driven out of Persia about 1,200 years ago,
and they are settled all along the west coast of India.   They are
extraordinarily active and well informed, industrious as well as
benevolent, so that you see among them no poor, far less beggars
and all appear prosperous.   The finest houses, in which the
Europeans live, belong mostly to them, and they drive about in
splendid equipages and with numerous trains of servants.   One
of the richest of them, Jamset-ize-jeejeebhoy, has had a hospital
built at his sole cost ; it is a very handsome building in the Gothic
style, attended by European physicians, and receives the sick of
all religions.   He has received the honour of knighthood from the
English government, and is certainly the first Hindoo on whom
such a distinction was ever conferred.

On my first arrival I went one morning on the Esplanade for
the purpose of seeing the whole body of Parsees in Bombay
assemble, as I had read in books they did, to greet the first ray
of the sun with prostrations and cries of joy.   I found, however,
only a few scattered singly here and there, and they were quietly
reading out of a book and murmuring a prayer in a loud voice.
Some even did not make their appearance till nine o'clock.   I was

equally mistaken about their mode of burial. I had been told they had the practice of placing their dead on the roofs of the houses that they might be devoured by the birds of prey ; but I found they had for this purpose enclosures surrounded by a wall four and twenty feet high ; inside this were three biers, for men, women, and children, and on these the bodies are laid and fastened with iron bands. The birds of prey, which are always in great numbers hovering about, then descend upon them, and in a few minutes tear the flesh from the bones; after which the bones are collected and thrown into a pit, also contained within the enclosure; and when this is full a new burial-place is taken. Many of the rich have private enclosures of this kind, over which is placed a covering of iron wire to keep off the birds: this mode of disposing of the dead is called "resigning them to the element of air." No one but a priest may enter or even look into these enclosures; and the priests, or rather the bearers who carry the bodies in, are rendered by that act so unclean that they are separated from all other society, and if another Parsee does but touch one of them accidentally he is obliged immediately to bathe and burn his clothes. The Parsees are no less jealous with respect to their temples : no stranger is allowed so much as a glance into them, so that I of course can give no account of the interior, except what I was told--that they are quite empty and unadorned, and that the sacred fire which burns in them is said to descend from that kindled by the prophet Zoroaster 4,000 years ago. It was carried with them when the Parsees were driven from Persia. During my stay in Bombay a Mr. Manuchjee was so kind as to invite me to his house, that I might see something of the mode of life of the Parsee families. I found their rooms fitted up very much in the European fashion, with chairs, sofas, looking-glasses, &c.; and the dress of the ladies differed very little from that of the rich Hindoo women, except that it was more decorous, as it con- sisted of silk stuff instead of transparent muslin. The silk stuffs were richly embroidered with gold, and this luxury extended even to children of three years old. Those still younger, and new- born infants, were wrapped in plain silk, but all had gold and silver embroidery on their little caps ; and even babies of eight months old had rings and armlets enriched with precious stones or pearls ; the dress of a Parsee lady on grand occasions is often worth as much as 100,000 rupees.

The dress of the men consists of trowsers and shirts of white silk, and long caftans of muslin; the turban is not like that of the Turks, but a kind of pasteboard cap ten or twelve inches high, and covered with some coloured stuff or wax-cloth. Both men and women wear round the body a double string, which they loosen when they are at prayer, and this is the most indispensable of all the articles of their dress. No engagement is binding if this string has not been worn at the time it was made; and the placing it on a child, which is done at the ninth year, forms an epoch in its life.

Before this, girls can go about with their fathers in public, and boys may eat of food prepared by Christians, but after the assumption of this string the girls must remain at home, and the boys eat at their father's table. Religion is concerned also in the form of a Parsee's shirt; it must have five seams and be laid in a particular manner over the breast. Mr. Manuchjee formed in many respects rather an exception to the generality of his countrymen. He has travelled much, has been in Paris, London, and Italy; and he has got into rather ill odour with his countrymen for his partiality to European customs, and his attempts to introduce some reforms, though he did not carry these so far as he would have wished, for fear of giving offence. His eldest daughter has been educated much as young ladies in Europe are; she plays the piano—sews, embroiders, and so forth, and her father would not consent to betroth her as a child, and even expressed a wish that her inclination might agree with his choice. It is however considered very doubtful whether in consequence of these innovations she will ever find a husband at all, especially as she has attained the age of fourteen, and as yet no bridegroom is forthcoming.

When I made my first visit, I found the mother and daughter engaged in needlework, and I was invited to remain to dinner, a favour which an orthodox Parsee would not have shown me. I was not however allowed to dine with the family, but the table was first covered for me only, and they brought me several dishes not greatly different from what I might have had in Europe. The whole family, servants included, and with the single exception of the master of the house, assembled to see me eat with a knife and fork, and after I had thus satisfied my appetite in the presence of the public, the table and every thing I had used was cleaned as carefully as if I had had the plague. After this they brought flat loaves or cakes, which were to serve instead of plates, and six or seven little dishes of the same kind as those which they had served to me. The family then washed hands and faces, the father said a short prayer, and all except the youngest child, who was only just six years old, sat down to table, and began to put their right hands into the different dishes; they tore the meat from the mutton and fowl bones, pulled off pieces of the fish, and dipped them into the broth and sauces, and flung the pieces into their mouths so cleverly as not to touch their lips. If they did, they would have to wash again, or to take the dish they were eating of at the time to themselves, and touch no other during the meal. They manage to drink also, by throwing the drink into the wide open mouths without allowing the lip to touch the vessel. This mode of eating is not very agreeable to look at, but it is not really dirty, as the hands are just washed, and do not touch any thing but the food.

Another ceremony which I had an opportunity of witnessing, was the funeral of an old Hindoo woman. From the time when she was known to be near death she was surrounded by a number of women, who set up periodically a dreadful howling and crying. Presently came other groups, and they set up the same noise as soon as they came in sight of the house; they then went in, but the men sat down quietly outside. In the course of a few hours the body was brought out and wrapt in a white linen cloth and laid upon the bier, to be borne by the men to the place of burning. One of the men carried a vessel with charcoal, and a piece of lighted wood, in order to kindle the funeral pile with the domestic fire. The women remained at home, and with the assistance of a hired mourning woman, kept up the above mentioned loud lamentation, striking themselves on the breast, and bowing their heads in time with one another, and with a jerking motion like that of a doll upon wires.

On the following morning the visits were repeated, the men remaining as before outside the house, – but every time a troop of women approached, going to the door and announcing them. The chief mourner then made her appearance to receive them. She threw herself on the ground before them with such violence that I feared she would not be able to get up again, the visitors then struck themselves vehemently with their fists, and carried their hands to their heads. In the meantime the chief mourner got up again, and then she fell on the neck of one of her visitors after the other, in the most stormy manner, drawing at the same time the cloth that covered her head also over that of her friend, and both howling one against the other. All these movements were made with great rapidity, so that a good dozen of embraces were given in almost no time. It was not till sunset on the second day that a good meal put an end to the ceremony, but during the whole two days, refreshments and toddy were plentifully distributed, so that with the addition of the price of the pile, a funeral becomes an expensive affair : the funeral I had witnessed was that of a poor woman. I once met the funeral of a child where the body was covered with fresh beautiful flowers ; and a man carried it in his arms as tenderly as if it slept, and he had feared awakening it.

The Hindoos have no weekly holiday, but only, at certain periods of the year, festivals which last several days. One of these, which I witnessed, was that of the new year, when the chief diversion is sprinkling each other with yellow, red, and brown paint, and smearing the cheeks and forehead with it. The noisy tam-tam and a few fiddles opened the procession, and then came larger and smaller parties laughing and singing from one house to another. Many of the company (amongst which of course there were no respectable women) appeared to have taken to the toddy rather too kindly ; in the evening there were in the houses parties of both sexes, where I was told things were not always conducted with the strictest propriety.

Among other sights which I saw in Bombay I should not omit to mention that of a martyr, who had held his hand and arm in the same position for three and twenty years. He had held the arm high up and the hand flat back, so that a flower-pot could stand on it. The flower-pot was taken off after the lapse of the three and twenty years, but the hand and arm could not then be placed in any other position, they were quite withered and had a very unpleasant appearance.

The island of Elephanta lies six or eight leagues distant from Bombay, and M. Wattenbach, the Hamburgh cousul, who had before shown me the most kind and hospitable attentions, took me to visit it.

The principal temple resembles the largest one at Adjunta,

only with the difference that it is separated from the living rock at the two sides, though connected with it above, below, and at the back.   In the sanctuary stands a gigantic three-headed bust, supposed to represent the Hindoo Trinity, which measures, including the head-dress, about eight feet.   On the walls and in the niches there are not only gigantic statues, but whole scenes from the Hindoo mythology, and the female figures I noticed all have the left hip out and the right one in.   The temple appears to have been devoted to the god Shiva.

Near this great temple stands another smaller one, the walls of which are also covered with divinities.   Both have suffered much from the Portuguese, who, when they conquered the island, went so far in their religious zeal as to plant cannon for the destruction of these dreadful works of the heathen, a work in which they succeeded better than in his conversion.   Several columns are lying in fragments, and almost all are more or less damaged.   The ground is covered with ruins ; and no one, even of the gods and their attendants, has remained uninjured.

From the façade of the great temple you enjoy a fine prospect over the wide sea, the extensive town, and the pretty hills around it.   We passed the whole day there, with the exception of the warmest hours, when we took refuge in the cool shade of the temple, and amused ourselves with reading.   Mr. Wattenbach had brought several servants ; and chairs, tables, a dinner service, books and newspapers, had been sent forward for our accommodation.   Indeed I thought we had quite a superfluity of conveniences and comforts ; but an English family whom we met here had, it seemed, found arm-chairs, sofas, and carpets necessary to their rural enjoyment.

Salsetta, also called Tiger Island, is connected with Bombay by a short artificial dam, and the distance from the fort to the village, behind which the temples lie, is about eighteen English miles, which, with relays of horses, we did easily in three hours.   The natural beauties of this island far exceed those of Bombay ; not rows of hills, but chains of mountains rise here, covered to the summits with wood, from the midst of which sometimes ascend masses of naked rock.   The valleys are full of luxuriant corn fields, planted with slender green palms ; but the island does not seem very populous, for I saw only a few villages and a single small town, which was inhabited by Mahrattas, just as poor and as dirty as those of Kundalla. From the village where we left the carriage we had three miles to walk to the temples. The principal one is surrounded by a lofty hall, in which stand two statues of gods twenty-one feet high ; and the second, adjoining it, contains cells for priests, and symbols of divinities, and reliefs. Some are not larger than a small room and without any sculptures ; and in general the temples of Elephanta and Salsetta are far inferior to those of Adjunta and Elora. I was told that those of Salsetta were little visited, on account of the dangers attending such an excursion. The district was full of tigers, and the wild bees swarmed so much about the temples that it was often scarcely possible to enter them ; and further, it was said that the temples were the abodes of robbers. We had, however, the good fortune to escape all these accidents ; and for myself, not being satisfied with one inspection, when my companions were taking their afternoon's nap I took the opportunity to slip away, and have a ramble alone. I climbed from rock to rock till I came to the temple farthest off, and there I was somewhat startled by finding the horns and skin of a goat that had been devoured by a tiger ; but I calculated on the unsocial habits of the beast, which in clear daylight will always rather shun than seek human society, and continued my ramble undisturbed.

We came back, as I have said, in perfect safety ; but two gentlemen, who visited the spot some days after, were not so fortunate. One of them was knocking at an opening he observed in the rock, when out rushed a mighty swarm of wild bees, and stung them both so violently on head, hands, and face that they had great difficulty in making their escape.

The climate of Bombay is healthier than that of Calcutta, and even the heat is, from the constant sea breeze, easier to bear than that of the former city, although Bombay is five degrees further south.

FROM BOMBAY TO BAGDAD.

Departure from Bombay.—Smallpox on board.—Muscat.—Bandr-Abas.— The Persians.—The Straits of Kishma.—Buschir.—Entrance into the Shat al Arab.—Bassora.—Entrance into the Tigris.—Bedouins.—Ctesiphon and Seleucia.—Arrival in Bagdad.

I HAD pretty well made up my mind to make the voyage from Bombay to Bassora in an Arabian boat, when Mr. Wattenbach brought me the welcome intelligence that a small steamer was about to make a trip thither. It was to sail on the 10th, and I by no means anticipated that it would not really take its departure till the 23d. It was only of 40-horse power, and had but two cabins, one of which had long been engaged by an English gentleman, Mr. Ross. The second was taken by some rich Persians for their wives and children; so that I had to content myself with a place on the deck, with the proviso that I was to dine at the table of the captain, who during the whole voyage overwhelmed me with attentions.

This small vessel, the "Forbes," was excessively overcrowded. The ship's company alone made 45 persons, and there were 124 passengers, mostly Persians, Mahomedans, and Arabs. Mr. Ross and I were the only Europeans. When this throng of people was assembled on the deck, there was not the smallest space left free to get from one part to another, and it was necessary to climb over chests, trunks, and other luggage, besides taking the utmost possible care not to tread on somebody's head or feet.

After taking a critical survey of the ground, I chose what seemed to me the most eligible spot under the circumstances; indeed one that possessed solid advantages. I took up my abode under the captain's dinner table, and rejoiced in my security that no one would tread on my hands, feet, or head.

It is true I was under the necessity at meal times of dragging myself out of my hole, in order to make room for the feet of the company, and I found this rather distressing, for I had left Bombay very unwell, and on the second day I was attacked by fever. I took no medicine, however, (I never carry any with me,) but gave myself up entirely to nature and Providence.

On the third day of our voyage a far more serious evil occurred than the malady that had attacked me. Smallpox broke out in the larger cabin, into which eighteen women and seven children were packed. They had less space than the negroes in slave ships; the air became poisonous in the highest degree; and the poor creatures dared not come upon deck because of the men there. The vapour that arose from the cabin was so pestilential that we were quite in dread lest it should spread through the open holes over the entire ship. It appeared that the disease had already existed among them when the women came on board, but no one could have discovered it, for they were brought late at night, and closely covered with veils and shawls. It was not till one of the children died that we discovered the danger. The body of the child was wrapped in a white cloth, fastened upon a plank, weighted with some pieces of coal and stone, and then let down into the sea. I know not whether any kindred or loving eye watched this melancholy funeral. I saw no tear flow ; but if the poor mother did mourn for her darling, she would not have dared follow it to its watery grave.

Two more deaths took place, and then the pestilence seemed to decline, and fortunately it had not extended beyond the cabin.

On the 30th of April we neared the Arabian coast, and saw some naked mountains. On the following morning the peaks of some fine groups of rocks showed themselves, with some small forts and watch towers, and soon a mighty mountain at the entrance to a bay.

We anchored before the town of Muscat, which lies at the end of the bay. It belongs to an Arabian prince, and is strongly fortified, besides being surrounded by several ranges of rocks, all guarded by towers and forts. The largest amongst them was once a convent of Portuguese monks ; but it was attacked in the night by Arabs, and all the inmates murdered.

The houses of the town are of stone with small windows and terraced roofs, and the two palaces are distinguished only by their superior size. Many streets are so narrow that scarcely two persons can pass in them. The heat is very oppressive, as the town lies in a hollow between rocks, and there is not the smallest sprig of verdure to soften the glare of the sunlight, which is consequently most painful to the eyes. Far and wide, no tree, no shrubs, no blade of grass even, refreshes the aching sight, and all who can any way afford it, as soon as they have finished their business, fly to the country houses by the sea side. European residents there are none, for the climate, it is said, is deadly to them.

At the back of the town is a rocky valley, and in that a village, which contains (oh, wonder!) a garden, with six palm trees, a fig, and a pomegranate. The village is larger and more populous than the town, for it counts 6,000 inhabitants, while the latter has but 4,000. It is, however, impossible to imagine the poverty, the dirt, and the foul smells which this village presents. The huts stand almost one upon the other. They are small; only made of cane and palm leaves, and every kind of filth is thrown before the doors. It really required some resolution to go through this village, and I could not help wondering that pestilential disease should be ever absent from it. Blindness and diseases of the eyes are excessively common.

From this valley we passed into another, containing the great marvel of Muscat, the aforesaid garden, which is maintained only by the most unwearied labour in watering. It contains some flowers and vegetables, besides the trees, and belongs to the prince. My guide appeared very proud of this wonderful garden, and asked whether in my country we had any as beautiful.

I took these walks in the full heat of the sun (41 deg. Reaumur), and when I was besides much weakened by my illness, yet I never felt any ill effect from them, although I have been repeatedly warned that in hot countries this exposure is fatal to Europeans, and brings fever and sun-strokes. But had I listened to all that was said I should not have seen much; so I took it quietly,—went out in rain or sun, just as it happened,—and always saw more than any of my travelling companions.

On the 2d of May we again weighed anchor, and soon came tolerably near to the island of Ormus, the mountains of which were distinguished by an uncommon variety of colour, and some glittered as if they had been covered with snow. They contain a great deal of salt, and many Arabian and Persian vessels come every year to take in cargoes. In the evening we reached the little town of Bandr-Abas, before which we anchored. It lies on low hills of rock and sand, and is separated by a sandy plain from some mountains. Longingly did I look towards the land, for I had a great desire to tread the soil of Persia, but the captain advised me not to think of it. He said the Persians were not so good as the Hindoos, and since in these remote regions the appearance of a European woman was quite an unheard of occurrence, it was not unlikely they would salute me with a shower of stones.

Fortunately there was on board a young man, half English, half Persian, (his father an Englishman, had married an Armenian woman of Teheran,) who understood both languages perfectly, and I begged him to take me ashore, which he willingly did. He took me to the bazaar, and through several streets, and the people streamed towards us from all quarters, and gazed at me with much curiosity, but did not offer me the slightest insult.

I found the houses in this town small, and the streets narrow, dirty, and mostly with few signs of life; the bazaar only was animated. Here I saw the bakers making their bread in a very rapid fashion in presence of their customers. They kneaded flour and water in wooden dishes to a dough, then parted it into small pieces, and worked it out into a thin strip, which they stuck to the inside of a round clay pipe about eighteen inches in diameter, and perhaps one and twenty in length; this was made hot, and then sunk to half its length in the earth, and burning charcoal placed in it, so that the bread or cake was baked on both sides at once; on one by the hot pipe, and on the other by the fire. I bought half a dozen of these cakes, and, eaten hot, they were very good.

The Persians are easily distinguishable from the Arabs by their appearance. They are taller and stronger built, with a whiter skin, harsher features, and a wild and robber-like aspect. Their dress resembles that of the Mahomedans. Many wear turbans, others conical caps of black Astrachan.

Of this half Persian, Mr. William Hebworth, my companion, I heard an instance of grateful conduct that I cannot omit to mention. When a lad of sixteen he was taken from Persia to Bombay, and there, in the house of a friend of his father's, met with the kindest reception, and through the same influence procured an appointment. One day his protector, who was married and the father of four children, had the misfortune to be killed by a fall from his horse, and thereupon William Hebworth took the really magnanimous resolution of marrying the widow, who was many years his senior, and whose only fortune was four children, in order to repay in some measure the services of his deceased benefactor.

In Bandr-Abas we took a pilot, in order to pass through the Straits of Kishma, and towards noon we set sail. This strait is avoided by sailing ships, and is not without danger for steam boats, for the passage is so narrow between the island of Kishma and the main land that with a contrary wind vessels may easily be thrown on one of the coast.

Captain Litchfield had talked much to me of the beauty of this island of Kishma, and of the luxuriance of the vegetation, and had spoken of places in the straits which were so narrow that the palm trees on the island and those on the main land touched each other ; but some extraordinary convulsion of nature must certainly have taken place since his last voyage, for the lofty slender palms have been changed into miserable dwarf shrubs, and the island nowhere approaches the continent within less than half a league distance. It was curious enough that I afterwards heard Mr. Ross telling the same story, having apparently trusted the captain's account more than the evidence of his own eyes.

In one of the narrowest parts of the strait stands the fine fort of Luft, and this spot fifty years ago was the chief haunt of the Persian pirates, but a regular battle took place between them and the English in which eight hundred of the pirates were killed, and the whole gang destroyed, and since then the strait may be traversed in perfect security.

In the Persian Gulf I noticed many varieties of sea weed, and molluscæ, some of a milk-white, others rose colour with yellow spots, and there were also sea serpents from two to five feet long.

The town of Buschir lies in a plain, but only six miles from mountains five thousand feet high   It is the best harbour in Persia, and has a population of 15,000, but it is a very ugly and dirty place.

The houses stand so close together that it is easy to pass from the terrace roof of one to the other.   Many of them are provided with square chimneys fifteen or twenty feet high called "wind catchers," which have apertures at the side, and whose purpose is to send cool air into the apartments below,   The men I observed all go armed ; even in the house they have knives and daggers, and in the street pistols also.   The women and quite little girls have their faces so closely wrapped up that I cannot understand how they can see their way along.   It had been my plan to land at this town, visit the ruins of Persepolis, and thence continue my journey by Shiraz, Ispahan, and Teheran ; but an important insurrection had broken out, and great bands of robbers were ravaging the district, and committing all kinds of outrages, so that I was compelled to give up my first intention, and go on to Bagdad.

On the 11th of May I had the good fortune to see and enter one of the most renowned rivers in the world, formed by the junction of the Euphrates, the Tigris, and the Kerah, called here the *Shat*

al Arab, or river of the Arabs.   We left the mountains behind us
with the sea, and now saw only boundless plains covered with
date woods, spreading out on both sides.   Eighty miles below
Bassora we entered the Kauran, in order to land some passengers
at the little town of Mohambra, which lies near the mouth of the
river, and it required much skill to turn the steamer safely in
this narrow space.   The whole population of the town ran to the
shore, for they had never seen a steamer before, and they watched
its adroit manœuvring with eager sympathy.   Six years ago
this town belonged to the Turks ; but it was attacked and taken
by the Persians, and five thousand of the inhabitants, nearly the
whole population, put to the sword.   Of Bassora or Bosrah, you
see from the river nothing more than some fortifications and date
woods, for the city lies behind these, six miles up the country.

The voyage from Bombay hither had, from the disadvantage of
the monsoon, taken us eighteen days, and it was the most wearisome sea journey I had ever had.   Constantly upon deck, in a
heat which even in the shade of the tent rose to thirty degrees
(Reaumur), in a perfect throng of human beings, and being able
only once, at Buschir, to change my linen and clothes I longed
intensely for the refreshment and purification of a bath.   The
landing of the Persian women was an amusing scene.   Had
they been princesses, and beauties of the very first rank, more
care could not have been taken to avoid the possibility of the
glance of a man's eye, and there was not really among them
(for my sex had procured for me the privilege of a peep into
their cabin) a single handsome woman.   Their husbands placed
themselves in two lines stretching from the cabin to the ship's
side, and held great cloths stretched out so as to form close move-
able walls.   Through these the ladies were marched by degrees
out of the cabin, and even then they were so closely enveloped
in shawls and veils that they had to be led along as if they were
blind.   As they reached the side they crouched down between the
walls till the others arrived, and when all were assembled the
still more difficult operation commenced of climbing down the
narrow ship ladder into a well-curtained boat.   The wall was in
motion again ; but first one tumbled, then another, and the landing
of this part of the cargo was not effected under a full hour.

Bassora is one of the largest towns in Mesopotamia, but it
possesses among its inhabitants only a single European.   The

English agent was an Armenian, a Mr. Barseige, and to him I had a letter; but when, as there is no such thing as an inn, the captain requested him to afford me an asylum for a few days in his house, the courteous gentleman flatly refused, and I had to be again indebted to the kindness of the captain, who invited me to remain in the steamer. By a fortunate chance for me, he found on inquiry that there was at present a German missionary staying in the town, who had an abode consisting of several rooms, one of which, when I had stated my case to him, he had the complaisance to give up to me. I took leave of my good captain with real emotion, and I shall never forget the friendly attention he showed me. He was really a thoroughly good-hearted man, and yet in his ship the Hindoos and Negroes were worse treated than in any other I have been in. Every word addressed to them by the crew was accompanied by kicks and cuffs, and at Mascat three of the unfortunate men deserted. Would that the Christian European excelled the Hindoo and Mussulman as much in kindness and benevolence as he does in learning and science.

Of the ruins of former days, beautiful mosques and so forth, Bassora shows few remains, but there are plenty of modern ruins, dating from 1832, when the plague carried away half the inhabitants. You pass through many streets and squares that consist of nothing but decayed and falling houses, and where twenty years ago men were busily at work there are now ruined walls and heaps of rubbish from which shrubs and palm trees are sprouting out. The situation of the town is very unhealthy, for it is surrounded by a plain intersected on one side with countless ditches half full of mud and filth, and exhaling the most pernicious vapour, and, on the other, covered with date woods that prevent the free circulation of air. The heat is so great that almost every house is provided with a room half under ground, in which the family spend the day. The greater part of the population consists of Arabs; the rest are Persians, Turks, and Armenians; and as there are no Europeans I was advised, if I went out, to envelope myself in a large shawl and veil. The first I agreed to ; but to the veil in such heat I could not submit, but marched out with my face uncovered, and even my great shawl I managed so awkwardly that my European clothing peeped out in various places. No one, however, offered me any offence.

I had been but a few days in Bassora when there arrived the English war steamer Nitocris, which during nine months of the year takes letters and papers to Bagdad, and the captain has generally the kindness to carry with him any stray European traveller who may have wandered so far as Bassora. This courtesy I also experienced, and he even gave up his cabin to me, without permitting me to offer any kind of payment. Had it not been for this favour the journey to Bagdad would have been most toilsome and difficult for me. The distance is about five hundred English miles, and any boat that I could have hired would have taken forty or fifty days to do it. By land, the distance is not more than three hundred and ninety miles, but the way leads through deserts traversed by hordes of robbers and wandering Bedouins, whose protection must be purchased at a high rate.

On the afternoon of the same day when we left Bassora we reached the Delta, where the Euphrates and Tigris unite their streams to form that to which (not knowing what else to call it, as both rivers are equally large,) they have given the name of Shat el Arab. This, according to some learned writers, is the precise spot where Paradise was situated. We entered the Tigris, and for several miles could still rejoice in the aspect of the beautiful date groves which had accompanied us almost without interruption from the sea. The country looked green and blooming on both sides, and fine corn-fields alternated with extensive pastures, sprinkled over with small trees and shrubs; but this fertility extends but a few miles inland; beyond it, and farther from the river, all is dreary desert. In several places we saw great hordes of Bedouins, who had pitched their tents in long lines close to the Tigris. Some of the tents were large and well covered; others, nothing more than a cloth or a few skins spread over two or three stakes, or perhaps a straw mat that scarcely shelters the head from the burning sun. In winter, when the cold often reaches the freezing point, they have no other dwellings, and the mortality is said to be very great among them. These people have quite the aspect of savages. They have no other clothing than some brown cloths; the men very little of that; and the children remain till the twelfth year naked. Their faces are a little tattooed; their hair plaited, and hanging down in four tails; and the women have large rings in their noses, and some other ornaments of shells and glass beads. They are all under the dominion of the Porte, to which they pay a tribute, but they are really obedient only to their own sheiks, many of whom have forty or fifty thousand tents under their authority. Some of the tribes practise agriculture, and they do not wander about.

Half way between Bassora and Bagdad we come in sight of the lofty mountain chain of Laristan, and with a clear atmosphere summits of ten thousand feet high may be seen. Every step of the ground calls up some historical recollection. The ground is here ;—but what has become of the cities ?—what of the mighty and powerful people who dwelt in them ? Fallen walls, hillocks of earth, and rubbish, are all that now remain. What were once prosperous and civilized empires are but naked and desolate steppes, trodden only by a few wandering Bedouins.

The agricultural Arabs are of course much exposed to the attacks of their nomadic brethren, and in order to preserve what they can of their harvests they carry it to little fortified places, a number of which exist between Bagdad and Bassora. We stopped near them several times to take in wood, for the well-armed and numerous crew of the steamer prevented any fear of attack. Once I was tempted, in pursuit of a beautiful insect, to venture a little way into the bush, and I was immediately surrounded by a swarm of women and children, who indeed did not offer me the least harm, but, considering their disgustingly dirty appearance, they excited in me no small terror, by pressing closely to me, touching my clothes, and endeavouring to try on my straw bonnet. The children looked dreadfully neglected ; many of them were covered with ulcers ; and old and young had their hands constantly in their hair. At the place where we stopped the people brought sheep and butter for sale. The sheep were large and fine ; had close long wool, and tails fifteen inches long and eight inches broad ; and they cost about *eightpence halfpenny* each.

The crew of our vessel, I noticed, was extremely well fed ; and what pleased me still better was the good treatment experienced by the natives on board, who were placed in all respects on a level with the English sailors, and as they were extremely clean and orderly I had an opportunity of convincing myself that cuffs and kicks are not, as I had been told, essential to their right management.

In the district we were now passing through, we heard, that lions often came from the mountains, and attacked cattle and sheep, but

rarely human creatures. I had myself the good fortune to see a
pair of these stately animals, but at so great a distance that I cannot say whether they excelled in size and beauty those in the
menageries of Europe.

MESOPOTAMIA.—BAGDAD AND BABYLON.

*Bagdad.—Climate, &c.—Festival at the English Resident's.—The Harem
of the Pascha of Bagdad.—Excursion to the Ruins of Ctesiphon.—The
Persian Prince Il-Hany-Ala-Euly-Mirza.—Excursion to the Ruins of
Babylon.*

THE ancient city of the caliphs rises grandly on the sight from
the distance. Its minarets and cupolas, inlaid with coloured tiles,
glitter in the sun ; palaces, city gates, and fortifications in endless
lines, embrace the shores of the yellow, turbid, Tigris ; and gardens,
with dates and other fruit trees, cover the country round for miles ;
but as you approach the effect declines. We had scarcely cast
anchor before the steamer was surrounded by a crowd of strange
little boats, round like baskets, made of palm leaves, and smeared
over with asphalte. They are called " *guffer ;*" are about six feet
in diameter, three feet deep, and very safe, as they never turn
over, and can go into the shallowest places. They are of very
ancient invention. The town lies on both sides of the river, and
nnmbers about 60,000 inhabitants ; three fourths Turks ; the remainder, Jews, Persians, Armenians, and about fifty or sixty
Europeans.

I had a letter to Mr. Rawlinson, the English resident; but
Mr. Holland, the first officer in the steamer, had kindly invited
me to his house, which was rendered especially agreeable to me by
the presence of a lady, as he was a married man. I found in
Mrs. Holland a very handsome, amiable woman (a native of
Bagdad), who, though only twenty-three years of age, was the
mother of four children, the eldest of whom was eight years old.

The first thing I had to do before attempting to see the town
was to get myself an immense shawl, called an *isar*, and a small
fez, with a shawl to wind round it. The sort of mask, made of
closely-woven horsehair, with which the women here cover their
faces, I would not submit to. It is impossible, indeed, to imagine

a more inconvenient walking dress. The isar is always trailing in the dust, and it requires no little skill to hold it together so as to make it cover the whole body ; and I could not help pitying the poor women when I saw them carrying a child, or perhaps going to wash in the river, with this troublesome dress to manage. They always came back dripping with water.

In order to have a good view of Bagdad, I climbed with some difficulty to the vaulted roof of the Osman-Chan, and from there I looked down on its countless houses, many of them lying in pretty gardens, with thousands on thousands of terraces, and the magnificent river flowing for five English miles through the far-stretching city, and then between groves of palm and fruit trees. The houses are but one story high, built of brick, burnt or unburnt, and having their backs, with perhaps one small grated window, turned towards the streets, which are narrow, and full of dust and dirt. The trades-people and mechanics, as in all oriental cities, are distributed into particular quarters. There are few mosques, and those not hand-some ; but the old bazaar is one of the few memorials of what Bagdad was in its days of grandeur in the ninth century, and shows traces of handsome columns and arabesques ; and the Chan-Osman, on which I was standing, has a beautiful portal and lofty cupolas that remind you of the city of Haroun al Raschid. The materials for nearly all the buildings are said to have been brought from the ruins of Babylon. Some of these ancient bricks which have been used in the fortifications are two feet in diameter, and more like blocks of stone. The fortifications, however, though very extensive, are seen, on a nearer inspection, to be extremely weak, and the guns upon them certainly not in the best con-dition.

The houses are handsomer inside than might be anticipated from the exterior, though not so splendidly fitted up as in Damascus. It is the custom, on account of the heat of the weather, to pass only the early morning in the common rooms ; towards nine o'clock you take refuge in subterranean chambers, which are like cellars, lying fifteen or twenty feet below ground, and here you remain till evening, when you ascend to the terrace, where people drink tea, gossip, and receive visits till a late hour in the night. The cool breeze is at this time very delightful ; and many maintain that the moonlight nights are much finer than with us, but I can-not say I thought so. It is very common to pass the night on the

terrace, under a mosquito net, but in winter the nights and mornings are so cold that people have fires in their rooms.

The climate is considered healthy, even for Europeans, although
there is an unpleasant disease prevalent which our young ladies
would feel a horror of, called the date or Aleppo boil.   It is a
kind of tumour, generally attacking the face, and which, beginning
with a spot not larger than a pin's head, spreads to the size of a
crown piece, and, even when healed, leaves an ugly scar behind it.
Among a hundred faces you scarcely find one without this dis-
figurement ; but those who have but one may be regarded as fortunate, for I saw many with two or three.   It is said that it usually
makes its appearance at the time when the dates are ripe, and
lasts till the same period of the following year.   No remedy for
it has as yet been discovered, and though inoculation has been
tried by the Europeans, it has not been with success.

It would seem that the disease is in some way connected with
the Tigris, as it is not found at a few miles distance from the river ;
but it can hardly be, as has been supposed, occasioned by some fog
or vapour rising from the water, for the crew of the English
steamer, who remained constantly on the water, escaped it ; though
it is possible it may arise from the deposit of mud on the banks.
One European, whom I knew, was a real martyr to it, having had
no fewer than forty of these boils ; and I myself, though I rejoiced
at the time of my stay in Bagdad in having escaped, as I thought,
with only one small one on the hand, was attacked by it most
seriously six months after my return to Europe.

On the 24th of May I received an invitation from the English
resident, Mr. Rawlinson, to a grand fête in honour of the birth-
day of the Queen of England.   At dinner we had only Europeans,
but of the evening party there was a large assembly of the Christian
part of the community of Bagdad, Armenians, Greeks, &c.   The
fête was held on the beautiful terraces of the house, which, as well
as the court-yards and gardens, were splendidly illuminated.   The
blaze of lamps made it as light as day ; and there were soft carpets,
elastic divans, and refreshments of the finest kind, that might have
made us fancy ourselves in Europe, but that the two bands of music
were so undoubtedly oriental in the style of their performance as
to prevent any such mistake.

Among the women and girls were some strikingly beautiful, and
all had such eyes as few young men could gaze into without pay-

ing the penalty. To the effect of these eyes art certainly contributes a great deal, for, besides that their brilliancy and beauty is much heightened by the mode of colouring the eyebrows and eye-lashes, every hair is carefully drawn out that could mar the perfection of their shape, and the place of any that may be wanting is carefully supplied by the pencil. This devout attention to the business of the toilette extends even to women of the lowest class; but, in one point, their taste is certainly defective, for it is the fashion to spoil their fine black hair by staining it with henna, which changes it into an ugly brown-red. The dresses were rich; much in the Turkish fashion, with wide silk trousers, fastened round the ancle, and over these garments embroidered in gold; girdles, heavy with gold and precious stones; small turbans wound round with gold chains; and arms, neck, and breast glittering with jewels.

Charming, however, as was the first sight of these beautiful women in their gorgeous attire, the lifeless stillness of their aspect made them after a time very stupid. No ray of thought or emotion beamed upon those fair faces; all the spirit and fragrance of life was wanting, for there was no kind of mental culture. A native girl is reckoned quite sufficiently educated if she can just read a few religious books in her mother tongue. She never sees any other. On this grand occasion they did not even gossip, but sat perfectly motionless; but at a visit I paid to the Pacha's harem some days afterwards there was giggling and chattering enough, —indeed almost more than I could bear.

My visit had been expected, and the women (fifteen in number) were as splendidly dressed as before, and much in the same manner, with the difference that their caftans were made of transparent stuff, and their turbans were adorned with ostrich feathers. The summer-harem, in which I was received, is a pretty, low building, in the most modern European taste, standing in a flower garden, surrounded by an orchard. When I had been there about an hour, a table was spread, and chairs placed all round it. There were excellent dishes of meat, pilaus, pastry, and fruit; and the first lady, having invited me to take a place, and seated herself, did not wait for the rest, but instantly plunged her hands into the dishes, and selected her favourite morsels. I had to use my fingers too, for no other instrument was offered to me, except towards the end of the meal, when they gave me a gold spoon. When we had done, the rest of the women seated themselves, as well as some of the chief attendants ; and afterwards came the turn of the slaves, amongst whom were some very ugly negresses. In conclusion, strong coffee, in small cups, on stands of gold enriched with jewels, and *nargilehs*, were handed round.

There was no other distinction between the women and the attendants and slaves than in their dress; their behaviour was precisely the same ; and they mingled in the conversation, seated themselves on the divans, smoked, and drank coffee all together. In general the treatment of slaves here is far better than it usually is among Europeans. But if it was pleasing to see this, it was on the other hand very painful to notice the tone of the conversation that goes on in these harems and in the baths. Nothing can exceed the demureness of the women in public, but when they come together in these places they indemnify themselves thoroughly for the restraint. While they were busy with their pipes and coffee, I took the opportunity to take a glance into the neighbouring apartments, and in a few minutes I saw enough to fill me at once with disgust and compassion for these poor creatures, whom idleness and ignorance have degraded almost below the level of humanity. A visit to the women's baths left a no less melancholy impression. There were children of both sexes ;—girls, women, and elderly matrons. The poor children! how should they in after life understand what is meant by modesty and purity, when they are accustomed from their infancy to witness such scenes, and listen to such conversation.

Among other lions of Bagdad is the monument of Zobeide, the favourite wife of Haroun al Raschid, but it has none of the beautiful minarets of the Mahometan mausoleums, being merely a moderate-sized tower, rising from a small octangular building, and much resembling those of the Hindoos. It is of brick, and contains three chambers, where other members of the family repose, and the whole has once been covered with coloured tiles and handsome arabesques. All monuments of this kind are regarded as sacred by the Mahometans, and they often come here to perform their devotions.

On my return from this place I made a small circuit to see the ruins of that part of the city that was desolated by the last plague ; and a Hungarian gentleman, Mr. Swoboda, gave me a terrible picture of the condition of the city during that time. He and his family had shut themselves completely up, with one servant, and a store of provisions, and took in nothing but fresh water. The doors and windows were pasted up, and no one was allowed to show himself on the terrace, or in the open air ; and to these precautions he attributed their exemption from the scourge, whilst whole families in the neighbourhood were carried off. As soon as the plague abated, the city was exposed to another visitation from the Arabs of the Desert, who plundered the empty houses, and overpowered, without difficulty, the few feeble inhabitants left in many others ; Mr. Swoboda agreed to pay a *tribute*, and so escaped further molestation. I was glad to make my escape from these mournful recollections, and this dismal quarter of the town, to the pleasant gardens of Bagdad, though they do not exactly answer to our idea of a garden, for they have neither flower beds, nor walks, nor lawns, nor grass at all, but many canals, and close thickets of fruit trees of all kinds, dates, peaches, apples, apricots, figs, mulberries, &c., surrounded by a brick wall.

I made from Bagdad two excursions, one to the ruins of Ctesiphon, the other to those of Babylon ; the first distant eighteen, the second sixty miles from Bagdad. On both occasions Mr. Rawlinson furnished me with good Arab horses, and a trustworthy servant ; and my kind and careful hostess, Mrs. Holland, wished to make for me a large store of provisions. But my rule in travelling is to do without all superfluities. Wherever human creatures are to be found, I carry with me no eatables ; what they can live on, I can, and if I do not like their food, it must be because I am not really hungry, and the remedy for that is to fast till I like any thing. I carried with me a leathern water bottle, but even this proved to be unnecessary, for we passed canals, and the Tigris itself, several times. The ride to Ctesiphon, if I did not mean to pass the night in the desert, had to be made between sunrise and sunset ; for in Bagdad, as in other Turkish cities, the gates are locked when the sun goes down, and the keys carried to the commandant, and they are never opened again till sunrise. When we had gone nine miles, we had to cross the river Dhyalab, in a large boat ; on the opposite side, in a sort of hole lined with brick, live some families, who maintain themselves by the ferry, and from them I was so fortunate as to procure some bread and buttermilk, which I found a most welcome refreshment. From this place I could already see the ruins of Ctesiphon, although they were distant still nine miles.

Of the once mighty city of Ctesiphon, the winter residence of the rulers of Persia, there remains now scarcely any thing but some fragments of the palace of the Shah Chosroes, a colossal arched gateway, a part of the façade, and some side walls ; but all these look so firm and solid, that they may stand there for many centuries yet.   The arch of the gate is, I believe, the highest in the world, as it measures ninety feet from the ground, though the wall is not more than sixteen feet high.   The façade is covered from top to bottom with small niches, arches and columns, and it has once been overlaid with a fine cement, in which the most beautiful arabesques were wrought.   Opposite to these ruins, on the western shore of the Tigris, lie some walls that are all that remains of Seleucia.*   On both shores there extend far around low hills, which are found at a small depth to contain ruins and brick rubbish.   Scattered about among these on the shore of the Tigris were some tents inhabited by Arabs of the Desert.   They looked by no means so wild as those I had before seen, and indeed I could have passed days and nights among them without any fear.   By the time I had paid my visit to these dirty acquaint- ances another and much more agreeable one was awaiting me. A Persian came towards me, and pointing to some handsome tents pitched at no great distance, addressed to me a short speech, which signified, as my interpreter informed me, that a Persian prince was residing in those tents, and politely requested through this, his ambassador, that I would pay him a visit.   I accepted the invitation with great pleasure, and met with a most courteous re- ception from his Highness *Il-Hany-Ala-Ealy-Mirza*, a handsome young man, who moreover, I was informed, could speak French ; but when we came to the trial, his Highness's stock did not extend further than " *Vous parlez Français ?*"   Fortunately, one of his people knew a little more of English, so that we could get on somehow.

I learned from the interpreter that the prince usually lived in Bagdad, but on account of the oppressive heat had come to reside

---

* The favourable position of Seleucia, where the Tigris and the Euphrates ap- proach each other so nearly, contributed to make this one of the greatest commer- cial cities of the ancient world.   It is said to have contained 600,000 inhabitants, of whom the most important part were Greeks, living under their own free constitution.   It was destroyed in the time of the Roman Emperor Verus.

for a short time in the open air. He was sitting on a low divan, and his suite reposed upon carpets around him; but, to my surprise, he had so much knowledge of our manners as to offer me a seat on the divan beside him. Our conversation soon became very lively, and his surprise on my telling him of my travels rose with every word. While we were talking, a *nargileh* of remarkable beauty, sky-blue enamel, richly ornamented with gold, turquoises, and other precious stones, was brought to me, and out of politeness I took a few puffs from it. Coffee and tea were also brought, and after that the prince invited me to dinner. A white cloth was spread upon the ground, and for the rest of the company large flat loaves, which were to serve for plates; but I was honoured with a plate, knife, and fork. The dinner consisted of several pilaus, a large roasted fish, and many dishes of meat, amongst which was a whole lamb with the head on, that had not, I thought, a very inviting appearance. Between the dishes stood cups with sherbet, and sour milk, and in each cup was a large spoon. An attendant cut up the lamb, and laid each person a portion upon his bread plate; they then tore off little bits, plunged them into the pilaus, kneaded them into a ball, and shoved them into their mouths. Some ate the fat meat without any pilau, and wiped off with their bread the grease that ran down their fingers after every bit. In drinking, the company made use indiscriminately of the spoons. At the end of the meal the prince, in spite of the Koran, ordered some wine to be brought, of which he poured me out a glass, and then drank two himself; one to my health, and the other to his own. When I told him I meant to visit Persia and Teheran, he offered to give me a letter to his mother, who belonged to the court and would introduce me there, and he immediately set about writing it, making use of his knee for a table. When he had done, he pressed his signet ring upon it and handed it to me, but cautioned me, laughingly, not to say anything to his mother, about his having drank wine.

When this business was settled, I asked the prince whether I might be permitted to visit his wife, as I was told he had one with him, and he complied with the request, and led me into a little building which had once been a mosque.

Here, in a cool vaulted chamber, I was received by a most beautiful young creature—incomparably handsomer than any I had seen yet. Her figure was of middle height, and most elegantly proportioned ; her features fine, of a true antique cast ; her complexion dazzlingly fair, with a delicate colour on the cheeks (though this was not pure nature), and her eyes were large and brilliant, with a slight expression of melancholy.   The poor young thing had no companions but an old servant and a young gazelle.   One ornament of her face, consisting of a broad blue stripe, which meeting over the nose, formed two arches to the temples, gave a very peculiar, and not very agreeable, character to the face : the hands and arms were also disfigured with tattooing—a custom not uncommon among the Mahomedan women of Bagdad.   The costume of this beauty was much the same as those of the Pacha's wives, only that, instead of a little turban, she had on her head a white muslin, which could be drawn over her face at pleasure.

As the interpreter could not enter this sanctuary with me, our conversation was of course not very animated ; indeed we could not speak at all, but were obliged to be satisfied with making signs, and looking at each other.   When I returned to the prince I expressed my admiration at the charms of his young wife, and asked what country had produced such a gem of loveliness.   He named the North of Persia ; but assured me that his other wives, of whom he had four in Bagdad, and four in Teheran, were much more beautiful than this one.

I was now about to take my leave ; but the prince begged me to remain a little longer, and ordered in two minstrels, one a singer, and the other a player on a sort of mandolin with five strings. They both kept good time, and seldom made false notes, and the singer made an amazing number of flourishes, though his voice was not pure or well cultivated.   The Persian songs and musical pieces have, however, great compass and variety ; and for a long time I had heard no such good musical performance.

I got into Bagdad again before sunset, and though I had had a ride of six and thirty miles, and had rambled about a great deal on foot, and the heat was tremendous, I was not immoderately fatigued ; and two days afterwards I set off for the ruins of Babylon.

The district in which these ruins lie is now called Irak-Arabi, the former Babylonia and Chaldea.   As we rode on, the palms and fruit tree gradually became scarcer and scarcer, the cultivated lands less and less, and the desert advanced more and more, spreading its deadly influence over all life and vegetation.

By the time we had gone twenty miles to Chan Assad the stunted herbage scarcely sufficed even for the abstinent camel. From Chan Assad to Hilla the way is one mournful and monstrous waste.

We came to the place where once stood the City of Borosipa, and where there is still one column of the palace of Nourhivan ; at least so it is said ; but I could nowhere find it, though the desert lay open before me, and a bright sunset gave me light enough. I had to content myself, therefore, with thinking of the great Alexander, on this the last scene of his exploits, where he was warned not again to enter Babylon. Instead of the column I saw the ruins of one large and several small canals ; the former connecting the Tigris with the Euphrates, and altogether serving for the irrigation of the country, but of course all now in a state of decay.

May 31*st.*—On the remote horizon I saw to-day what I took for groups of trees, but, like Macbeth's wood, it advanced to meet me, and gradually as it came closer developed itself into long legs, humps—in short a vast herd of camels, as much, certainly, as seven or eight thousand, many of them carrying burdens of women or children, but most going empty, so that this was probably the migration of a wandering tribe in search of new pastures. Among them I saw a few of those snow-white camels which are so highly prized, almost worshipped, by the Arabs. I saw also this day a new kind of bird, much like a green parrot, only that the beak was slenderer and less crooked, and which nestles in holes in the earth. The place where they were was one of the most dreary in the whole desert, and far and wide not a single blade of grass was to be seen.

The heat had now risen to 45 (Reaumur), and was still more insupportable from a glowing hot wind that accompanied it, and drove clouds of sand in your face. This day also we passed many canals, now half filled up.

The chans met with on this road are the finest and most secure that I have anywhere seen ; they are like little fortresses. A lofty gateway leads into a great court-yard, surrounded by spacious halls, with brick walls of considerable thickness. In these halls you find long ranges of alcoves, every one of which is large enough to form a sleeping place for three or four persons. Before the alcoves are places for the cattle, and in the court-yard there is a

terrace five feet high, on which travellers may sleep in the hot
nights, and rings for tethering the cattle, that they also may, if it
is desired, remain in the open air.   These chans are intended for
the great caravans, and are capable of accommodating five hundred
travellers at a time, with their cattle and baggage.   They are
sometimes maintained by the government, but more frequently by
rich people, who think by this means to gain a step in their ascent
to Heaven.   Every chan has ten or twelve soldiers for a guard;
the doors are locked at night ; and for all the security and accommodation afforded him the traveller has nothing whatever to
pay.   Near the chan, too, some Arabian families have usually
taken up their abode, who furnish the travellers with camel's milk,
bread, coffee, and often camel's or goat's flesh.   The camel's milk I
found rather heavy, but the meat good, and a good deal like beef.
Travellers provided with a firman from a Pacha are allowed to
take with them one or two of the mounted soldiers from one chan
to another, and as I enjoyed this advantage I made use of the
privilege when we were travelling at night.

   It was afternoon when we arrived at a spot whence we could
see the fine date groves beyond which lie the ruins of Babylon,
part of the site of which is occupied by the town of Hilla.   Four
miles from it we turned to the right from the road, and soon found
ourselves between enormous masses, like hills of bricks and rubbish.
The largest of these is 140 feet high, and above 2000 feet in
circumference.   The date usually assigned to the building of the
city is about 2,000 years before the birth of Christ, and 2,000,000
men and all the architects and artists of the vast Assyrian empire
were called to take part in the work.   The town wall was 150
high and 20 feet broad, defended by 230 towers, and closed by 100
gates.   It was divided by the Euphrates into two parts, and on
either bank stood a magnificent palace connected by a bridge.
According to tradition, there was even a tunnel beneath the bed of
the river, and three colossal figures of wrought gold adorned the
tower of the Temple of Belus.   Six hundred and thirty years before
Christ, Babylon was still flourishing in splendour.   The Temple
of Belus was destroyed by Xerxes, and Alexander wished to
restore it ; but as it took 10,000 men two months,—some say two
years,—merely to clear away the rubbish, he got tired of the work.
Of the two palaces, one is conjectured to have been a castle, and
the other the residence of the monarch; but they are fallen so

completely to ruins, that there is nothing to afford the antiquarian any clue. An English mile from them you come upon another vast mound of rubbish, El Kasr, and here the Temple of Baal is supposed to have stood. There are still some massive fragments of walls, and columns, and a lion of dark-coloured granite, so large that I at first took it for an elephant. It is much mutilated, and to judge from what remains not the work of a very skilful artist. The bricks in all these ruins are of a reddish yellow colour, a foot long, and the same in breadth, and three and a half inches thick. In the ruins of El Kasr stands a single withered tree of the fir kind, which is quite unknown in these regions, which the Arabs regard as sacred, and of which many wonders are told, — how it utters melancholy sounds when the wind moans through the branches, and so forth. Of course it is considered to date from the days of ancient Babylon ; but that a crippled looking tree, scarcely eighteen feet high and nine inches thick, should last 3,000 years, does seem, with all possible inclination to believe, somewhat too marvellous. The environs of Babylon, once so fertile that they have been called the Paradise of Chaldea, are now entirely barren and desolate, and the only way of crossing the river is by a wretched bridge made of boats, planks, and trunks of trees, which sway up and down at every step ; it is scarcely broad enough for two horsemen to go abreast, and there is no kind of handrail to keep you from the water. Along the banks of the river there is still some trace of rich vegetation, and a few mosques and handsome buildings belonging to Hilla serve a little to re-animate the landscape. In this town I was received into the house of a rich Arab, who, as it was just sunset, invited me, not to a room but to a place on the magnificent terrace. For supper he sent me roast lamb, vegetables, some delicious pilau, and for drink, water and sour milk. This terrace had no walls round it, to my great satisfaction, as it enabled me to get some insight into the doings of my neighbours. In the courts I saw the women occupied in baking bread of the same kind that I had seen in Baudr-Abbas, and in the meantime the men and the children spread straw mats on the terraces, and brought up pilau vegetables and other dishes. When the bread was ready the meat was served up. I saw the women, too, sit down, and I was really in hopes that the Arabs had made such progress in civilisation as to allow my sex a place at table ; but, alas ! the poor women did not touch the dishes, but only took up straw fans to wave off the flies from the heads of their lords and masters. I presume they got a meal afterwards inside the house, but neither on the terrace nor in the court-yard did I see them eat anything. When the time came for going to rest, men and women enveloped themselves entirely, from head to foot, in coverings, and lay down on the terrace, but neither took off a single article of dress.

Six English miles from Hilla, in what was once called the plain of Shinar, lie the ruins of Birs-Nimrod, and to visit these I engaged the services of two Arabs for an escort and two fresh horses. There is a mound near the Euphrates of 265 feet high, and a part of a wall of between twenty and thirty. Most of the bricks are covered with inscriptions, and near these walls lie some great black blocks, which might be taken for lava, but that on a nearer inspection there are traces of masonry to be seen on them, and it is therefore to be presumed that their present condition is the effect of lightning.

From the summit of these hills you get an immense prospect over the desert, the town of Hilla and its beautiful palm groves, and over countless mounds of brick and earth. Not far from where I stood was a Mahomedan house of prayer, said to be on the spot where Shadrach and his companions were flung into the fiery furnace for refusing to worship the idols.

Towards evening the family of my obliging host paid me a visit, accompanied by several other women and children, their natural good sense and delicacy having prevented them from disturbing me on the day of my arrival, when they knew me to be wearied by my long ride. I cannot say but that I would willingly have excused the visit now, for Arabs, rich or poor, have but little idea of cleanliness, and the very filthy little children insisted upon sitting on my lap or in my arms, and I knew no way to decline that pleasure. Many of them had Aleppo boils, and others sore eyes and cutaneous diseases, so that I was very glad when the women and children left me and were replaced by my host, who was at least clean, and had more knowledge of the world.

The next day I left Hilla at sunrise, and rode without stopping sixteen miles to Scandaria, where I rested for some hours, and then went on another sixteen to Bir-Yanus. At one o'clock in the morning I set off again, escorted by a single soldier. We had gone about four or five miles when we thought we perceived, at no great distance some very suspicious sounds, and my servant signified to me that I should remain quite still, that our presence might not be observed, and the soldier then alighted from his horse, and crept rather than walked through the sand to reconnoitre. My weariness was so great, that, though alone in the dark night, in the dreary desert, I could not help falling asleep on my horse, and only waked up when the soldier, with a joyful shout, came back to say there were no robbers, but a sheik, who, with his suite, was going to Bagdad. We immediately gave our horses the spur, and joined the procession. The chief saluted me by pressing his hand on his brow and his breast; and moreover, as a sign of good intentions, presented arms to me, his weapon being a club, with an iron knob at the end, furnished with many points, exactly like our well-known "morning star," a weapon that sheiks only are allowed to carry.

Until sunrise I remained in his company, and I then urged on my horse, and at eight o'clock was once more seated in my room at Bagdad, after having ridden 132 miles in three days and a half, besides rambling about a great deal on foot.

I had now seen every thing there was to be seen in Bagdad, and was beginning my preparations for continuing my journey to Ispahan, when I received a letter from Prince *Il Hony Ala Euly Mirza*, to say that he had had bad news from his country. The province of Ispahan was in a state of insurrection, the governor had been murdered, and my going to Persia at present was out of the question. I therefore took the resolution to go first to Mossul, and there await till circumstances should determine my further course.

MOSSUL AND NINEVEH.

Caravan Journey through the Desert.—Arrival at Mossul.—Things to be seen.—Excursion to the Ruins of Nineveh and the Village of Nebryanis. —Second Excursion to Nineveh.—Tel-Nimrod.—Arabian Horses.—Departure from Mossul.

In order to travel safely and without too great cost from Bagdad to Mossul, it is necessary to join a caravan, and I begged Mr. Swoboda to recommend me to a trustworthy leader. He endeavoured to dissuade me from trusting myself entirely to the

Arabs, and thought I ought at least to take· with me a servant of my own. But this would have occasioned too heavy expenses for my very slender means, and besides I knew the people tolerably well, and believed that I could trust them.

A caravan was to set off on the 14th of June, but a caravan leader is in this respect like the captain of a ship, and one must always give him a few days grace ; so the 14th turned out to be really the 17th. The distance from Bagdad to Mossul is about three hundred English miles, which usually takes twelve or fourteen days. The mode of travelling is on horseback or on mules, and, in the hottest season, during the night. I hired for myself and my trifling luggage a mule, for which I was to pay the low price of seven and a half florins (12s. 6d.), and to have no further expense or trouble about his keep, and we were all to assemble in the caravansera before the city gate at five o'clock in the afternoon. Mr. Swoboda accompanied me thither, recommended me to the particular care of the leader, and promised him a good bachsheesh on his return if he should have been properly attentive ; and then without any other protection I commenced my toilsome and dangerous journey through steppe and desert.

I was now travelling like the poorest Arab, and would have to make up my mind, as he would, to endure the glowing heat of the sun, to live on bread and water, or a handful of dates or cucumbers, and to content myself with the scorched ground for a bed. I had written out a short list of Arabic words for articles of the first necessity ; but the language of signs was quite familiar to me, and by these means and that of the words together I got on wonderfully. I got indeed so much into the habit of making signs, that even in places where I knew the language perfectly well I found myself, if I did not take care, having reeourse to my hands to speak for me.

Whilst Mr. Swoboda was taking leave of me, some bread and a few other needful provisions had been placed in two bags, and hung across the back of my mule. My cloak and a pillow formed a soft convenient seat, when I was once upon it, though the climbing up was rather difficult, as I had no stirrups. Our caravan was small at present, counting only six and twenty animals, most of them carrying burdens, and twelve Arabs who walked on foot.

At six o'clock we were in motion, and some miles beyond the town we were joined by other travellers, traders with beasts of burden, so that our procession soon amounted to sixty, but the number varied every evening, some going and others coming. Sometimes we looked like a regular rabble; and I was more afraid of our own company than the robbers; indeed I thought they might happen to be identical, for thieves often join caravans in order to find opportunities for pursuing their profession. In any case I could reckon nothing on the protection of such a caravan consisting of traders, pilgrims, and so forth, most of whom had never drawn a sword or fired a pistol in their lives. A few dozens of well-armed robbers could with ease have put to flight hundreds of them.

We rode on the first night for ten hours till we reached Yeugitsché. The country was flat and barren; there were neither men nor houses nor cultivated lands. Some miles after we passed Bagdad indeed all culture seemed to be suddenly cut off; and it was not till we reached Yeugitsché that we again saw stubble fields and palms, which showed that the industry of man was still able to wring something from nature.

Caravan travelling is very wearisome. You go always at a walk, and nine, even twelve hours, at a stretch. You lose your rest at night, and in the daytime the heat, the flies, and the mosquitoes make it almost impossible to recover any of your lost sleep.

The chan at Yeugitsché by no means equalled in beauty and cleanliness those on the road to Babylon, but it was surrounded by a little village into which hunger drove me in search of food. I went from hut to hut, and at last was lucky enough to make the conquest of three eggs and some milk, with which I proudly returned to my chan, after having filled my water-bottle at the Tigris. The eggs I baked in hot ashes, and ate immediately; the milk I put by for the evening; and I certainly felt more satisfaction in my hardly-earned meal than many do at the best furnished tables.

On my foraging expedition through the village I observed that it had formerly been a place of more importance, as there were many fallen houses and huts; but the plague had carried off all but a few families. I saw here a new mode of making butter, by merely shaking the cream in a leathern bottle; but the butter so made was as white as snow, so that if I had not seen it made I should have taken it for lard.

At ten o'clock at night our caravan got under weigh again, and we rode without stopping for eleven hours. The country through which we passed appeared to be less desolate than that nearer to Bagdad, and the barking of dogs and the groups of palm trees intimated the existence of villages, though we could not see them. At sunrise we rejoiced in the sight of a low range of hills that relieved the continued monotony of the plains.

June 19*th.*—Yesterday I was finding fault with the chan of Yeugitsche, but to day I should have been thankful for a much worse, that would have afforded me some protection from the scorching beams of the sun, which streamed down upon me with intolerable fierceness. But we halted on a stubble field far from any human dwelling. My caravan leader threw a cloth over a couple of sticks, and endeavoured so to procure me a little shade, but the place was so small, and this imitation of a tent so slight, that I had to remain constantly in a sitting posture, and quite still, lest by the slightest movement I might bring it down. How I envied the missionaries and naturalists who make their difficult journeys with pack-horses, tents, provisions, and servants. For refreshment I had only lukewarm water, bread so hard that I could not possibly eat it without soaking, and a cucumber without salt or vinegar. But my courage and patience did not desert me, and I never for a single moment repented having exposed myself to these hardships.

At Deli-Abbas, where we stopped at eight o'clock in the morning, we found a chan, but in such a ruinous state that we had to encamp outside it, for fear of the snakes and scorpions which are apt to harbour in such places. Near the chan lay some dozens of dirty Arab tents, and the wish to obtain some other food than bread and cucumber drove me to overcome my disgust, and to creep into several of them. The inhabitants offered me butter-milk and bread, and they also possessed fowls, one of which I would have gladly purchased, but I could not make up my mind to kill it myself, so I was obliged to put up with the simpler fare. In this district there were wild flowers growing that reminded me of my dear country. At home I should have scarcely thought them worthy of a glance, but here I re-joiced at the sight of them; indeed I am not ashamed to confess that I bent over them as friends, and found my eyes dim with tears.

This day we set off again at five o'clock in the evening, as we had the most dangerous part of the journey between this and the next station, and we meant to try and reach it before a very late hour. The vast flat sandy desert now changed a little its character; hard flints rattled under the hoofs of the horses, and rocks, and rocky hills alternated with mounds of earth. Had this tract continued longer I should have taken it for the dried up bed of a river; as it was, it looked like a piece of ground left bare by the retiring of the sea. In many places there were crystals of salt that glittered in the sun.

Our leader urged on the beasts, for this spot is regarded as dangerous, because the rocks and hills afford places of concealment for robbers, and the poor animals had to hurry on over stock and stone at a much sharper pace than they are accustomed to; so that before it was quite dark we had passed that tract, and could pursue our journey more at leisure. Towards one in the morning we came in sight of the small town of Karatappa, and took up our quarters on a stubble field about a mile or two from it. Here the weary desert plains were at an end, and henceforth we were to travel through a cultivated country intersected by hills. The next day we got to Kuferi.

All these Turkish towns are much alike, and there is little to be said about them. The streets are dirty, the houses built of mud or unburnt brick, the shops wretched booths, the people disgustingly dirty, and the women increase their natural ugliness by dying their hair and nails red-brown with henna, and tattooing their hands and arms. At five and twenty they look quite old.

On the 25th of June we reached a village which was the home of our leader, and his house lay, with several others, in a large dirty court-yard, surrounded by a wall that had but a single entrance. This court resembled a regular camp, for all the inhabitants, as well as their horses and asses, were lying sleeping about it. Our animals recognised their own places, and trotted so fast by the sleepers that I was quite in fear for them. However, these creatures are very careful, and the men knew it, and remained quietly where they were.

My Arab had been three weeks absent, and had returned now for a very short time, and except one little old woman no one of his family got up to greet him.   Even the said old lady, whom I took for his mother, did not speak to him a word of welcome or attempt to help him, but merely trotted along by his side, so that I thought she might almost as well have lain sleeping with the rest.

The Arab's house consisted of one large lofty apartment, divided into three portions by two middle walls that did not reach quite to the front.   Each of these divisions was thirty feet long by about nine feet broad, and served as the dwelling of a family. The light came through the common entrance, and two holes at the top of the front wall.   In one of these compartments a place was assigned to me where I could remain during the day; and my first study was directed to ascertaining the relations of the family with whom I was to live.   I wanted to ascertain the degree of kindred, and at first this was very difficult, for no one showed any affection for any but the little children, who seemed to be regarded as common property.   At length I made out that in the whole house there were three families related to each other; the grandfather, a married son, and a married daughter.   The grandfather was a stout vigorous old fellow, the father of my caravan leader.   I had discovered this on the way, for he had been in our party.   He was horribly quarrelsome; disputed about every trifle, and constantly contradicted his son, who took it very quietly, and did what his father liked.   The animals of the caravan belonged to them both, and were also attended to by a grandson of fifteen and some servants; but when we had once got home the old man gave himself no further concern about them, but enjoyed his rest, and merely gave his orders.   It was easy to see that he was the patriarch of the family.

On the first impression the character of the Arab appears cold and reserved.   I never saw either husband or wife, father or daughter, exchange a friendly word; they spoke to each other only when it was absolutely required.   For the children there was much more feeling shown; they might romp and riot as much as they would, not a word was ever said to them, nor anything they did taken amiss.   As soon as the child is grown up, however, it comes to his turn to bear with the weaknesses of his parents, which he generally does, treating them with much patience and respect.

To my great surprise I heard the children call their mother *mama* or *nana*, and their father *baba*.

The women lay the whole day on their lazy sides, doing nothing whatever, and only towards evening they made up their minds to get up and make some bread. Their costume was certainly very ill adapted to work of any kind. The sleeves of their chemises were so wide that they hung down half an ell from their arms; and directly they went to do anything they had to wind them round their arms, or tie them in a knot behind their backs. Of course they continually got loose, and were a constant hindrance, to the work. As they were not very punctilious about cleanliness, the good ladies used to make these sleeves serve in the capacity of pocket handkerchiefs, as well as to wipe the spoons and other utensils. The covering of their heads consisted of no less than two, three, or sometimes four large handkerchiefs, wound one round the other.

I had, alas, two days to pass in this family circle. The first was almost intolerable, for all the women in the neighbourhood came to stare at me. They began by examining my clothes ; then they wanted to take my turban from my head, and after that they became so outrageously troublesome that I was obliged to deliver myself by a *coup de main*.

I suddenly took one of them by the shoulders, and turned her out of doors, and that so quickly that she scarcely knew what had happened. To the other I signified that I would certainly do the like if she did not behave better. Probably they supposed me much stronger than I really was, and they therefore drew off their forces ; and I then described a circle round my place, and forbade any one of them to step over it, and in this they thought proper to obey.

The worst of my tormentors was the wife of my leader. She besieged me the whole day, kept coming close up to me, and worrying me to give her things. I gave her a few trifles, but I had little of any thing with me, and she would certainly not have left off till she had got all. Fortunately her husband came home, and I complained to him of her behaviour, and affected to be about to leave his house, and seek elsewhere for a shelter, which the Arab would regard as the greatest disgrace. He immediately set to work, and gave his wife a thorough good scolding, and then I got a little peace. I always insisted on having my own way, for energy and fearlessness impose on all people,—Arabs, Persians, Bedouins,—or whatever else they may be called.

Towards evening, to my great joy, I saw a large pot set on the fire with a quantity of mutton. For eight days I had eaten nothing but bread, cucumbers, and a few dates, and I really longed for some warm and nourishing food. But how did my appetite decline when I observed the cooking operations. The old mother threw in a few handsful of red grain, along with an immense quantity of onions, into a potfull of water. After half an hour she stirred them round with her dirty hands, and mixed and squeezed them together, then took out a portion, chewed it into small masses, and *spat it back again* into the pot. Then she took a dirty rag, strained this delicate sauce through it, and poured it over the meat in the larger vessel. I had firmly resolved not to touch this dish, but when it was ready my desire of food was so great, and the smell was so savoury, that I reflected that I had most likely already eaten what was not a whit cleaner ; in short, I became unfaithful to my resolution. " I did eat, and was filled," and felt greatly strengthened by these untempting viands. I had gone through much fatigue in the journey from Bagdad, and really required support.

On the morrow I supposed that before setting off again we should have had a similar meal, but the Arab is too frugal a housekeeper to have such a feast twice running, and I was obliged to put up with bread and cucumbers, without salt, oil, or vinegar.

We left the village at nine o'clock at night, and by sunrise we had a magnificent prospect of a majestic chain of mountains, which forms a wall of separation between Kurdistan and Mesopotamia.

In the valley that lay between these were the loveliest wild flowers,—among others, blue bells, amaranths, and a remarkable kind of thistle that produces bunches of delicate blue flowers the size of a man's fist, and which covers large tracts. The country people cut it and use it for fuel, as wood is here very scarce.

We saw here also some troops of gazelles that came merrily past the caravan.

On the 28th of June we reached the small town of Erbil, once Arbela, where Alexander met the army of Darius. It is a fortified town, and lies on a single hill in the middle of a valley. We encamped in the suburbs, and, as I found to my great vexation that we should remain till the next evening, I had to seek some place where I could obtain shelter from the sun, and I found a hut where there were already several people, two asses, and a large number of cocks and hens. The proprietress, a particularly unpleasant looking old Arab woman, allowed me for a small consideration to lie down in a corner where, at least, the burning rays could not reach me, but beyond this I had not the smallest accommodation; yet this hut appeared to be considered a desirable place of residence, for from early morning till late in the evening there was always a crowd of company present. Some came to gossip only, others brought their flour to knead into bread in order to enjoy the gossip at the same time. In the background children were bathed and cleansed from vermin, and in the midst of all this the asses brayed, and fowls flew upon and dirtied everything. To the honour of the people, however, I must state that though there were among them men of the poorest classes constantly going in and out, no one of them offered me the slightest insult; even the women left me at peace.

In the evening, before our departure, a meal of mutton was boiled, in a kettle that had previously been filled with dirty linen: this was emptied out, and without the ceremony of washing, the mutton put in, and then the cookery went on in exactly the same style as on the former occasion.

On the following day we had to cross a large river, and this was effected on a raft, probably of a very ancient kind; inflated skins were fastened together by means of some poles, and on these were laid boards, reeds, and canes. There were eight and twenty skins, and the raft was seven feet broad, and the same length, and carried half a dozen men and three horse burdens at a time; but, as our caravan consisted at this time of two and thirty animals, we took nearly half a day to get across. The horses were tied four or five together, and led by a man seated astride on a skin; the feebler ones, as well as the asses, had skins tied on their backs.

Most striking is in this part of Mesopotamia the entire want of trees; for the last five days I had not seen one, and I believe there must be many people who have never seen one in their lives. There were tracts of twenty or thirty miles where there was not so much as a shrub, though there is no want of water, for no day passed in which we did not cross one or two rivers, large or small.

The town of Mossul came into view twenty miles before we reached it; it lies on a low hill in a very large valley on the western shore of the Tigris, which is here considerably narrower than at Bagdad.

We reached Mossul at seven o'clock in the morning, and I was in perfect health, though in the fortnight past I had only twice had a warm meal, had had no opportunity of changing my clothes, and had been almost constantly exposed to tremendous heat.

I alighted first at the caravansery, and then got some one to take me to the English vice-consul, Mr. Rassam, to whom my coming had already been announced in a letter from Mr. Rawlinson, and who had had a room made ready for me.

My first walk was through the town, but there is little to be said concerning it ; it is surrounded with fortifications, and has about 2,500 inhabitants, but amongst them scarcely a dozen Europeans ; there are many coffee booths, and extensive, though not handsome bazaars. The entrances to the houses are low and narrow, and furnished with strong doors, as in former times the town was frequently exposed to hostile attacks ; but, when you get inside, you find beautiful court yards, lofty airy rooms, with large windows and doors, and the walls of the ground floors mostly of marble, of which there is a rich quarry directly before the town. Here also it is the custom to pass the hot hours of the day in the subterranean chamber or sardab ; and in the month of July, even there, the temperature will rise to ninety-nine degrees, when the burning simoom comes sweeping across the Desert. During my stay several people died suddenly, it was said of the heat, and even the birds suffered much, and kept their beaks wide open and their wings stretched out from their bodies. The eyes are often greatly affected here, but the Aleppo boil is less frequent than in Bagdad.

Amongst my sufferings from the heat at Mossul, however, I cannot at all events count that of a decrease of appetite ; probably it might be in consequence of the severe regimen on which I had lately been kept ; but I really think I could have eaten at every hour of the day.

During my stay at Mossul, a great body of Turkish troops passed through the country. The Pacha rode out to meet them, and then marched into the city at the head of the infantry. These troops were infinitely better dressed than those I had seen in Constantinople in 1842 ; they wore the fez,—had white trowsers and blue spencers with red facings, and looked very well. The cavalry remained outside the town, and pitched their tents along the Tigris.

As soon as I had in some measure recovered from the fatigues of my journey, I begged my kind host to furnish me with a servant to accompany me to the ruins of Nineveh,—but instead of a servant, a Mr. Ross and the sister of Mrs. Rassom were good enough to bear me company. We viewed on the first morning, the ruins that lie nearest, on the opposite side of the Tigris at the village of Neby-yunis,—and the next day the more distant, eighteen miles down the river, at a place called Tel-Nimrod.

According to Strabo, Nineveh was still larger than Babylon,—and the greatest city in the world ; the circumference of its walls was three days' journey, and the wall was defended by fifteen hundred towers. Now all is covered with earth, and only occasionally when the peasant's plough makes a furrow in the field does a fragment of brickwork or marble come to sight. Whole ranges of hills that extend across the boundless plain on the left bank of the Tigris, and lose themselves in the distance, cover, as is now known with certainty, the ruins of the city. In the year 1846, the celebrated Mr. Layard began here the excavations which have been crowned with such distinguished success. Passages were dug in the hills, and soon the excavators came to large and stately apartments whose walls were of marble covered from top to bottom with reliefs. There were kings with their crowns and sceptres, gods with vast pinions, warriors with their arms and shields ;—there were representations of hunts, of battles, of the storming of fortresses, of triumphal processions,—but, unfortunately, proportion, perspective, and correct drawing are wanting. The hills are scarcely three times higher than the men, the fields reach to the clouds, the trees are no bigger than the lotus-flowers, and the heads of men and animals are all after the same models, and all in profile. On many walls is that club-shaped sign or letter which distinguishes what is called the cuneiform character, and which is only found on Persian and Babylonian monuments.

Among all the chambers that were brought to light, only one had walls, not of marble, but of fine painted cement. But these walls, notwithstanding the utmost care, could not be preserved. As soon as the air reached them, the cement cracked, and fell off. The marble also had in many places been changed into lime by the terrific conflagration which laid the whole city in ashes. Many marble slabs with reliefs and cuneiform inscriptions have, however, been taken from the walls, and sent to England. When I was in Bassora, a whole cargo of these antiquities, including a sphynx, lay ready to be sent off.

On our return, we visited the little village of Neby-yunis, which lies near the ruins on a slight elevation, and which is celebrated on account of a mosque where, according to tradition, the remains of the prophet Jonas lie buried, which every year are visited by thousands of devout pilgrims. On this excursion, we passed many fields where the people were separating the corn from the straw in a quite peculiar manner, with a machine consisting of two wooden tubs, between which was a roller with ten or twelve broad, long, blunt knives, or choppers. The whole was drawn by two horses or oxen over the bundles of corn, and when it had all been chopped up it was flung up into the air with shovels, in order to separate the corn from the chaff.

As we came home we saw near the walls of Mossul two sulphur springs, betrayed from a considerable distance by their smell. They rise in natural basins, and though they have been surrounded by high walls, every one is at liberty to bathe in them,—the women at certain hours, the men at others,—without putting his hand in his pocket. People here are not so envious and niggardly with the free gifts of nature as they are in Europe.

Tel-Nimrod lies, as I have said, eighteen miles down the Tigris; here the earth mounds lie thickest, and here the principal excavations are being made. To visit them we seated ourselves one evening on a raft, and glided in the moonlight along the desolate shores. After a voyage of about seven hours, we landed at one o'clock in the morning at the miserable village that bears the proud name of Nimrod; we awakened some of the inhabitants, who were all lying asleep outside their huts, got fire made, and some coffee; and then lay down on some carpets we had brought with us, to wait for the morning light.

At dawn we mounted horses, which are always to be had, and rode a short distance to the excavations. We saw a number of hills opened, but there were not, as at Herculaneum, whole houses, streets, and squares, but only single chambers, at the utmost three or four connected together; and even then the outer walls were not free from earth. The articles brought to light perfectly resemble those discovered at Mossul, but they are in greater number. I saw also here figures of gods, as animals with human heads, and of a colossal size. There were four of these, but two of them considerably damaged; the others were not in the best preservation, but sufficiently so to show that the art of sculpture had not reached any high degree of perfection when they were made. A small sphynx undamaged, and an obelisk of inconsiderable height, had just been sent off to England; but when Mr. Layard returned to his country the excavations had to be again closed up, as the wandering Arabs had begun to injure the antiquities. Mr. Rawlinson, of Bagdad, has occupied himself so much with the cuneiform character that he can now read it well, and to his industry we are indebted for many of the translations.

Our return to Mossul was made on horseback in five hours and a half. The horses had only a quarter of an hour's rest, and nothing but water to refresh them ; and they would have the whole distance back again to do in the greatest heat of the day. It is wonderful what these Arab horses can endure, for Mr. Ross informed me that the post stations sometimes lie seventy-two miles apart. The finest horses are found about Bagdad and Mossul, and they fetch a high price. Some, which had just been bought for the Queen of Spain, and which Mr. Rassam had in his stable, had cost a hundred and fifty pounds each. Their long narrow heads, fiery eyes, and slender beautifully formed legs, would have thrown a connoisseur into raptures.

After remaining some time at Mossul I found I could, without great risk to my life, venture to undertake the journey to Persia, although I was compelled to take a circuitous route. A caravan was going to Tebris, and Mr. Rassam undertook to arrange my route as far as Ravandus, and furnish me with some letters to natives of that place. I was warned that I should not, on the entire way, meet with a single European, and as I could not feel very confident that my undertaking would have a happy issue, I first sent off my papers to Europe, in order that if I should be robbed or killed my journal at least might reach the hands of my sons.

PERSIA.

Caravan Journey to Ravandus.—A Kurd Family.—Continuation of the Journey.—Sauh-Bulok.—A Happy Family.—Oromia.—The American Missionaries.—Kutschié.—Three chivalrous Robbers.—The Persian Chan and the English Bongolo.—Arrival at Tabreez.

IN the evening of the 8th of July, the caravan leader came to fetch me, but his appearance was so little prepossessing that had

I not been assured he was a man well known in the place I should scarcely have ventured to go a mile with him. His dress was a mere collection of rags, and his physiognomy appeared to me precisely that which would suit a robber. He told me that the people and the goods had already been sent forward and had encamped at Neby-yunis, about a mile off. The journey was to commence before sunrise. I found at the place mentioned, the beasts of burden, and three other men,—Kurds, whose countenances were no more agreeable than that of the leader, Ali, and I saw that I could not promise myself much good from my company.

I took up my quarters for the night in the dirty court-yard of the Chan, but I could sleep very little for I could not help feeling rather anxious. In the morning to my surprise there were no preparations for departure. I asked Ali the reason of this, and was told it was because the travellers were not all assembled, and as soon as they came we should move. I could not, short as was the distance to Mossul, venture to leave the miserable shelter lest they should arrive in my absence, but the whole day passed in waiting, and the people did not arrive till towards evening. There were five of them, one of whom, apparently a man of some opulence, as he had two servants with him, was returning from a pilgrimage. At ten o'clock at night we started, and after a march of four hours crossed some ranges of hills, which form the boundary between Mesopotamia and Kurdistan. In the morning we reached Secani, but Ali did not halt at the village, which lay on the fine river Kasir, but on a hill where there were a few dilapidated huts. I hastened into one of the best, and found a place where at least the sun's rays did not pierce through the sieve-like roof; but the pilgrim who came in after me did not seem inclined to leave me in peaceable possession. I threw my cloak down, seated myself upon it, and would not move from the place, knowing well that a Mussulman would not use any violence towards a woman, even though a Christian, and so it proved. He left me my place, though he went away grumbling : but the behaviour of one of the traders was still better. When he saw that I had nothing to eat but dry bread, while he had cucumbers and sweet melons, he gave me one of each, and positively refused to take any money for them. The pilgrim also, I noticed, took no better food, though he needed only to have sent one of his servants to the village to buy eggs and poultry. The moderation of these people is really astonishing.

At six o'clock in the evening we were again in motion, and during the first three hours we were constantly ascending. The ground was barren, and covered with masses of stone resembling old lava ; but towards eleven we entered a fine valley, into which the full moon threw a soft and brilliant light. We wished to halt here instead of travelling through the night, as our caravan was small, and Kurdistan has a very bad reputation ; but as we were jogging on over a stubble field past some high heaps of corn, all at once, half a dozen stout fellows armed with strong cudgels sprung out, and seizing our horses bridles, poured out upon us, with uplifted sticks, what seemed a volley of bad language. Seeing that we had fallen into the hands of a band of robbers, I rejoiced at having had the happy idea of sending away, before entering on this journey, my papers and various treasures that I had collected in Babylon and Nineveh ; my other effects would have been easily replaced. In the meantime one of the travellers had sprung from his horse, seized one of the assailants by the throat, and held a loaded pistol to his head, threatening to blow his brains out. This had an immediate effect ; the highwaymen desisted from their attack, and were very shortly engaged with the travellers in quite a friendly conversation ; nay, at last they even pointed us out a pleasant place to encamp in, for which service they received a trifling bachshish, collected from the whole caravan except myself, from whom, as a woman, they asked nothing. We passed the night in the spot indicated, though not without setting a watch, for we had not perfect confidence in the treaty of peace.

We passed through many villages on the following day which had a very wretched appearance ; the huts were only of cane and reeds, and looked as if a puff of wind would blow them down. The people wore almost entirely the oriental costume, but in a most dirty and ragged condition. The surrounding hills were barren, and trees were still great rarities ; at most there grew in the vallies some amaranths, wild artichokes, and thistles. The noble pilgrim thought proper, when we halted, to point out to me a place among the lowest of our company; but without giving him any answer I went and deposited myself under a fig tree. Ali, who was really a better fellow than he looked, brought me a pot of buttermilk ; and so this day, on the whole, I may be considered to have fared well.

Several women came out of the village and begged of me, but I gave them nothing, for I knew, by experience, that if you give to one you may to all. I had once only given a little ring to a child, and immediately I had the mother and grandmother importuning me to make them also a present, and I had great difficulty in preventing them making their way, by force of arms, to my pocket ; since then I was more cautious, but one of the women here soon changed her begging tone into one so threatening that I was heartily glad I was not alone in her company.

At four in the afternoon we broke up our camp, the pilgrim left us, and the caravan now only consisted of five men. After an hour and a half's travelling, we reached a height whence we had a prospect over an extensive and well-cultivated hilly country. The soil in Kurdistan is incomparably better than that of Mesopotamia, and the country is therefore more populous, and villages, occur more frequently. Before night-fall, we reached a valley where there were some fresh-looking rice plantations and fine shrubs, and a pretty little brook was murmuring along a bed set with canes and green rushes,—a most welcome and refreshing sight after the heat of the day. Our satisfaction did not however last long,—for one of our party,—the tradesman, suddenly became so ill that he nearly fell from his mule, and remained lying on the spot. We covered him with carpets, but could do nothing more for him, as we had neither medicine nor any other requisite. Fortunately after a few hours he fell asleep, and we could only endeavour to do likewise. In the morning he felt well again, which we were particularly glad to hear, as we had that day a most fatiguing and mountainous road before us. We had to go constantly up and down hill, along the side of a valley following the course of the river Badin, which winds like a serpent from one side to the other. In the valley pomegranate trees and oleanders were in full bloom, and wild vines hung their draperies on tree and shrub. After a dangerous ride of six hours, we came to a ford, but our raft was so small that it could hold little luggage and only two people at a time, so that it took us four hours to get across the river.

The next day our road became still worse, for we had to cross a considerable mountain ridge. Far and wide we had only rocks and stones ; but I remarked to my astonishment that in many places the stones had been removed in order to make use of every little spot of ground capable of cultivation. I saw, nevertheless, no villages, but they must have existed, for on many of the heights there were large burial places.

Our halt on the following day was in the romantic valley of Halifan, which is surrounded by lofty mountains, rising on one side precipitously, and on the other sloping gradually down. Everything looked blooming and verdant, and we passed between plantations of tobacco and rice, meadows and stubble fields. There was a village pleasantly situated at the foot of a hill, and surrounded by poplars, while a stream, bright and clear as crystal, rushed impetuously from the mountains, but flowed more gently through the valley; and away over the hills, towards the west, I saw numerous herds of cattle, and flocks of sheep and goats.

We encamped, however, far away from the village, and I could get nothing to eat but dry bread, and no couch but the hard ground of the stubble field. I counted this evening, nevertheless, as among the most delightful I had had, for the lovely landscape around me made ample amends for the want of any other enjoyment.

Ali granted us only half a night, for at two o'clock again the word was " to horse." Scarcely a hundred paces from where we were lying there was a magnificent mountain pass. The lofty walls were cleft to leave a passage for the stream, and a narrow foot-path beside it. The moon shone in her fullest splendour, otherwise it would have been difficult even for these practised animals to keep their footing along the narrow and dangerous way, among rolling stones and fallen masses of rock.

The good creatures scrambled along the steep mountain-side like chamois, and carried us safely past dreadful precipices at the bottom of which the river dashed along from rock to rock. This night-scene was so wild and striking that even my uncultivated companions were involuntarily silent, awe-struck, and as we moved along no other sound was heard than the clatter of the horses' hoofs and the noise of the stones which, set in motion by them, rolled down into the abyss. Nothing else disturbed the death-like stillness.

We had been going along thus for about an hour, when the moon all at once became covered with thick clouds, and the darkness was so total that we could scarcely see a step before us. Our leader kept constantly striking fire with a flint, in order that the sparks might enable us to see in some measure where we were going; but this was not sufficient, and the animals began to stumble and slip, and soon there was nothing for it but to halt and stand motionless one behind another—as if we had suddenly been changed to stone—till morning. But with the dawn of light our life returned again, and we cheerfully urged on our steeds, and soon found ourselves in an indescribably beautiful circle of mountains. Right and left, before and behind, they rose one above another, and far in the back-ground towered above all a mighty giant crowned with snow. But the pleasure I had in contemplating this scene met with a sudden shock.

A short distance before we reached the plateau we noticed, at several places on the ground, spots of blood, to which we paid very little attention, as a horse or a mule might have scratched themselves against the rocks and left those traces behind. But soon we came to a spot that left no doubt of the origin of these stains, it was covered with a complete pool of blood, and looking down into the abyss below, we saw two human bodies, one hanging scarcely a hundred feet below the ledge on which we were—the other, which had rolled further, half hidden by a projecting crag. This told its own tale, and we hastened away from the hateful scene of murder. I could not get it out of my mind for days together.

In the valley on the other side of the plateau we found grapes, and further on came to a village of huts covered with leaves, near which, on the summits of two neighbouring mountains, we perceived fortifications. Here the rest of our travelling companions stopped, but Ali went on with me a couple of miles more, to the town of Ravandus, which we did not see till we were nearly upon it.

The aspect of this town is very singular. It lies on a steep round hill, perfectly isolated, but surrounded by mountains, and the houses lie in terraces one above another so completely that their flat roofs, covered with hard-trodden clay, look like little squares, and really serve the houses lying above them for a passage, so that it is often hard to tell which is roof and which street. Upon many of them there are also leafy arbours, where the people sleep.

I did not feel much pleased at the sight of this eagles' nest, for I could not help thinking it was no place for opportunities of travelling further, and every step strengthened me in the opinion. Ravandus was one of the most wretched places I had seen. Ali led me across a deplorable bazaar into a dirty court that I took for a stable, but which turned out to be the chan. When I had alighted I was conducted into a dark hole where the merchant to whom I had been recommended was sitting on the ground before his shop. This Mr. Mansur was nevertheless the first of his class in Ravandus.

He was a full quarter of an hour spelling through the note I had brought with me, though it consisted only of a few lines ; and after that he saluted me with repeated salams, which were meant to signify that I was welcome.

The good man probably guessed that this day not the smallest morsel had passed my lips, for he ordered breakfast to be immediately served up, consisting of bread, lean cheese, and melons, to which I did ample justice.

With the conversation I did not get on quite so well, for he knew no European tongue—I no Asiatic one ; but I managed to make him understand by signs that I wished him to forward me as soon as possible on my journey, and he made it intelligible to me on his side that he would do so, and moreover that he would provide for my comfort during my stay ; and as he was not married himself, would take me to the house of a relation.

He kept his word, and conducted me, after breakfast, to a house that precisely resembled that of the Arab at Kerkoo, only that the court-yard was smaller and full of puddles.

Under the gateway, upon some very dirty carpets, sat some especially nasty-looking women playing with little children, and I was obliged to crouch down beside them and undergo the customary curious investigations. I endured this for a time, and then I got up and left the charming company to look for some place where I could bring my toilette a little into order, for for six days, in a heat equal to that under the line, I had not changed my clothes.

I found at last a dark dirty hole of a room, which, besides the disgust its appearance occasioned, gave me no small apprehension of vermin and scorpions. I had always been afraid of the latter, and at first fancied I should meet with them everywhere in this country, as I had read in books of travels that they were here in countless numbers. But subsequently my fears rather diminished, for even in subterranean chambers and among ruins I had never seen one. Indeed in my whole long journey I never saw but two.

But I suffered much from vermin—indeed there is often no way of freeing yourself from them but that of burning your clothes.

I had scarcely taken possession of this very uninviting apartment, where at least I thought I should enjoy quiet, when one woman presented herself, then another, and then another ; the women were followed by the children, the children by the neighbours, who had heard of the arrival of an *Inglesi* (for here they have no notion of any foreigner that is not an Englishwoman), and at last I found I was worse off than under the gateway.

At length one of my visitors hit on the happy idea of offering me a bath, and I accepted the offer with great joy. They got the hot water ready and made me a sign to follow them; I did so, and came into a sheep-pen, and one that had not been cleaned for as many years perhaps as it had stood. Here they pushed together two stones, and intimated that I was to stand upon them and have the water poured over me, and that in the presence of the whole company who had followed me like my shadow. I desired them to go away, explaining that I would do what was necessary myself, and they complied ; but, alas ! the pen had no door, and they all turned round at the entrance and stood looking in.

My delightful hope of a bath faded away—for it is hardly necessary to say that I did not choose to bathe in the presence, and for the entertainment of a large party.

Four days did I pass among these people ; the days in the dark hole—the evenings and nights upon the terrace. Like my hostess, I had to crouch upon the ground; and if I wanted to write to make use of my knees for a table. Every day I was told, To-morrow a caravan will go ; but it was said only to tranquillize me, for it was easy to see I did not like my abode. The women lounged idly about the whole day, and slept or gossipped or quarrelled with the children, liking much better to go in dirty rags then to wash or patch them. The children were allowed completely to tyrannise over them. They did not indeed, exactly strike their parents, but if they did not get all they wanted immediately, they flung themselves on the ground and kicked and screamed till their will was obeyed. During the day there were no regular meals, but women and children were perpetually eating bread, cucumbers, melons, and buttermilk. In the evening every one bathed and washed hands, face, and feet,—a ceremony that was often repeated three or four times before the prayer, but they had no hesitation

in gossiping all the time it was going on. Perhaps, among ourselves, however, there might sometimes be seen at prayers very
little more of true devotion.

Notwithstanding the great faults of these people they were not
deficient in good nature, and when I noticed any thing amiss in
their behaviour they were very willing to acknowledge themselves
in the wrong. A little girl of seven years old, for instance, named
Ascha, was particularly naughty. The moment anything was
refused her, she would fling herself on the ground, howl with all
her might, and even roll herself purposely in the dirt, and then
come and lay her hands on the bread and melons. I tried to
make her understand the impropriety of this proceeding, and I
succeeded beyond my expectations.

The only plan I could think of was to imitate her behaviour as
closely as I could, and do just what she did. The child gazed at
me for a moment in speechless astonishment, and I then managed
to ask it how it liked me to do that; it saw the error of its ways,
and I seldom had occasion to repeat my lesson. I endeavoured
in the same manner to give it a little instruction in cleanliness, and
very soon it would go and give itself a good washing, and then
come jumping to show me its hands and face.

In few days the little creature grew so fond of me that she was
constantly at my side, and tried in many ways to do what she
thought would please me.

No less fortunate was I with the women ; I used to point to
their torn clothes, and then fetch needle and thread, and show
them how they might be mended. They were quite pleased with
the discovery, and very soon I had quite a sewing school round me.
What good might not any one do among such people who should
set about it in earnest, and who understood their language ; what
a beautiful field would be here opened to the labours of a missionary who would submit to live among them, and endeavour
by kindness and patience to overcome their faults. But the missionaries who come here devote to them at the utmost only a few
hours in the day, and make their scholars come to them instead of
seeking them in their own homes.

The women and girls in the Asiatic countries have no kind of
instruction, and those in the towns have scarcely any employment,
but remain the whole day abandoned to idleness. At sunrise the
men go to the bazaar, where they have their booths and work-

shops; the elder boys go to school or accompany their fathers, and neither return home till sunset. Then the husband expects to find the carpet spread on the terrace, the meal prepared, the nargileh ready; and when he comes he plays a little with the younger children, but they and the mothers must go away during the meal. The women in villages have more freedom and more occupation, as they generally take an active part in the house-keeping. It is said also that a better state of morals is found in the country than in the cities.

The costume of the Kurds is, with the wealthier classes, entirely oriental; that of the people varies from it a little. The men wear wide linen trowsers, and over them a shirt confined by a girdle, as well as sometimes a woollen jacket without sleeves, made of stuff of only a hand's-breadth wide, and sewed together. Some, instead of white trowsers, have brown ones, which are excessively ugly, and look like sacks with two holes to thrust the feet through. Their *chaussure* consists of boots of red or yellow leather, with large iron heels; or sometimes shoes made of coarse white wool, and adorned with three tassels. On their heads they wear the turban.

The women have the red and yellow boots, with iron heels, and loose trowsers like the men; but over this they wear a long blue garment long enough to reach half an ell below the feet, but which is tucked up under the girdle; and a large blue shawl hangs down below the knee. Round their heads they wind black shawls in the turban fashion, or they wear the red *fez*, with a silk handkerchief wound round it, and on the top of that a sort of wreath made of short black fringe, put on like a diadem, and leaving the forehead free. The hair falls in narrow braids over the shoulders, and from the turban hangs a heavy silver chain. It is not easy to imagine a more becoming head-dress.

Girls and women go with their faces uncovered, and I saw here several exquisitely beautiful girls, with really noble features. Their complexions are brown, and the eyebrows and eyelashes black, or dyed with henna. Nose-rings are only seen among the women of the very lowest class.

My friend Mr. Mansur entertained me very well. In the morning I got buttermilk, bread, and cucumbers, and sometimes even dates fried in butter; a dish however that I did not much relish. In the evening, mutton with rice, or barley, maize, onions.

and chopped meat,—all very good; and I had not to complain of any deficiency of appetite. The buttermilk and water is taken cold, besides the luxury of a piece of ice thrown into it; for as it can be procured from the neighbouring mountains ice is to be had here in every village, and the people may often be seen eating large pieces of it. But in spite of the endeavours of Mansur and his relations to make my abode with them endurable, nay perhaps in their opinion even agreeable, I was glad enough when one morning Ali came to me with the information that he had got a small cargo for Sauh-Bulok (70 English miles off) which lay on my route. The same evening I went to the caravansera, and on the following morning before sunrise we were once more in motion. Mansur remained to the last friendly and hospitable, and besides furnishing me with a letter to a Persian settled at Sauh-Bulok, he provided me with a stock of bread, melons, cucumbers, and sour milk. The latter I found particularly useful, and I advise every traveller to make use of this refreshment; it is carried here in bags of thick linen; the watery part trickles through, and one can at pleasure take out the thicker portion in spoonsful, and thin it with water. In the hot season indeed it will dry up to cheese on the fourth or fifth day; but this cheese is very good, and in four or five days one generally comes to a place where the stock may be renewed.

On the first days of our journey we passed through narrow valleys between high mountains. The roads were extremely bad. On the second evening we came to a half-ruined citadel, and scarcely had we pitched our camp before there appeared half a dozen strongly-armed soldiers, under the command of an officer, who took a place at my side, pointed to a written paper, and made me several signs. I soon understood that he meant to tell me I was on Persian ground, and he required my passport. I did not however wish to open my trunk in presence of the whole village now assembled around us, and therefore pretended I did not know what he meant, and persisted in being stupid, till at last he left me, saying to Ali, " What can I do with her ? she does not understand me,—she may go on."* In what European state should I have been treated so mildly ?

---

* I had picked up enough of the language between here and Mossul to understand this much.

In almost every village we passed through I had had half the population assembled round me, and it may well be imagined what a swarm had gathered while this was going on, and I must own that this everlasting staring is to be counted amongst the greatest sufferings I had to endure in my travels. Sometimes when the women and children would not keep their hands off me, and my clothes, I was driven to take my riding whip, and distribute a few cuts among them. This always procured me some alleviation, and they at least drew back, and formed a larger circle. On this occasion a lad of sixteen tried to punish me for my boldness, and when I went down to the river, as I was accustomed to do to fill my water bottle, wash my hands and face, and bathe my feet, he followed me, and lifted up a stone. As it would not do to show any fear, I went down composedly into the river, and he flung the stone ; but I thought from the manner in which it was thrown, it had been intended more to frighten than to hurt me ; and after he had tried a second and a third, and I still took no notice, he got tired, and went home.

It was not quite without reason that I had felt fear of this journey, for few days passed in undisturbed tranquillity. This day I was much alarmed to see come galloping towards us a troop of seven well-armed, and five unarmed men. The first carried lances, sabres, daggers, knives, pistols, and small shields, and were dressed like the common people, with the exception of their turbans, round which they had wound Persian shawls. I took them, when they stopped us, for robbers ; but after asking several questions,—where we came from, where we were going to, what we carried, and so on,—they allowed us to pursue our way ; and as in the course of the day we were stopped several times in the same manner, I concluded they were soldiers on service.

The next day matters seemed to be taking a still more serious turn. Whether Ali had given any incorrect replies to their queries, I know not—but they seized on his two pack-horses, threw their burdens on the ground, and commanded the animals to be led away. Poor Ali begged and implored most piteously, and then he turned and pointed to me, saying, that all belonged to me, and that they certainly would have compassion on a helpless woman.

The soldier turned to me, and asked whether this was true, but as I did not consider it advisable to confirm the statement, I pretended not to understand. Ali began to cry, and our situation really seemed desperate,—for what could we do in this desolate uninhabited country without the horses? but at last the soldier allowed himself to be softened, sent for the animals, and gave them to us back.

It was late in the evening when we arrived at the town of Sauh-Bulok. As it was not fortified we were able to get in, though it cost some trouble to get a chan opened to us; it was handsome and spacious, and had a basin of water in the middle of the court, round which were booths for the traders, and alcoves for sleeping in. The company assembled in it,—all men, had already mostly gone to rest, — and their astonishment may be imagined when they saw me, a woman, enter alone with the caravan leader. It was too late to deliver my letter, so I seated myself in resignation by the side of my modest package, and thought to pass the night thus ; but a Persian came up to me, pointed out to me a place in an alcove where I could sleep, and afterwards brought me some bread and water. This charity was so much the greater since the Mahomedans have, as is known, an aversion to Christians.

The next day I delivered my letter, and the merchant to whom it was addressed introduced me to a Christian family, and promised to provide for my further journey. In this little town of Sauh-Bulok there are about twenty Christian families, who are all under the care of a French missionary, and have a very pretty little church. I rejoiced at this intelligence, as I thought I should now again have an opportunity of speaking a language with which I was well acquainted; but, to my vexation, I learned that the missionary was just now gone on a journey, and I was therefore just as awkwardly situated as at Ravandus, for the person with whom I was to lodge, and his family, spoke nothing but Persian.

This man, who was by trade a carpenter, had a wife, six children, and an apprentice. They all lived in the same room, and also with great apparent pleasure made room for me in it. The whole family was uncommonly good and complaisant towards me. They shared with me honourably every morsel they had, and if I bought fruit, eggs, or any other trifle, and offered some to them, they partook of them with great modesty. But it was not only towards me that they showed themselves thus benevolent: no poor person ever appealed to them in vain, or left their threshold without relief; and yet the abode with them was dreadful, and I had really a horror of them. The mother was a silly quarrelsome woman, who was the whole day wrangling and fighting with her six children, (from four to sixteen years of age). No ten minutes ever passed in which the children were not quarrelling amongst themselves, and exchanging cuffs and kicks, or tearing each other's hair, so that I, in my corner, had not a single moment's peace, and not unfrequently ran great risk of getting my share of what was going on when they were spitting at each other or throwing lumps of wood at each other's heads. Several times the eldest son would seize his mother by the throat, and hold her till she was black in the face. I did what I could to keep the peace, but, unfortunately, I very seldom succeeded, for, from my ignorance of their language, I could not represent to them the sinfulness of their behaviour. It was only in the evening when the father came home that anything like peace and order was restored.

Among no nation on the earth—among the poorest and lowest of the people, did I ever see such a specimen of behaviour, nor did I ever before see children lift their hands against their parents. When I left *Sauh-Bulok* I left behind me a letter for the missionary, in which I called his attention to the condition of this family, and entreated him to do what he could for their reformation. Religion does not consist wholly in praying and fasting, in reading the bible, and going to church. My stay at this place was rendered so unpleasant to me by these circumstances, that I daily worried the Persian merchant to find means of sending me on ; but he shook his head, and made me understand that, in his opinion, if I persisted in travelling alone, I should be shot or have my throat cut.

At last, however, I really could bear my domestic *Inferno* no longer, and begged the merchant, at whatever risk, to get me a horse and a guide, and determined, let the danger be what it might, to go at least to Oromia—a place about fifty miles off, where I knew I should find an American missionary, and I did not doubt, some means or other of getting on.

The merchant came to me on the following day in company with a wild-looking fellow, whom he presented to me as my guide. I was obliged, on account of the risk of travelling without a caravan, to agree to pay him four times the ordinary price; but I would have done anything to get away. The treaty was concluded; and the guide bound himself to set off on the following morning and to take me to Oromia in a three days journey. The one half of the money promised I was to pay him in advance, the other not till I got to Oromia, in order to keep some check upon him if he hesitated about fulfilling his engagement.

Joy and fear together took possession of my mind when the business was settled; and, in order to compose myself a little, I went out to take a walk in the bazaar and outside of the town, and I found not the slightest obstacle to my free locomotion, though I wore no veil, but merely the isar thrown round me.

The bazaars are not so poor as those of Ravandus, and the chan is large and pleasant; but the aspect of the common people I thought repulsive, if not terrific; they are large and strongly built, with harsh features, which are disfigured by an expression of wildness and cruelty, and they all looked to me like robbers and murderers. In the evening I took care to see that my pistols were in order, and made up my mind that if I were attacked I would not give my life for nothing.

It was towards noon, instead of sun-rise, as had been intended, when we left *Sauh-Bulok.* The way was very desolate, and I could not help a feeling of alarm when we occasionally met a stranger, but, thank God, no harm happened to me, and we met with no other enemy than enormous swarms of locusts, which passed in masses like clouds; they were nearly three inches long, and had large wings of a red or bluish colour. All the grass and plants in this district had been devoured by them, and though I have heard that the people try to indemnify themselves by eating them, I have never been able to meet with any such dish. After a ride of seven hours we reached a valley that was populous, large, and fertile; villages were frequent, and people were at work in the fields, wearing the high black Persian cap, which had a very odd effect with their ragged attire. We stopped for the night at a village called Mahomed-Jur, and had I not been too idle I might have prepared myself an excellent meal of turtle, for I saw many in the brooks, and even on the fields, and needed only to stoop and pick them up; but then I must have got some wood, have made a fire, and cooked; and I preferred contenting myself with a bit of dry bread and a cucumber, and eating it in peace and quietness.

The next day when we halted, I saw to my surprise that my guide was making preparations for a longer stay, and on my urging the continuation of our journey, he declared he could not go on without a caravan, as the most dangerous part of the way lay before us. He then pointed to a few dozen of horses that were grazing in a stubble field near, and endeavoured to make me understand that in a few hours a caravan would arrive. But the whole day passed, and there were no signs of a caravan. I considered that my guide had deceived me, and was very angry, when in the evening I saw him making up for me with my cloak a bed on the floor. It was now necessary to summon all my moral strength, and make the man see that I would not be treated like a child, and kept there as long as he thought proper; but the mischief was that I had no words wherewith to scold him. I therefore snatched my cloak from the floor, flung it at his feet, and signified that if he did not take me to Oromia to-morrow or the next day, I would give him no more money. I then turned my back upon him (which is considered one of the greatest affronts), sat down on the ground, and leaning my head on my hand, gave way to a very melancholy mood; for what was I to do if the guide should not regard my *demonstration*, or leave me waiting here till a caravan should chance to go by?

Some women of the village who had come up during my dispute with the guide, now came to me and brought me some milk and warm food; sitting down by me, and asking why I was so angry. I managed to explain the matter to them, and they seemed to take my part, pouting with their countryman, and doing what they could to console me the stranger. They would not move from my side, but begged me so cordially to partake of the food they had brought me that I could not refuse, and ate a little, though I was not much inclined to it. The dish consisted of bread, eggs, butter, and water boiled together, and vexed as I was I thought it very good. I wished to give them a trifle in return, but they would not accept it; but seemed quite pleased to see me a little more tranquil and happy.

All at once, at one o'clock in the morning, my guide got up, saddled my horse, and desired me to mount him. I was thrown into some consternation by this move, for I saw no appearance of any caravan, and the thought flashed across my mind that perhaps the man was about to revenge himself on me. Why should he wish now in darkness, in the middle of the night, to go through a district that he had avoided in bright daylight? I had not Persian enough to ask for an explanation, but I would not leave him any excuse for not fulfilling his contract, and so I agreed to go.

I mounted my horse with some anxiety, and commanded my guide, who wished to remain behind me, to ride on, and I kept my hand on my pistol, listening to every sound and watching every movement he made ; but I would not turn back.

But after all my fears were groundless, for in half an hour's rapid riding we came up with a large caravan, and one that had the additional advantage of being protected by a dozen well-armed peasants. The way, it seemed, really was dangerous, and my guide had received information of the passage of the caravan.

I could not help wondering on this occasion at the persistance of this people in whatever is matter of custom. Because they are in the habit of travelling in the night, they would do the same even in the most dangerous regions, where the peril would be greatly diminished by daylight.

In a few hours we came to the lake of Oromia, which henceforward remained always on our right hand. On our left lay for many miles a tract of naked hills, mountains, and ravines, which composed the dreaded part of the road ; but the morning brought us to a beautiful fertile valley, the sight of which with its inhabited villages, gave me courage to leave the caravan, and push on to Oromia.

The lake of Oromia, from which the town has its name, is above sixty miles long, and in many places above thirty broad. It appears to be quite closely surrounded by high mountains, but in reality there are large tracts of level land between them and the water. The lake and its environs are both beautiful, but its waters have a somewhat melancholy aspect, as no sail or boat enlivens its surface ; it is, in fact, a second Dead Sea, for its waters are so salt that no fish or mollusk can live in them ; it is said that the human body will not sink in the lake for the same reason ; and there are on its shores large spaces covered with a thick white incrustation of salt, which the people have nothing to do but to scrape up.

Since leaving the sandy wastes around Bagdad I had seen no camels, and did not expect to see them any more, as my way lay towards the north ; but to my surprise we here met with several troops, and I found that they serve the Kurds as beasts of burden as well as the Arabs. This affords a sufficient proof that they are able to bear a cold climate, for even in the valleys the snow often lies here several feet deep.   They appeared to me stronger made than those I had before seen; their legs are thicker, and their hair closer and longer, the neck shorter and not so slender; their colour is generally darker, and I saw no quite light ones. Besides these animals, the Kurds use a kind of waggon to assist in bringing home their harvests, but they are of the coarsest and simplest construction, being in fact nothing more than slender trunks of trees fastened together, with a shorter one for the axle, and two rude wheels.   They are drawn by four oxen, and have a driver for each pair, who in an odd manner sits upon the shaft with his back to his cattle.

Late in the evening, after riding sixteen hours, I arrived at Oromia in perfect safety.   I had no letters to any of the missionaries, who I found lived with their families some miles in the country, and were all absent but one—Mr. Wright.   He indeed received me with true Christian kindness, and once more, after many weary days, I tasted of comfort and cheerfulness.   The first evening I could not help laughing when he told me how I had been announced to him.   Since I knew too little of Persian to explain what I wanted, I had merely pointed to the stairs when I came in, to intimate to the servant that he should go up to his master, and he immediately went with the intelligence that a woman was below who spoke no language at all; but a moment after, when I asked another for a glass of water, he rushed up stairs to correct the statement, and declare that I could speak English.   Mr. Wright informed the other missionaries of my arrival, and they were so kind as to invite me to spend some days with them in the country. I accepted the invitation, however, only for a single day, as I was anxious, having already lost so much time, to go on.   These gentlemen would have dissuaded me from going on alone, but they admitted that I had already passed the most perilous part of the road, and they recommended me at all events to take with me some armed peasants as an escort across the mountains of Kutschié. Mr. Wright had the kindness to provide me an honest and safe guide, and I paid him double the usual price, that he might take me to Tabreez in four days instead of six.   In order to make the guide believe that I was a poor pilgrim, I gave Mr. Wright the half of the sum I agreed for, and begged him to pay it for me, and tell the man he would get the other from Mr. Stevens, the English consul.

Of the day I spent in Oromia, I made the utmost possible use. In the morning I saw the town, and afterwards I visited with Mrs. Wright some families both of the rich and poor, in order to see something of the manner in which both classes live. The town contains 22,000 inhabitants, and is surrounded by walls, but not closed at night, so you can get in or out at any hour. It is built like most other Turkish towns, with the exception that the streets are tolerably broad and clean. Before the city lie many large fruit and flower gardens surrounded with high walls, and with pretty dwelling-houses in the middle of them. In the streets the women go very closely veiled, covering head and breast with a white cloth, and having even the places left for the eyes covered with a close impenetrable net-work.

In the houses of the poorer classes three or four families live under one roof ; they have little other property than straw mats, cushions, blankets, and some cooking utensils ; not to forget a large wooden chest, containing the store of flour, which is their chief treasure ; for here, as in all countries where it is cultivated, corn is the chief food of the common people. Families here bake twice a day—morning and evening.

Many of the small houses have very pretty little courts, in which are grape vines, trees, and flowers, so that they have quite the appearance of gardens. The dwellings of the rich are spacious, lofty, and airy ; the reception rooms with many windows, and the floors covered with carpets, on which you sit, as there are no divans. We made our visits without any previous notice, so that we found the ladies in quite simple coloured cotton dresses, made of course in the fashion of their country.

In the afternoon I rode out in company with the missionaries to their large summer house, which lies six miles from the town, upon a low hill. The valley through which we rode is very large, fertile, and beautiful, though it lies 4,000 feet above the level of the sea. Cotton, wine, tobacco, and all the fruits of Southern Germany are raised here—as well as the castor-oil plant. Many of the villages lie almost hidden in the groves of fruit trees ; and I came at a fortunate time, when the magnificent peaches, apricots, apples, grapes—all the fruits of my native country, were ripe.

The house of the missionaries commands a view over all this lovely valley, as well as the lower ranges of hills and mountains. The house itself is large, and furnished with so many conveniences and comforts that it seemed to me as if I were not under the roof of simple followers of Christ, and teachers of the Gospel—but in that of some wealthy private gentleman. Here were four ladies—their wives—and a whole troop of children, large and small, amongst whom I spent some most delightful hours, and greatly regretted when nine o'clock compelled me to take my leave.

A few native girls were presented to me who were instructed by the wives of the missionaries. They spoke and wrote English, and had some knowledge of geography.

I cannot help here making some remarks on the mode of life of the missionaries which I have had in the course of my travels so many opportunities of observing. In Persia, China, India, every where I found them living quite differently from what I had imagined. I had represented to myself, missionaries as half, if not whole, martyrs ; and supposed them to be animated with such zeal for the conversion of the heathen, that like the Apostles of Jesus Christ, they forsook all personal indulgence—all conveniences and comforts of life—lived with the people under one roof, ate out of one dish, and so forth.

Ah ! those were ideas that I got out of books ; things were in reality quite different. They live quite in the manner of opulent gentlemen, have handsome houses fitted up with every convenience and luxury. The missionaries repose upon swelling divans—their wives preside at the tea-table—their children feast on sweatmeats and confectionery—in short, their position is one incomparably pleasanter and freer from care than that of most other people—and they get their salaries punctually paid, and take their duties very easily. In places where several missionaries are settled, they have what are called " meetings," three or four times a week, supposed to be devoted to business, but which are little else than parties at which their wives and children appear in tasteful dresses. At one of the missionaries' houses the meeting will be a breakfast, at another a dinner, at a third a tea party ; and you will see several equipages and servants standing in the court-yard. There is indeed, on this occasion, some little talk of business, and the gentlemen remain together perhaps half an hour discussing it ; but the rest of the time is passed in mere social amusement.

I cannot believe that this is the proper method for gaining the affections of the people or effecting the objects of a mission. The foreign dress, the elegant mode of life, leaves the poor man at too great a distance, and induces him rather to draw back in awe, than to approach in confidence and affection. He does not venture to look up to this grand rich gentleman, and the missionary has great difficulty in overcoming the reserve and timidity thus occasioned.

The missionaries themselves say that they must appear in this halo of splendour in order to create respect ; but I cannot but think the kind of respect they should seek would be better purchased by noble behaviour and the dignity of virtue, than by any external display.

Many of the missionaries think they do much good by travelling through the towns and villages, preaching in the language of the country, and distributing religious tracts, and they draw up the most captivating reports of the number of people that have thronged to hear them, and get their tracts, so that one might suppose that at least one-half of their audience were ready for immediate conversion to Christianity. But alas ! this listening to sermons and taking tracts is no proof at all.

Would not Chinese, Indian, or Persian priests draw immense audiences to hear them if they should come in their national costume to preach in French or English ? Would they not have plenty of people to receive books and pamphlets that they gave away for nothing, even though no one could read them ?

In all places where I have been I have made close enquiries on the subject of the conversions made by these missionaries, and it always appeared that they were excessively rare. The few Christians in India, small scattered communities of twenty or thirty families, have arisen from fatherless children which the Missionaries have brought up, provided afterwards with employment, and kept under vigilant superintendence, that they might not fall back into the errors of heathenism.

Preaching sermons, and distributing tracts, do not make up the whole duties of a missionary. Any one who takes on himself this sacred office should be willing to live amongst and with the people, to share their toils, their joys, and their sorrows, and by a modest and exemplary course of life to gain their affections, and then communicate some simple and intelligible doctrine. It would be better too, it appears to me, that a missionary should not be married to a European woman ; firstly, because European girls are seldom willing to adopt this mode of life, except for the sake of an establishment ; and secondly, that a young European woman who has children in this country generally becomes sickly, and can then no longer fulfil the duties of her station, but stands in need of change of air, or of a voyage to Europe. The children, too, grow up weakly, and require at least till their seventh year to be kept away. The father will often accompany them, and take the opportunity to spend some time in his native country ; or if this is not to be managed, the family will go to the mountains in search of a cooler climate, or they go to a *Mela*, a religious festival of India, at which thousands of people assemble, and where the missionaries often preach. On all these occasions, too, they do not travel in a humble and simple manner, but surrounded by luxurious accommodations,—with palanquins carried by men, pack horses, or camels,—with tents, beds, cooking utensils, dinner services, &c.,— with male and female attendants in suitable numbers. And who pays for all this ? Often poor well-meaning believing souls in Europe and America, who perhaps deprive themselves almost of the necessaries of life that the good seed may be sown in these distant regions of the earth.

Were the missionaries married to native women, few of these expenses would be requisite. There would be few sickly wives and children, and no need for voyages to Europe ; and the education of the children might be provided for in schools established in the country, though perhaps not such luxurious ones as those in Calcutta.

I trust that these remarks will not be misunderstood. I have great respect for the missionaries, whom I have known to be worthy men, and good fathers of families. I believe that there are among them also very learned men, who could furnish most valuable contributions to history, geography, and ethnology. Whether by all this they fulfil the object of their appointment, is another question. For myself, I owe these gentlemen many thanks, for they every where received me in the most friendly and hospitable manner. Their mode of life surprised me only because I had to give them the name of missonary ; for I could not help remembering the men who, with no promise of support from their country, went out into the world to preach the Gospel of Jesus Christ, and took nothing with them but a staff.

On leaving Oromia (which, by-the-bye, I should mention was the birth-place of Zoroaster,) I rode for ten hours to the village of Kutschié, which also lies not far from the lake, though we seldom got a glimpse of it. During the whole journey, not only from Mossul, but from Bagdad, I had had no such agreeable day as this. My guide was an excellent fellow, full of attention for me, and anxiously careful about every thing. In the village of Kut-schié he led me to a very clean peasant's house, inhabited by most obliging people, who spread a beautiful carpet for me upon the terrace, brought me immediately a basin of water to wash myself, and large black mulberries for refreshment. Afterwards they served up to me nourishing soup, with meat, rich sour milk, and good bread, and moreover all in cleanly utensils. But what crowned this good treatment was, that when they had brought me my food they did not stop to stare at me, as if I had been a strange animal, but went away. After all, they actually refused to receive any compensation, and at last I only managed it in a round-about way, by taking two of the men of the family as an escort to the mountains, and giving them double the usual pay-ment. They thanked me with really touching earnestness, and wished me all happiness and blessings for the rest of my journey.

The dangerous passage across the mountains, of ill repute, lasted three hours ; and my two armed men would have afforded me but little protection against a band of robbers ; but, at least, they ren-dered the journey less terrible to me, than if I had made it alone, with my old guide.

When we had ascended the mountains, we came to some vast vallies, that seemed to have been forsaken by man and forgotten by nature ; and I could not help thinking that, though our escort had left us, the dangers of the journey were not altogether over, and so it proved : for, as we were passing some ruinous huts, several fellows rushed out upon us, and, seizing the bridle of our horses, began rummaging my luggage. I expected a command to alight, and already looked upon my small package of worldly goods as lost and gone. But they spoke with my guide, who told them the fable I had arranged for such occasions, namely, that I was a poor pilgrim, and that the English consuls or missionaries every-where paid the expenses of my journey. My dress, my insignifi-cant baggage, my being alone, all agreed perfectly with this story ; they believed it, had compassion on my supplicating looks, and let me go on, unmolested ; nay, they even came to me, and asked whether I wanted any water, which is very scarce in these vallies. I begged them for a draught, and so we parted excellent friends, though for some time I felt a little uneasy lest they should repent of their magnanimity.

We now approached the shores of the lake, and the oppressive feeling of fear passed away as we found ourselves again among pleasant inhabited vallies, and saw people at work in the fields, corn being carried home, cattle grazing, and so forth. During the heat of the day we remained at Dise Halil, a considerable little town, with very clean streets. The principal one is intersected by a silvery stream of water, and the courts of the houses are like gardens. There are also, outside the town, many neat gardens enclosed within high walls.

To judge from the number of the chans, this town must be much frequented by caravans, for only in the small street we passed through I counted half a dozen. We alighted at one of them, and I was quite astonished at the accommodations I found in it. The stalls for the cattle were covered in, the sleeping-places for the drivers were neat paved terraces, and the rooms for the travellers were perfectly clean, and furnished with fire-places. These chans are open to every one, and nothing whatever is to be paid for the use of them ; at most, you may give a trifle to the keeper, who, in return, will attend to any little commission for you.

In this respect, the Persians, Turks, and others whom we consider as uncultivated nations, are far more liberal and magnanimous than we Europeans are. In India, for instance, when the English erect bongolos, you must pay a rupee for the privilege of spending a night in one, or even taking an hour's rest ; and there is no provision for the driver or his beasts,—they may sleep in the open air as they can. In many of the bongolos no traveller is allowed to enter who is not a Christian, or, at all events, he must only remain till a humble-minded Christian comes to turn him out. Even though it should be in the middle of the night, the poor heathen is expelled without mercy.

But in the infidel countries, the first comer has the place, let him be Christian, Turk, or Arab ; nay, I am convinced that if the chan were already in the occupation of these infidels, and a Christian should arrive, they would crowd themselves together to make room for him.

At Ali Schach, which we reached in the following afternoon, we met three travellers, who were also going to Tabreez, and my guide agreed to journey in company with them, and that we should set off in the middle of the night; but, I must own, this addition to our party was not particularly welcome to me, for the men looked very wild, and were completely armed. I would much rather have set off at day-break, without these companions, but the guide declared they were very worthy fellows ; and so, trusting, perhaps, more in my own good fortune than in his word, I mounted my horse at one o'clock, and away we went.

The feeling of apprehension with which I had set out gradually wore off, however, as we met on the road parties of two and three persons, who would not probably have been travelling in the night had there been any danger. After this we met great caravans, with several hundred camels, which blocked up the road so completely that we had often to wait half an hour to let them pass. Towards noon we reached a valley, where we came in sight of a great town, but the nearer we came to it the more ruinous and desolate it appeared. The town walls were decayed, the streets and squares full of heaps of rubbish, and many of the houses lay in ruins, as if an enemy had destroyed it, or the plague committed fearful ravages. I at length inquired the name of this melancholy place, and thought I could not have heard rightly when I was told it, was Tabreez. My guide took me to the house of the English Consul, Mr. Stevens, who, to my terror, I found did not live in the town, but ten miles off in the country. A servant, however, said that he would go directly to a Dr. Casolani, who could speak English. In a very short time this gentlemen arrived, and his first questions were, How came you here alone ? Have you been robbed ? Have your companions been murdered, and you alone escaped ? When I gave him my passport, and explained how the matter stood, I think he scarcely believed me. It appeared to him absolutely incredible that a woman, without any knowledge of the languages, could have made her way alone through such countries ; indeed, I felt myself that I could not be sufficiently thankful for the Divine protection that had been accorded me in such circumstances. My mood now was perfectly joyous, for it seemed that life had been bestowed on me a second time.

Dr. Casolani assigned me some rooms in Mr. Stevens's house, and told me he would immediately send a messenger to him, and in the meantime I should apply to himself for any thing I required. When I expressed to him my wonder at the deplorable condition of this the second city in the country, he explained to me that from the side on which I had entered the town had indeed a wretched aspect, but that I had ridden through an old and mostly forsaken suburb that was not reckoned to the town at all.

TABREEZ.

Description of the Town.—The Bazaar.—Behmen Mirza.—Anecdotes of the Persian Government.—Presentation to the Viceroy and his Wife.— Behmen Mirza's Women.—Visit to a Persian Lady.—The People.— Persecution of Jews and Christians.—Departure.

TABREEZ, or Tauris, is the capital of the province of Aderbeidschan, and the residence of the heir to the throne of Persia, who bears the title of Viceroy. It lies in a treeless valley, on the rivers Platscha and Altchi, and counts 160,000 inhabitants. It is a handsomer town than Teheran or Ispahan, has many silk and leather factories, and is considered one of the chief commercial places of Asia. The streets are tolerably broad and clean, and subterranean conduits are carried along them, with openings at certain distances for drawing water. Of the houses you see from the street, as usual in an oriental city, nothing but high walls, without windows, and low entrances. The fronts are always turned towards the court-yard, which is planted with flowers and small trees, and frequently opens into a handsome garden. The reception rooms are large and lofty, and furnished with such long ranges of windows as to make perfect walls of glass. They contain, however, little or no furniture, except carpets, for European articles of luxury seldom find their way here.

Of beautiful mosques, palaces, monuments, either of ancient or modern times, there are none but the half-ruined one of Ali-Schach, which can bear no comparison with the mosques of India; but the new bazaar is very handsome, and its lofty streets and covered passages reminded me vividly of the bazaar of Constantinople, except that it looks newer and pleasanter. The goods displayed in it are, perhaps, not quite so costly; but as the stands of the merchants are larger, they are laid out with more taste, especially the carpets, fruits, and vegetables. Even the cook-shops had an inviting appearance; the eatables were excellent, and often diffused a most savoury and tempting odour. The shoe-making department was certainly very inferior, for only articles of the commonest kind were exhibited, whilst in Constantinople you see behind glass cases the most costly shoes and slippers, embroidered with gold, and even ornamented with precious stones.

It was at a most unfavourable time in which I had come to Tabreez, for it was the month of the great fast, and from sunrise to sunset no one goes out, or receives a visit, or takes anything to eat. People do nothing whatever but pray. These fasts are observed by the Persians so strictly, that many sick people fall victims to them, as they will not even take medicine, for a single mouthful would be enough to forfeit the benefit of the fast. The more enlightened, indeed, make an exception in case of illness, but not without permission from a priest, which can only be obtained by a written declaration from the physician that such a medicine or drink is positively necessary. The priest then puts his seal on the declaration, and the indulgence is granted. Whether this practice of indulgences has been borrowed by the Mahomedans from the Christians, or that the reverse has happened, I know not. The girls begin the practice of fasting in their tenth, the boys in their fifteenth year.

To the especial courtesy of Dr. Casolani, and his great connexions, I was indebted for being introduced at court, as well as into several Persian families, notwithstanding the Fast.

The viceroyalty of the province of Aderbeidschan dates only from about six months before my arrival. It had been created by the then reigning Shah, for the eldest son of the monarch, and future heir of the empire. The last governor of Tabreez, Behmen-Mirza,* the Shah's brother, was a very honourable and intelligent man, who had brought the province, in a few years, into a most flourishing condition, and established order and security in every part of it. But this only awakened the envy of the first minister, and he urged the Shah to recal his brother. For a long time he resisted these insinuations, but the minister did not rest till he had effected his purpose. Behmen-Mirza, who understood the whole business, came immediately to court to justify himself, and then the poor Shah declared his entire love for and satisfaction with his brother, and entreated him only to try and gain the favour of the

---

* *Mirza*, when it stands after a name, signifies Prince; when before it, merely *Mr.*

minister. But Behmen-Mirza learned through his friends that the hatred of the minister was implacable, and that, if he remained, he was in imminent danger of having his eyes put out, or being murdered, and he was advised to lose no time in making his escape from the country. He returned to Tabreez, therefore,—hastily got together his valuables, and took refuge, with a part of his family, on the Russian territory. There he wrote to the emperor, begging his protection, which was immediately granted, and the emperor wrote with his own hand to the Shah, declaring that the prince was now no longer a Persian subject, and that every persecution of him or his family *must* cease. He then assigned the prince an elegant palace at Tiflis, sent him costly presents, and, I was told, settled on him a yearly pension of 20,000 ducats.

This minister, Haggi-Mirza Agasi, entirely ruled over the Shah, whom he had even found means to make venerate him as a prophet or a saint, and obey without hesitation every one of his behests. On one occasion he related to the Shah how, the night before, he had been awakened in the night by feeling his body floating upwards in the air, and that he had gone higher and higher, till at length he had reached Heaven, and had had an interview with his deceased father, who had required from the minister a report of the government of his son. The deceased monarch had expressed himself extremely well satisfied with the behaviour of his son, and advised him by all means to go on as he had begun. The Shah, who had been much attached to his father, was in raptures, and then the adroit minister took occasion to suggest that, in some few particulars, his royal parent had desired alterations,—that he had wished that this or that should be done or not done,—mentioning, of course, certain schemes of his own, and forthwith it was done as he desired.

It must be added, however, that the minister does sometimes apply his power to a good purpose, and stand between the wrath of his highness and its victims; for his said highness is very passionate, and will sometimes proceed briskly to the instant execution of any one who has incurred his displeasure. The minister has therefore given orders that in such case he shall be immediately sent for, and the preparations for the execution proceeded with slowly. He then makes his appearance, *quite accidentally*,—asks what's the news; and when the angry monarch declares he is about to punish a criminal, the minister goes to the window to observe the heavenly bodies, and commonly finds the conjunction unfavourable, so that the execution (if it should take place) might involve some damage on the illustrious head of the state himself. The order is then given to delay it till the next day, and by that time the passion of the Shah is over, or he has forgotten the whole affair.

On one occasion the minister saved a friend who was a governor of a province from strangulation, by declaring that he had adopted him as his son ; and that if it should be his sovereign's pleasure to put him to death, which of course he did not oppose, he must go to Mecca to find another in his stead. The journey to Mecca lasts a year, and the king could not do without him for so long a time ; and as he was not going to differ with his favourite about such a trifle as a man's life, he promised that he would let the offender remain unstrangled, and, moreover, let him keep his place. These anecdotes I had on the best authority.

My presentation at the court of the Viceroy took place a few days after my arrival. I was requested one afternoon by Dr. Casolani to accompany him to a summer-house lying in a small garden, and this again in another, both surrounded by high walls. In the first, besides grass, fruit-trees, and dusty roads, there were many tents occupied by soldiers, who wore the ordinary Persian dress, with the difference that the officers had a sword girded on, and the common men carried a musket on their shoulders. It seems they only appear in full uniform on rare occasions, having the same objection to it that our military men often have.

At the entrance of the small garden we were received by several eunuchs, who led us into an unpretending one-storied house that lay at the end of a parterre of flowers. Certainly, from its appearance, I should never have guessed it to be the residence of an heir to the Persian throne, yet so it proved. In the narrow entrance were two flights of stairs, one of which led to the reception-rooms of the Viceroy, the other to the apartments of his Queen ; and Dr. Casolani was led up the first, while some female slaves attended me to the latter. At the top of the stairs I pulled off my shoes, and entered a pleasant little room, the side walls of which were entirely composed of lofty windows. The Vice-queen, a young lady of fifteen, was seated in a simple arm-chair, and one of the same kind was placed opposite to her for me, whilst not far from the princess stood a matron whom I took for the duenna of the harem.

I was so fortunate as to meet with a particularly favourable reception, for Dr. Casolani had not only introduced me as an authoress, but mentioned that I was going to publish an account of my travels. The princess inquired whether I would mention her; and as I replied in the affirmative, she determined to show herself to me in all her finery—she said, to give me an idea of the rich costume of her native country.

The youthful princess wore trowsers of silk so rich and heavy, and made so full, that they seemed as if they could have stood quite alone. I am told they are often not less than twenty or five-and-twenty ells in width. Over these was worn a jacket fitting closely to the figure, and elaborately and tastefully embroidered in gold. Under this was a chemise of white silk; on her head a white crape handkerchief, worked in coloured silk and gold, falling down on the shoulders, and fastened under the chin; and the whole dress, as well as the arms and hands, was richly ornamented with jewels of great size and beauty, but which lost much of their effect from being merely strung on a gold wire, instead of being properly set. The wearer could not be called positively handsome, but she had large fine eyes, a pretty figure,—and only fifteen years. Her face was painted red and white, and she had the usual blue stripe over eyebrows and eyelashes, which to me did not appear at all a beautifier.

Our conversation was carried on in dumb show, for Dr. Casolani, who speaks Persian very well, was not admitted to-day, as the princess was in gala dress and unveiled. I found some amusement in looking at the prospect from the windows, which commanded a fine view of the town; and here first I perceived how extensive it is, and how many gardens it possesses. They are, it is true, its only decoration, for it has no fine buildings to show, and the valley in which it lies, as well as the surrounding mountains, is naked, treeless, and destitute of any attraction. I expressed to the Vice-queen my surprise at the extent of the town, and the beauty of its gardens, and she seemed much pleased. Towards the end of my audience fruits and sweetmeats were brought upon large plates, but for me only, on account of the fast.

I was afterwards taken to be presented to the Viceroy, who was only two years older than his Queen; and to the name of authoress, which the Doctor had bestowed on me, I was again indebted for the honour of an arm-chair. The largest of these saloons was wainscotted, and had looking-glasses in gilt frames and several paintings of heads and flowers. In the midst of this apartment stood—two great empty bedsteads! The prince was dressed in the European style, with a blue coat,—the collar, cuffs, and edges richly embroidered in gold,—and white silk stockings and gloves ; but on his head he wore the Persian fur cap, very nearly a yard in height. This, I was told, was not his common costume ; but it would be difficult to say what that is, as he changes his fashions oftener than his wife, and appears sometimes in the Persian cos- tume, and sometimes entirely enveloped in Cashmere shawls. I should have taken his highness for several years older than he really was, for his complexion had a pale, yellowish, sickly cast, and his glance is not open ; on the contrary, he seems never to look any one in the face, and from the whole expression of his physiognomy I could not help pitying all who should be subject to his authority.

He put several questions to me, which were interpreted by Dr. Casolani, who stood a few paces off ; but none of them shewed any intelligence, they were merely common-places about my travels. The Viceroy can read and write only his mother tongue, but he takes some European papers and periodicals, from which his inter- preters have to make extracts. At the accounts of the recent revolutions in Europe, he is said to have declared that the Euro- pean sovereigns must be good, but extraordinarily stupid, to allow themselves to be driven so easily from their thrones. If they had set to work vigorously, strangling and beheading, things would have turned out better. In the application of these remedies he is said to be far more energetic than his father, and unfortunately he has not even the advantage of a minister of the character of Haggi Mirza to control him. His government is quite that of a child. He orders a thing one minute, and countermands it the next. But what can be expected from a boy who has had very little education, who has been married at seventeen, and placed as the unlimited ruler of a large province, with an income of a million of tomans, and to whom every means and temptation to sensual indulgence is at command.

The prince has at present only one lawful wife, though he is entitled to four ; but he finds no deficiency of fair friends, who supply their places. In Persia it is the custom, if the king or the heir to the throne hears of any of his subjects having a beautiful daughter or sister, for him to desire the girl to be sent to him; and the parents and relations are delighted at the honour, for even if the royal lover grows tired of her after a little while, she is provided for, as he makes a present of her to his minister or some other rich man; but should she have a child, she is regarded as a lawful wife, and remains at court. On the other hand, it sometimes happens that when the damsel is presented she does not find favour in the eyes of the monarch, but is sent back again,—a terrible misfortune, for her reputation for beauty is damaged, and her market injured accordingly.

The Vice-queen, young as she is, is already a mother, but unfortunately only of a girl, and if any other wife should produce a boy she will take her place, become Vice-queen in her stead, and be honoured as the mother of the heir to the throne. One consequence of this custom is, that the poor infants are continually exposed to be poisoned or murdered in some way, for the envy of all the childless women is immediately awakened towards a mother, more especially if her child is a boy. When the princess followed her husband to Tabreez, she left her infant daughter to the care of its grandfather the Shah, in order to secure it from her rivals. When the wives of the prince go out, not only are they closely veiled and surrounded by eunuchs, but several others hasten onward and announce their coming, when all men must leave the street through which they are to pass, and fly into the houses or bye lanes.

When the wives of Behmen Mirza, who had been left behind, heard from Dr. Casolani of my intention of going to Taflis, they begged me to come to them; and as their husband had not been among the most fanatical on this point, Dr. Casolani, as his friend and physician, was allowed to accompany me, and remain in the room, though the ladies wrapped themselves up very much in consequence.

Most of these women looked much older than they really were; one who was only two-and-twenty looked at least thirty. They presented to me the latest addition to the harem,— a plump, brown, little beauty of sixteen; and they seemed to treat their new rival with great good nature, and told me how much trouble they had been taking to teach her Persian.

Among the children there was a beautiful little creature of six years old, whose face was not yet disfigured by white and red paint. I perceived on this occasion, what I had before been told, that the Persian costume is not particularly modest; for at every rather quick movement the jacket flies back, and the silk chemise is displaced, so that the whole form down to the waist is displayed. I noticed this also with the female attendants when they were preparing the tea, or performing any other service. Some part of the dress was every moment opening.

Another more interesting visit that I paid was to Haggi-Chefa-Hanoom, one of the most distinguished and cultivated women in the city. At the very entrance into the house there were signs of the presence of a superior spirit in its greater cleanliness and taste. My visit had been expected, and I found quite a large party of women and girls drawn together by curiosity to see a European woman. Many of them were very handsome, though, like the Vice-queen, they had too high cheek bones. The greatest beauty of the Persian women is their eyes.

As compared with the women in most Oriental houses, I was told this might be considered as quite an educated and refined society; and I conversed with the lady of the house, in the French language, through the medium of her son, a lad of eighteen, who had received what was thought a liberal education in Constantinople ; and even the girls, Dr. Casolani assured me, could all read and write. In this respect the Persians are greatly in advance of the Turks.

The mistress, her son, and myself, were seated upon chairs, the rest crouched upon the carpet. But here, for the first time in a Persian house, I saw a table. It was covered with a beautiful cloth, and loaded with fruits, sweatmeats, and sherbet, the latter prepared by the lady herself. The peaches and melons were so magnificent as to shew that Persia is their native country. The latter were, if possible, sweeter than sugar itself, and fit to eat almost to the outermost skin.

Before I leave Tabreez I must say a few words about the common people. Their colour is browner than can, I think, be accounted for by the mere effect of the sun, though among the higher classes the white skin is common with both sexes. They have black eyes and hair, and features strongly marked, especially the nose, and with a somewhat fierce aspect. The women of the poorer classes do not seem to be severely treated ; I saw very few at work in the fields, and I observed that in the towns all the hard work is done by men.

In Tabreez, as in Persia in general, the Sunnite Mahomedans, the Christians, and the Jews, are equally hated. Only three months before my visit, the two latter had been exposed to great danger. A tumultuous mob assembled, and traversing the quarter of the town where they live, plundered and destroyed the houses, threatened the inhabitants with death, and in some instances fulfilled the threat. Fortunately the governor was informed of these terrible scenes, and, being a bold determined man, rushed out at once into the thickest of the mob, and with a brief energetic speech induced them to disperse.

From the intelligence which I received while I was at Tabreez, I had at first very little hope that I should be allowed to continue my journey, as I had intended, across Natchivan and Erivan, to Tiflis; for since the late political occurrences in Europe, the Russian government has excluded strangers from its territory as jealously as the Chinese could do. Mr. Stevens promised, nevertheless, that he would use his influence with the Russian consul; and to this powerful intercession, as well as to my sex and age, I owed the consent to make an exception in my favour. I received from the Consul also several good letters of introduction to Erivan, Natchivan, and Tiflis. I was advised to take post horses and a servant as far as Natchivan (155 wersts); and several gentlemen, whose acquaintance I had made in Tabreez, accompanied me the first few miles. Before we parted we took a luncheon together on the banks of a beautiful rivulet, and then I went on my way in good heart, for now I thought I was entering a Christian country, beneath the sceptre of a civilized, European, law and order loving monarch.

ASIATIC RUSSIA.—Armenia, Georgia, and Mingrelia.

Sophia Marand.—The Russian Frontier.—Natchivan.—Caravan Journey.— A night in Prison.—Continuation of the Journey.—Erivan.—The Russian Post.—The Tartars.—Arrival in Tiflis.—Residence there.—Kutais Marand.—Voyage on the Rione.—Redout-Kale.

THE stations between Tabreez and Natchivan are very unequal; but one of the longest is the first, to a village called Sophia, for which we took six hours.   The road led mostly through barren and uncultivated vallies.

Since it was three o'clock when we arrived the people did not wish to let me go on further.   They pointed to the sun, to signify that it was late, and performed a good deal of expressive pantomime to intimate that I should be plundered and probably murdered. But representations of this kind never have much effect on me ; and after I had, with much trouble, made out that it was only four hours journey to the next station, I ordered my servant, to his great vexation, to saddle fresh horses for the continuation of our journey.   Immediately on leaving Sophia we entered a narrow wild valley, which my guide declared to be very dangerous ; and perhaps it might not have been quite safe to go through it in the night, but just now the sun was shining in full splendour, and I urged on my horse, and enjoyed the sight of the magnificent colouring and grouping of the rocks.   Many gleamed with a pale grass green, others were covered with a semi-transparent white substance, and many terminated in crags and peaks of such wildly fantastic forms that they looked at a distance like groups of stately trees.   There was so much to see, in short, that I had no time to think of fear.

About half way to Marand we came to a pretty village, and after this again had to climb a steep mountain, from whose summit I obtained such a glimpse into a grand mountain world, as kept me long rivetted to the spot.   We did not reach Marand till eight o'clock, but we brought in our luggage, to say nothing of our necks, perfectly safe and sound.

This is the last Persian town that I saw, and it is an extremely pleasant and pretty place.   It has broad clean streets, houses and gardens well kept, and several little squares with springs encircled by trees.   I cannot bestow quite such unqualified praise on my quarters, for I had to pass the night in the court-yard with the post horses ; and my evening meal consisted only of roasted eggs, burnt, and quite spoiled with excessive salting.   To-day we had but one stage, to Arax the Russian frontier town, but it was a stage of eleven hours long.   We followed the course of a brook that wound through valley and ravine.   No village met our eyes, and, except some little mills and the ruins of a mosque, I saw no building more in the Persian dominions.   It is a country which, from the scarcity of water, is very thinly peopled ; no country in

the world has fewer rivers or more mountains, and for that reason
the air is very dry and hot.

The valley in which Arax lies is large, and very picturesque
from the remarkable form of the rocks.   Far in the background
rise lofty mountains, amongst which is the Ararat, towering to a
height of 16,000 feet ; and in the valley itself walls and towers
and peaks, of which the chief is the so-called Serpent Mountain.
Near its foot flows the river Aras or Araxes, separating Armenia
from Media, and forming the limit between the Persian and
Russian frontiers.   We crossed the river in a boat, and on the
opposite bank we were detained to prove that we were not
robbers or murderers, or, what is worse, politically *dangerous*
persons.   Besides this, if it is supposed that the plague or the
cholera is to be found anywhere in Persia, you have to be shut
up to perform quarantine.

I had scarcely set my foot upon Russian ground before the
shameful begging for *drink money* began.   A fellow was sent to
me by the officer at the station to ask my wishes (the letter from
the Consul procured me this civility) ; and though he had pretended he spoke German, he knew in reality as much of it as I
of Chinese,—at the utmost three or four words.   I consequently
had to decline his services, but he nevertheless stretched out his
hand for money all the same.

Natchivan lies in a large valley among the mountains of the
Ararat, which, though not unfertile, is, like most of the country,
very bare of trees.   In no place in the world have I ever had so
much trouble to find a shelter.   I had brought with me two
letters, one to a German physician, and the other to the governor ;
but I did not wish to present myself to the latter in my travelling
dress (for I was now in a civilised country, where of course
people are judged of by their clothes), and therefore, as there was
no such thing as a hotel, I thought I would beg the hospitality
of the doctor.

His address had been written for me in the language of the
country, and I thought it would be easy to find him ; but every
one I showed it to, shook his head, and bade me inquire further.
By this time we had reached the custom-house, and my trifling
luggage had to be examined by the inspector, who ordered me
into a room, whither to my surprise, for I supposed it to be out
of civility, the inspector's wife and sister accompanied me.   I

soon found, however, that the ladies had another motive than civility. They sent for chairs, seated themselves before my trunk, and I had scarcely opened it before *six* hands were rummaging in it,—those of the two ladies and the inspector. About a dozen folded papers, containing coins, dried flowers, and other articles from Babylon and Nineveh, were immediately snatched up and scattered about. Every cap, every ribbon, was pulled out; and it was very evident that it cost the lady inspectress a struggle to let the ribbons again out of her grasp. I really thought that now, for the first time, I was in the hands of savages.

When the trunk had been sufficiently scrutinised, the turn came for a small box, which contained my greatest treasure, a head in relief that I had brought from Nineveh. The inspector snatched up a hatchet in order to break open the lid, but that was more than I could bear. I flung myself upon it, and just at that moment came in a third woman, who proved to be a German. I explained to her that I had no intention of refusing to open it; but that it must be cautiously done with proper tools; but, behold, at the custom-house, where daily similar cases occur, there were no tools for the purpose but the hatchet; and the utmost I could obtain was, that they should break the cover as carefully as possible into three pieces. Notwithstanding my anger, I could not help laughing at the foolish faces of the inspector and the two ladies when they saw that the box contained nothing but some fragments of brick, and a rather damaged head. They could not at all understand how any one could be at the trouble of carrying such things.

My countrywoman, Mrs. Henriette Alexandwer, invited me to take a cup of coffee with her, and when she heard of my embarassment with respect to a lodging, politely invited me to take up my abode with her. But on the following day, when I paid my visit to the Governor, he overwhelmed me with attention, and insisted on my moving to his house. He put my passport in order, provided it with the due amount of *visés*, of which it seemed, short as was the time which I had yet spent in this civilised dominion,—half a dozen at least were required,—and then arranged for my further progress with a Tatar, whose caravan was going to Tiflis.

I viewed the half decayed little town, and what is called the tomb of Noah, in company with Mrs. Alexandwer. According to Persian report, this Natchivan was once one of the largest and handsomest towns of Armenia, and its founder, moreover, was no less remarkable a person than Noah. It is built mostly in the oriental style, but here and there are houses with their windows turned towards the street. The costumes also present the same mixture of styles; for the people wear the Persian dress, while the authorities are dressed as Europeans. Noah's tomb is merely a small vaulted chamber, without a cupola. It seems as if there had once been one; but there are so few ruins lying round, that it is impossible to tell with certainty. In the interior is neither a sarcophagus, nor any other appearance of a grave, nothing but a stone column in the middle which supports the roof. The whole is surrounded with a low wall, and many pilgrims, both Christian and Mahomedan, come here. They seem all to have a singular superstition connected with it, namely, that if they press a pebble on the wall, and think of something at the time, or form a wish, the wish will be fulfilled, or the thought prove true, if the pebble remains sticking where they placed it, which sometimes happens, as the cement is mostly damp.

Not far from this tomb is another very handsome monument, though I could not make out of whom, which is covered inside with mathematical figures, and has two half decayed towers like minarets at the entrance.

When the evening came, on which I was to set off again, I was excessively unwell. For several days I had not been able to eat anything, and I was now lying on a sofa, extremely weak; but I got up when the time came, and managed to mount my horse, as I thought perhaps change of air might be the best restorative.

The caravan was carrying only goods, and the guides were Tatars. The distance to Tiflis is two hundred and fifty miles, which would take, I was told, twelve or fourteen days; but to judge by the rate at which we commenced our journey, it seemed likely to last six weeks; for in the first night we went only three miles, and in the second little more than twelve. I could have walked on foot faster.

The next day it was almost worse. The whole day long we lay on a stubble field, exposed to the burning rays of the sun. It was not till the evening at eight o'clock that we started, and then halted again at one. The only good thing about the caravan was that we got better food than before, for the Tatars do not live so frugally as the Arabs. Every evening a magnificent pilau was prepared, which was enriched with plums or dried raisins ; and almost every day splendid water-melons were brought us for sale, and a nice piece was always offered to me as a present.

The road led along the foot of Mount Ararat, through large fertile vallies. The mighty mountain rose so clear and vast in its proportions that it appeared not more than eight or ten miles off ; and from its superior size it seems to stand alone, though it is, in fact, connected with the Taurus by ranges of hills. Its highest summit is cleft, so that between the two peaks there is a small plot or hollow space ; and here it was, according to tradition, that the ark rested ; indeed, there are many people here who maintain that if the snow were scraped away, it would be found there still ; and below, where now stands the convent of Arakilvank, is the very spot where Noah built his first house.

After several days travelling we still remained in the neighbourhood of Ararat, passing, however, several Russian and German colonies, but along a very rugged and stony road. Near Sidin a very disagreeable adventure befel me. The caravan had encamped close to the high road, and about eight o'clock in the evening I trotted out upon it for a walk, and was just about to return when I heard the sound of the bells of post horses. I stood still to hear who the travellers were, and soon saw a Cossack with a musket, and a gentleman seated beside him on an open car. As soon as they had passed, to my great surprize, the car suddenly drew up, and almost at the same moment I felt myself seized by two powerful arms. It was the Cossack who was dragging me to the car. I struggled to get loose ; pointed with my free hand to the caravan, and screamed that I belonged to it. But the fellow immediately placed one hand over my mouth, and flung me upon the car, where the *gentleman* held me fast. The Cossack then sprung up, and the driver received the order to go on as fast as the horses could gallop. This all passed so quickly that I scarcely knew what had happened. The men, however, held me with a strong grasp, and my mouth was not uncovered till we were so far from the caravan that my cries could not be heard.

I did not, fortunately, feel much afraid, for it immediately occurred to me that these two amiable Russians must, in their zeal, have taken me for some dangerous person, and imagined they had made an important capture. As soon as they allowed me to speak, they commenced a long list of questions, concerning my name, country, and so forth; and I understood Russian enough to answer them, but they were not satisfied, and required to see my passport. I told them to send for my trunk, and I should then be able to give them full satisfaction; but when we came to the post-house, they placed me in a room as a prisoner, and the Cossack mounted guard over me with his musket on his shoulder, keeping his eye constantly upon me. The gentleman also, whom by his green velvet collar and cuffs, I took for an imperial officer, remained some time in the room. In half an hour, the post-master, or whatever he might be, came to take a view of me, and hear the heroic exploit of my capture narrated.

I had to pass the night, under strict superintendence, on the wooden bench, without either blanket or cloak to cover me, and without food or drink ; and if I only attempted to rise up from the bench, and walk a little up and down the room, the Cossack ordered me back, and desired me to remain quiet.

Towards morning my effects were brought. I showed my papers, and was set at liberty ; but instead of making any apology my captors laughed in my face, and when I came out into the court-yard all the people pointed their fingers at me, and joined in chorus.

Oh you good Arabs, Turks, Persians, Hindoos! How safely did I pass through your heathen and infidel countries ; and here, in Christian Russia, how much have I had to suffer in this short space.

By the time I reached Erivan I had fully made up my mind to leave the caravan with the first opportunity, for it never travelled more than four hours a day ; and I thought, as I had some letters to the town physician (a Dr. Muller) and to the governor, I might be able by their assistance to find means of getter rather more quickly to Tiflis, and I was not disappointed.

Erivan, which lies on the river Zenqui, is the capital of Armenia or Trans-Caucasia, and, according to tradition, was of all the earth the spot first peopled after the deluge. It lies in a large plain encircled by mountains, as well as by some fortifications. Here begins the completely European style of building, but the town is neither handsome nor clean. The bazaar I found very amusing, not that the goods I saw there were handsome, but that there were so many costumes of nations to me entirely unknown, Circassians, Georgians, Mingrelians, Turcomans, &c.,—and the wearers were fine handsome looking men, with noble expressive features. The costume of the Tatars was extremely like that of the common Persians, except that they wore lower caps, and had pointed toes to their boots, often as much as four inches long. Of the female sex of all these races little is to be seen in the street, as they are much wrapped up, but at least they do not veil their faces. The Russians and Cossacks have coarse Calmuck features, and their behaviour shows that their features do them no injustice. I have nowhere else met with people so rude, covetous, and servile in disposition.

I was strongly advised not to travel with the Russian post, since, as a solitary woman, I should have infinite trouble with the noble-minded official personages whom I should have to deal with ; but I was resolved nevertheless to take my chance, and begged Dr. Muller to see to whatever was necessary for me.

In order to obtain permission to travel in this pleasant Russian empire, I found it was necessary to take no less than six walks,—first to the treasurer, then to the police, then to the commandant, then again to the police, then again to the treasurer, and lastly, once more to the police.

In the *padroshne* (permit) that you receive, it must be exactly stated how many miles you mean to travel, and the postmaster must not allow you to go a single werst further. For every horse you must pay half a copek the werst, which seems at first little enough, but when you consider that a werst is only half a mile, and that you always travel with three horses, it amounts at last to a considerable tax.

It had been arranged that the horses were to be at the door at four in the morning, but the clock struck six, and nothing was to be seen of them. Dr. Muller was so good as to go himself to look after them, and so at last I started at seven, a pleasant foretaste of the punctuality I was to expect. We drove fast enough, but whoever has not a well-stuffed spring carriage, or a body of cast iron, would prefer often on these rough roads to go a little more gently.

The post-chaise, for which you pay ten copeks a station, is nothing more than a very short uncovered wooden car on four wheels ; and instead of a seat some hay is put in the bottom, and a

small box, on which the postilion sits. Of course these machines
jolt horribly; and the bells, hung to a wooden arch over the neck
of the middle horse (they are harnessed three abreast), keep up
a constant abominable jingling. These with the creaking of the
car, the screaming of the driver to his horses, make so much noise
that when, as has sometimes happened, the traveller has been
flung out on the road by the violent motion of the car, the driver
has gone on, and never missed him till he arrived at the station.

Between the second and third stage of my journey, I came to a
short tract, on which I found a kind of lava which perfectly resembled the fine shining glassy lava of Iceland called obsidian,
which, it has been supposed, could be found nowhere else.

August 27th.—To-day, I had again some experience of the pleasures of travelling in Russia. I had in the evening ordered and
paid for everything that I should want on the following morning,
yet when the morning came I had to go myself to awaken the
postmaster, to find the driver, and, in short, run about after every
one of the people wanted. At the third stage, I had to wait four
hours for the horses, and at the fourth they would give me none
at all, and I was obliged to stop the night, although in the whole
previous day I had gone only twenty-seven miles.

August 28th.—Perpetual torment with the post people. I am in
general a great enemy to harshness and severity ; but to these
fellows I really would rather have spoken with the stick ; their
rudeness, stupidity, and want of feeling really exceed belief. You
find officers and men lying asleep and drunk at every hour of the
day, and if you succeed in raising them they will perhaps only
laugh in your face, instead of helping you. It is not till after
endless scolding and disputing that you can induce one to get out
a car, another to grease the wheels, and a third to feed the horse,
which besides often has to be shod ; then, perhaps, the harness is
not in order, and has to be patched and mended, and over all these
operations as much time is lost as possible. When I expressed in
the cities my surprize at the miserably defective arrangements of
these post stations, I was told it was because these countries had
been so short a time under the Imperial sceptre,—because the
Imperial city was so far off,—and, moreover, as a single woman
travelling without a servant, I might think myself well off to have
been served no worse.

I could only answer that in countries belonging to the English, which lay much further away from their capital than these did from St. Petersburgh, I had found the arrangements excellent, and that there it was supposed that a woman who paid for attendance had as much claim to it as a man, or even an official gentleman.

Now, in Russia, the moment an official personage of any sort makes his appearance every one flies at his bidding, and all vie with one another who shall most humbly bow before him; for this is the privileged caste ; and though, according to law, those who are not travelling on official business have no rights beyond those of other travellers, they who should be the first to show an example of respect for the law, pay not the smallest attention to it. They send a servant, perhaps to mention that on this or that day they will require ten or twelve horses ; should anything induce them to delay their journey,—a dinner, a hunting-party, or a headache of the lady,—they simply put off the journey for a day or two, and desire the horses to be kept till they are wanted ; and, in the meantime, any private travellers arriving at the station must await their pleasure. It may easily happen, therefore, with all these hindrances, that though the Russian rate of travelling is very rapid when you do get into motion, you do not, on the whole, get on faster than in a caravan. Many a time, in the course of my journey through Russia, I have not been able to do more than a single stage in a whole long day ; and every time I saw a uniform it threw me into a fright, lest I should not be able to get any horses.

Waiting at the post stations is of course extremely disagreeable. There is a room for you to wait in, and a Cossack and his wife, who are supposed to wait upon you ; but it is often hard to get for your money either civil treatment or food,—eggs, milk, or whatever it may be that you require. With all its dangers I greatly prefer travelling in Persia.

Among the interesting incidents of this part of my travels I must count the meeting several migrating hordes of Tatars. They were seated on oxen and horses, and had their tents and household utensils packed up ; the cows and sheep, of which there were always great numbers, were driven near them. The dresses of the Tatar women were often rich, though ragged,—crimson silk, sometimes embroidered in gold, wide trousers, a long caftan, with a short one over it, and on their heads something that looked like a bee-hive, and which is made from the bark of a tree, but covered

with red silk, and oramented with corals, coins, and metal plates;
and their dresses also, down to the waist, exhibit a profusion of
buttons, bells, rings, and amulets. They had large shawls wrapped
round them, but their faces were uncovered. Amongst their
household goods I saw handsome carpets, vessels of copper, iron
kettles, and so forth.

The villages of the settled Tatars have a most singular appearance ; they lie mostly on the declivities of hills, in which
chambers are hollowed out, with no other light than from the
entrance ; and this is protected by projecting eaves of planks supported on trunks of trees. You see neither walls, windows, nor
doors, nothing in fact but these penthouse roofs. Those who
have their abode in plains build huts of stone or wood, and cover
them over with earth, so that they look like large molehills.

August 29*th.*—To-day I had a variety in my Russian travelling
pleasures. It had been raining all night, and rained still, and the
wheels of the car flung up such a mass of mud, that I sat in a
thick puddle, and found my head and even my face crusted over.
Some small boards fastened above the wheels would easily have
prevented this annoyance ; but who in this country troubles himself about the comfort of a private traveller ?

We came in sight of Tiflis during the latter half of this day,
and I was much struck by its European aspect, as I had seen no
city in this style since Valparaiso. It is in the capital of Georgia,
and counts about 50,000 inhabitants. Many of the houses are
built on hills, or even on high steep rocks, and from these you get
a magnificent prospect over city and valley. The latter, however,
had not, at the time of my arrival, a very attractive appearance, as
the harvest had robbed it of all colour, and it is not rich in
gardens and groves ; but the river Kurry (mostly called Cyrus)
meanders beautifully through it, and far in the distance glitter
the snow crowned peaks of the Courasus.

In the interior of the city, the old houses are everywhere being
pulled down to make way for new ; and the Greek and Armenian
houses will soon be the only memorials of the oriental style of
building. The churches are far behind the other edifices in size
and grandeur ; the towers are low, and mostly covered with green
glazed tiles. The oldest Christian church stands on a rock within
the fortress, at the entrance of the town, and it is only used as a
prison. The town possesses many warm sulphureous springs,

which is partly indicated by its name, since *Tiflis* or *Ibilissi* signify *warm town;* but of the numerous baths there are scarcely any that are not in a bad condition. The buildings containing the springs are small domes covered with windows, and the basins, floors, and walls are of stone. Marble is very scarce.

Not far from the baths you find the Botanic Garden, which has been formed, at great expense, on the side of a mountain on a series of terraces which have to be supported by masonry.

Why a place so unsuitable has been chosen I could not make out, especially as there are few rare plants, and indeed little else than vines. The most remakable things in the garden were two vines, one of which has a stem a foot in diameter; they are carried to an immense distance, and walks and arbours formed out of them. From these two only, more than eighty dozens of wine are obtained every year. On one of the uppermost terraces of this garden a very spacious lofty grotto has been cut in the rock, in which, in the summer evenings, there is music and dancing, and even sometimes dramatic performances. On Sundays and holidays the governor's garden is opened to the public, and there you find swings and running at the ring, and two bands of music; but the performance of these Russian musicians I found still more intolerable than that of the blacks in Rio de Janeiro.

I entered an Armenian church, and there saw the dead body of a young man, lying in a rich open coffin, lined with crimson velvet, and trimmed with gold lace. The body was adorned with a sort of crown, scattered over with flowers, and covered with fine white gauze, and priests in magnificent robes were performing the ceremony, which was very like that of the Catholics.

The poor mother, at whose side I accidentally knelt down, sobbed aloud, as they prepared to carry away the dear remains. and I too could not refrain from shedding tears, not for the death of the youth, but for the deep sorrow of the afflicted mother.

Leaving this place of mourning I went to visit some Greek and Armenian families. The ladies were in simple Greek dresses, and the rooms, though spacious, were almost destitute of furniture. There were only painted wooden chests running along the walls, and partly covered with carpets; on these they sit, eat, and sleep. In the streets the mixture of European and Asiatic costumes is so common that neither the one nor the other attract the least attention. The newest to me was that of the Circassians.

It consists of wide trousers, and over this a very full garment fastened by a girdle, worn by the wealthy of dark blue cloth, trimmed with gold or silver lace, and in the breast pockets of these are carried from six to ten cartridges.   The Circassians are, as is well known, celebrated for beauty, though I have myself seen far more striking beauties among the Persians.

I have not much to tell concerning the domestic life of the Russian government officers here, for though I had letters to two of them it did not appear to me that I found favour in the sight of either of these gentlemen ; probably on account of my expressions concerning the last regulation of the post-stations, the wretched roads, and my own capture and imprisonment, which I told with the addition of a few marginal notes.   What was worse, I said, it had been my intention to cross the Caucasus, and go by Moscow to St. Petersburg, but after what I had seen of the Russian dominions I should certainly take the shortest way, and get out of them as soon as possible.

Probably, had I been a man speaking thus, I should have paid for my boldness with a short excursion to Siberia.   As it was, they only teased me about my passport, for which I had to apply again and again, and at last did not get it, till the sixth day ; and yet I had letters to the chief officers.   How the poor travellers get on who do not enjoy this advantage I know not.

One of my most agreeable visits was that to the Persian prince Behmen-Mirza, to whom I had letters and news of the family he had left behind him at Tebris; although he was very ill at the time, and received me in a great hall which looked like an hospital, for there, on carpets and cushions, lay *eight* sick people— the prince, four of his children,and three of his wives— who were all ill of fever.

The prince is a remarkably handsome, powerful looking man of about five and thirty, and his open eye is full of intelligence and goodness.   He spoke with deep melancholy of his country, and a mournful smile played over his features as I mentioned his lovely children (it would have been contrary to Mussulman etiquette to have mentioned the wives), and told how well and safely I had travelled through the provinces which had been under his government.   How fortunate would it be for Persia if this man should come to the throne instead of the young Viceroy.

The most interesting, and at the same time most useful,

acquaintance that I made was that of a countryman of my own, a Mr. Salzmann, of whom every one speaks with the highest honour. He has a beautiful house, fitted up with every possible convenience, where he receives travellers, especially his own country people, with the most hospitable kindness ; and he has also, five miles from the town, a large fruit garden, near which are some naptha springs that I went to see. The naptha is drawn in wooden tubs out of a deep square pit, but it is of the commonest kind, of a dark brown colour, and thicker than oil. From this is made asphalt, cart grease, and so forth ; but the fine white naptha, which can be used for light and fire, is got from the neighbourhood of the Caspian Sea.

Mr. Salzmann offered to accompany me on an excursion to the German colonies which lie around Tiflis, but from the accounts I had heard of the sad degeneracy of the Germans who have emi-grated to Russia—of their idleness, drunkenness, uncleanliness, and dishonesty—I felt little wish to visit them.

On leaving Tiflis, I noticed just outside the town a pedestal of polished granite, surrounded by an iron railing, and on which stands a metal cross with an " Eye of God," and an inscription, stating that on the 12th of October 1837, his Imperial Majesty was here upset, but that he had escaped unhurt, and that this monument was placed there by his most grateful subjects. It is to be recollected, that this monument could not have been placed there without the express permission of the illustrious personage himself.

I made this day but one stage, but it was so long a one that it took me till the evening, and going on was out of the question, as it is not safe to travel in the night without an escort of Cossacks, of which there is for this purpose a small division kept at each station. The country was not unpicturesque ; there were pleasant valleys and hills, on whose summits stood ruins of castles and for-tresses ; for here, as in the German empire, there was a time when every noble might make war upon the other, and lived in a strong dwelling within which his vassals could take refuge in case of hostile attack. It is said there are still people who wear shirts of mail and iron helmets, but I never saw any of them.

As we went on to the small town of Gory the scenery became more wildly romantic, hill and valley was covered with wood, and in the town itself an eminence crowned with a citadel rises abruptly from the very midst of the mass of houses. In clear weather the Caucasus, which like a triple chain is drawn across between the Black Sea and the Caspian as the limit between Europe and Asia, is constantly in sight. Their highest points, from the recent estimates, are 16,800 and 14,400 feet. They were now covered far down with snow.

September 7th.—To-day I made but one stage, as far as Suram. They could not allow me to go on further, as an officer, with his lady and her companion, &c. were returning from a bathing place, and would require twelve horses. In order to drive away my ill-humour a little I took a walk to an old castle that lay mostly in ruins, but where you could still see, from the numerous walls and spacious vaulted apartments, that the knights who had their abode there must have lived in rather grand style. On my return home through the fields I was much struck by the teams used for ploughing. The ground was a beautiful plain, and almost without a stone, and yet there were twelve or fourteen oxen harnessed to a plough.

September 8th.—The mountains are now drawing closer together, and nature is becoming more and more luxuriant. All sorts of parasite plants,—wild hops, wild vines, twining from tree to tree,—enwreath them to their highest summits, while the under-wood grows so thick and rich that I am reminded of the forests of Brazil. The third stage led mostly along the banks of the river Mirabka, and the road between the river and the rocky wall is often so narrow that there is not room for a second carriage, and we had repeatedly to wait for ten or twenty minutes for the cars laden with wood to pass ; and that is called a post-road !

Georgia has been now fifty years under the Russian rule, and it is not till quite lately that there have been any roads made at all, or rather begun. Perhaps in another fifty years they may be finished, or, what is more likely, fallen again into decay. Another want, besides that of roads, is of bridges. The deep rivers are crossed in wretched boats, and the shallower you must walk through how you can. In rainy seasons, or after a thaw, when the snow has melted on the mountains, a traveller may have to wait for many days, or cross at the utmost hazard of his life. What a vast interval between the colonisation of Russia and of England !

Late in the evening, wet through, and covered with mud, I arrived at the station, which lies about a mile from Kutais ; for, among other inconveniences, it is to be mentioned that the post stations usually lie one or two wersts from the towns and villages, so that you cannot easily provide yourself from them with anything you may require.

Kutais has about 18,000 inhabitants, and lies in a natural park; all round it is verdure and luxuriant foliage. The houses are neat and pretty, and the green painted church steeples and barracks have a pleasant effect. The costumes of the people are just as various here as about Tiflis. What struck me most was the comical hats of the Mingrelian peasants, which are large, round, flat pieces of felt, tied with a string under the chin.

I had now only two stages to go to the village of Marand, on the river Ribon or Rione, for there you exchange the post car for a boat, which carries you to Redout-Kalé, on the Black Sea.

The first part of the way lay through beautiful woods; the second commands a free prospect over field and meadow, but the houses still lie hidden among trees and shrubs. We met many peasants, who, if they were but carrying a few eggs, fowls, &c. to the town, were on horseback. There was abundance of pasture, and, consequently, no want of horses or horned cattle.

There was no kind of inn at Marand, so that I had to alight at the house of a Cossack. These people, who live here as colonists, have pretty little wooden houses of two or three rooms, and a piece of land which they cultivate as field and garden. Some of them receive travellers, and know how to make high enough charge for the wretched accommodation that they offer. For a little dirty room without a bed I paid twenty silver copeks, and for a chicken the same sum. I got nothing more, for the people are too lazy to fetch anything, and if I had wanted bread, milk, or anything else, I should have had to go for it myself. At the utmost, they would take such trouble only for an officer or official person.

In the morning of the 11th of September the boat started for Redout-Kalé. It was bad weather, and the Rione, otherwise a beautiful river, cannot be navigated at night or in a gale of wind, on account of the many trunks of trees and other obstructions. The country was enchanting. The river flowed on between groves and fields of maize and millet, and the eye, wandering over hills and promontories, reverted at last to the grand peaks of the

distant Caucasus. Before and behind, on the right and the left,
according to the windings of the watery road, they appeared in all
their endless variety of form, dome, peak, horn, and table land.
We often stopped and landed, and then everybody hastened
towards the trees, to pluck the tempting grapes and figs; but the
grapes were sour as vinegar, and the figs small and hard. I found
only a single ripe one, and this I flung away as soon as I tasted it.
The fig-trees were of a size that I have never seen in Italy or in
Sicily, and it seems probable that the whole vigour of the plant
shoots into wood and leaves, and the same cause may act on the
grapes, for the vines are of immense height, though the grapes are
so small and poor. With cultivation much might be done with
them. We had to go out to sea, and be rocked about for a few
hours, in order to pass round from the main arm of the river into
the smaller branch on which Redout-Kalé is situated. There is,
indeed, a canal between them, but it is now so blocked with sand,
that it can only be passed when the water is unusually high.

In Redout-Kalé I had again to give myself over to the miseries
of a speculative Cossack, who keeps three rooms which he lets to
travellers. I was uncertain how long I might have to stay, as
I was to leave with one of the government steamers which go
twice a month from this town to Odessa, calling by the way at
eighteen forts and military stations. They take with them any
traveller who may wish to go without making any charge,
though he must content himself with a place on the deck, as the
cabins are kept for the military officers, who frequently go from
one station to another. No places are to be obtained by
payment.

I did not know when I might be summoned, as the steamer
when it comes, stays only two hours, so I hastened to get my passport put in order, and I certainly cannot complain of having got
nothing for my money, for instead of a simple *visé* I got a whole
page of writing, and of this copy after copy was taken, till I
thought there would never be an end of it. I packed my goods
ready, and scarcely ventured to have a dinner cooked, lest I should
be called away before I could eat it; yet, after all, I had five days
to wait.

From what I saw during this time of Redout-Kalé and Min-
grelia, it seems to me that the country, beautiful and luxuriant as
it is, is damp and unhealthy. It rains very frequently, and the

sun draws up heavy mists, that remain floating four or five feet from the ground; and these are said to be the cause of many diseases, especially of fever and dropsy. Besides the unhealthy influences to which they are unavoidably exposed, the people are unwise enough to build their huts and houses, not in open, airy, sunny places, but deep in the woods, and under a canopy of foliage. You may go through a village and scarcely see a house, so concealed are they by trees. The people look thin and sallow, and appear both stupid and indolent, and they very seldom, I was told, reach the age of sixty. For strangers the climate is still more injurious; and yet I cannot but believe that for industrious colonists, and good economists, the country would offer the finest opportunities. There is land enough to be had; for certainly three fourths of it is lying unemployed, and by clearing the woods and draining, the climate would lose much of its insalubrity. Its fertility is almost boundless, and would be, of course, greatly increased by judicious management. The finest grass grows everywhere in abundance, mingled with rich herbs; the fruit grows wild; the vines, as I have said, shoot up to the highest branches of the trees; and during the wet season the earth is so soft that only wooden ploughs are used. The wine is prepared by the inhabitants in the simplest manner. They hollow out the trunk of a tree, and in this tread out the grapes, and they then take the juice in earthenware vessels, and bury it in the earth. The Mingrelians bear generally a very bad character; they are said to be given to drunkenness, to disregard the ties of marriage, to be commonly thieves, and not unfrequently murderers; but of the truth of these allegations I can, of course, know little from personal experience. Of their idleness I can, however, speak with some confidence, for during the five days I stayed there I could not, either for money or good words, induce any one to get me either grapes or figs. I went daily to the bazaar, but never found one to sell, for the people are too lazy to go into the woods to gather them. They will do no manner of work until they are driven to it by dire necessity, and then they require immoderate payment. I had to give as much for eggs, milk, and bread as I should have done in my native city of Vienna.

Another thing that displeased me in the Mingrelians was the senseless multiplication of external religious ceremonies. You are required to cross yourself every moment for something or other;

on putting the first bit in your mouth at dinner, before you drink, before you put on or off any of your clothes, on going into another room ; in short, the only thing their hands find to do is the making everlastingly the sign of the cross. When they pass a church they will stand still and keep bowing and crossing as if they would never have done ; and if they are in a carriage they will stop it to go through the same performance. While I was at Redout-Kalé a ship was going to sea, and then the priest had to be fetched to bless, first the ship in general, and then every part in particular. In and out he went, and up and down, and creeping into every hole and corner, and at last he blessed the sailors, who laughed at him when his back was turned. I have always found that where there was most show of it there was least real religion.

EUROPEAN RUSSIA.

A Voyage on the Black Sea.—A Case of Cholera.—The suspected Vessel.— Kertsch.—The Museum.—Tumuli.—Continuation of the Journey.—The Castle of Prince Woronzow.—The Fortress of Sebastopol.—Odessa.

On the night of the 19th of September, amidst a violent storm of wind and rain, I found myself on the Black Sea, in the Russian government steamer. Although my place was on the deck, I begged permission, as the weather was so bad, to sit upon the cabin stairs, and it was with some shrugging of shoulders granted to me ; but after a few minutes there came an order from the commander to put me in a place of shelter. I was rather surprised at this politeness, but less so when I saw where I was to go to, for I was conducted into the great cabin, filled with sailors, who smelled so horribly of brandy, and in some instances too had been tasting it to such an extent that I was soon glad to go back to the deck and endure rather the fury of the elements than their company.

The next day the Caucasian mountains had disappeared, and the thick forests had given place to great open spaces ; but wind and storm and rain continued unabated. Fortunately for me, however, there was an Englishman on board, a Mr. Platts, the engineer of the steamer, who now presented himself to me, offered me the half of his cabin during the day, and then made interest for me with one of the officers, and got me a small one for myself, near that of the sailors, indeed, but separated from them by a door. I was very grateful to both for this kindness, and it was so much the more deserving of gratitude as I was a stranger, and there were at least half a dozen Russian officers for whom no accommodation had been found, and who had to encamp on the deck.

The next night was a dreadful one. One of the sailors, who had eaten his supper with a good appetite, appearing perfectly well, was suddenly attacked by the cholera. His cries and groans went to my heart, and I fled again to the deck to escape from them; but the violent rain and the piercing cold were scarcely more bearable. I had nothing but my cloak to protect me, and it was almost immediately wet through; my teeth chattered, the frost seemed to penetrate quite through me, and I had no resource but to return to the cabin, hold my ears closed, and pass the remainder of the night by the dying man. He died in the course of eight hours, notwithstanding all that could be done for him; and in the morning, when we stopped at Bschada, the body was wrapped in sailcloth and sent away, the cause of his death being kept carefully concealed from the rest of the passengers on board. The cabin was then well washed with vinegar, scoured, and no second case occurred. It was certainly not surprising that there should be illness on board, but I should have expected that it would have appeared among the poor soldiers, who lay day and night upon the deck, had no other food than dry black bread, and were not even provided with cloaks or covering. I saw many of them, dripping wet and half frozen, gnawing a piece of dry bread. In winter the sea is so rough that they are often for days together opposite a station without being able to reach it, and the voyage to Kertsch will last frequently twenty days. It is really wonderful if they reach the place of their destination alive, for on the Russian system there is nothing done for the comfort of the common soldier. The sailors are a little better off; they get at least brandy with their bread, and a little meat, and twice a day a sort of cabbage soup called bartsch.

The number of officers, with their wives and children, on the deck, increased at every station, and very few were landed. The deck was consequently soon so encumbered with household goods, as well as chests, trunks, or boxes of all kinds, that I could find no other place to sit down than on a pile of these effects. The ship was a complete camp.

In fine weather all this life and bustle was amusing, for every one looked cheerful and contented, and as if they all belonged to one family ; but when the rain came down, or a heavy sea washed over our deck, then there was crying and lamentation—"Oh ! my flour will be quite spoiled !" " Ah ! how can I protect my sugar ?" Here was a woman mourning for her spoiled bonnet, and there another for her husband's damaged uniform. At some of the stations we took up sick soldiers, to carry them to the hospital at Kertsch, not so much that they might be better taken care of as for the sake of security, as all the villages, from Redout-Kalé to Anapka, are liable to the incursions of the Circassians, who burst unexpectedly from the mountains and plunder and murder all in their way. Not very long ago they got a cannon, and fired upon a Russian steamer.

The poor sick men were laid upon the deck, and all the care that was taken of them was, that a sail was spread so as to shelter them from the wind on two sides ; but when it rained heavily, the water streamed in upon them from all quarters, so that they soon lay quite in the wet.

After passing Anapka the shore no longer presented the beautiful variety of wooded hills and mountains, but the dreary monotony of the steppe, but I was amused by an incident that occurred to-day. Our captain perceived a vessel lying quietly at anchor in a little bay, and immediately, stopping the steamer, sent out an officer to see what it was doing. ' This was not surprising, for in Russia they would like, if they could, to prohibit so much as a foreign fly from crossing the frontier ; but when the officer came up to the ship, he did not attempt to board, or require that papers should be shown to him ; he merely bawled to the captain to ask what he was doing there. The other answered that he had been detained by contrary winds, that he had been compelled to cast anchor, that when he got a wind he was going to so-and-so ; and with this answer the officer returned quite contented, which seemed to me much as if you were to stop a suspected person in the street, and ask him to tell you whether he really was an honest man or a rogue, accepting his own assurance as sufficient proof.

September 23d.—Another wet and stormy night ! How I pitied the poor sick, and even the healthy, who were on deck exposed to this weather ! Towards noon we reached Kertsch.

The town lies in a semicircle on the shore, and looks very well from the sea. Behind it rises the Hill of Mithridates, and on it, higher than the town, lies the museum, in the style of a Greek temple, with columns all round. The summit of the hill terminates in beautiful rocky peaks, amidst which lie obelisks and monuments belonging to an ancient cemetery. Around the town the steppe is covered with *tumuli*, which contain memorials of bygone ages. The town of Kertsch is now considered the capital of the government of Tauria, and has a population of 12,000, a secure harbour, and a tolerably important trade. The streets are broad, and furnished with side pavements for foot passengers; and on the two squares there is a great deal of lively bustle on Sundays and holidays, as a market is then held of all possible articles, but chiefly eatables. But the rudeness and coarseness of the common people was very striking to me; I heard nothing but screaming, scolding, and cursing.

The Mithridates Hill, the only public walk, is provided with stately flights of steps and abundance of winding paths. It is about 500 feet high, and must have served the ancients as a burying place, for wherever the upper soil has been washed away sarcophagi are discovered. From its summit the prospect is almost boundless, but very unattractive, for on three sides is nothing but the dreary, treeless steppe, whose monotony is only broken by the many grave hillocks before mentioned; on the fourth, indeed, is the sea, which always has its charms, and here so much the more as you see at the same time the Black Sea and the Sea of Asoph. There were, too, many ships in the roads, though by no means the five or six hundred that I had read of in newspapers.

On my return from visiting this hill I went to the Museum which consists of a single saloon, containing some interesting, antiquities from the tumuli ; but all that was most valuable has been sent to Petersburg. The statues, though damaged, indicate a high degree of art ; and one sarcophagus, in white marble, is covered with exquisite reliefs—especially a figure in the form of an angel, holding two garlands of fruits and flowers above his head. On the lid are two figures in a recumbent position, the heads of which are wanting ; but the bodies, the attitude and the draperies are all masterly. Another wooden sarcophagus shows great skill in the arts of wood carving and turning.

A collection of earthen pots, lamps, and vessels for water reminded me vividly of those I had seen in the Museum of Naples. The pots are burnt and painted in the same manner as those dug up from Herculaneum and Pompeii. The water pitchers have two handles, and are so pointed at the bottom that they cannot stand without being supported against something ; in Persia, pitchers of this form are still in use. There were some coarsely made gold ornaments, bracelets, rings, and crowns of wreaths of laurel leaves ; copper chains and kettles ; and ugly caricature faces in plaster of paris ; besides finely executed coins and ornaments that seemed to have been used for the outsides of houses. On some of the coins I saw remarkably beautiful impressions.

The tumuli are monuments of a very peculiar kind. They consist of passages sixty feet long, fourteen feet broad, and twenty-five feet high, and built with long thick slabs of stone, and with a very small chamber at the end, of a long shape, and the walls of which, like those of the passage, incline together towards the top. It appears that when the sarcophagus was deposited in its place the whole monument was covered with earth. The fine marble sarcophagus now in the British Museum was taken from a tomb near the Quarantine Building, and is considered to be that of King Bentik.

Most of the monuments have been already opened by the Turks, and the remainder by the Russians, and they have found many of the bodies with golden crowns and trinkets as well as coins.

September 26th was a great religious festival for the Russians; and the people brought bread, pastry, fruit, and so forth as offerings to the church, which were all laid up at first in a heap in a corner ; but after the service the priest blessed them, and then gave a few small fragments to the poor who surrounded him ; but the greater part he had packed up in baskets and sent to his own abode.

In the afternoon almost the whole population turned towards the cemetery, whither the common people also took provisions which were blessed by the priest, but consumed with right good will by themselves.

Among the people I saw but few in the genuine Russian costume, which, for both men and women, consists of a long wide garment of blue cloth ; and for the former, low felt hats with broad brims.

The next point of my journey was Odessa, to which I had two ways to choose between. The land route promised much that was beautiful and interesting; but that by sea offered the inducement that I should escape so much of the Russian post roads, and this was to me irresistible.

On the day following that on which I left Kertsch the steamer arrived at a village called Yalta in the Crimea, where it was to stay four and twenty hours, and I employed this time for an excursion to Alapka, one of the estates of Prince Woronzoff, and celebrated for a castle which is one of the sights of the peninsula. The road led over low hills close to the sea-shore, and through a beautiful natural park, in which only here and there the helping hand of man had been called in. Among groves and woods, vineyards and gardens, open glades and slopes, lie elegant villas and castles belonging to the Russian nobility, and so lovely a scene is presented to the eye that one could almost think only happiness and concord could find admittance into it.

The first of these charming abodes that strikes the eye is that of Count Leo Potocki, lying close to the sea-shore, and remarkable for its extent rather than its beauty. It was intended to serve the Empress of Russia as a bathing-place, but has not yet been used as such. Then comes the extremely pretty seat of the Princess Mirzewski, in the midst of a superb park, and commanding a grand view of sea and mountain; and then the villa of the Princess Gallitzin, built so entirely in the Gothic style that one takes it at first for a church, and looks about for the town belonging to it.

After going about thirteen wersts, the road turns to the right round a stony hill, and the princely castle of Woronzoff comes into view in all its extent. Its aspect is however not so striking as I had expected, perhaps because the freestone of which it is built is of exactly the same colour as that of the surrounding rocks; when it comes to be encircled by a fine park it will appear to more advantage. There is a fine garden now, but every thing is still too young, though the head gardener, Mr. Kebach, a German, is, it must be owned, a master in his art.

The castle is built in the Moorish-Gothic style, full of towers and turrets, and battlemented walls and points and corners. The principal front is turned towards the sea, and two lions of Carrara marble, by the hand of a celebrated artist, lie reposing at the top of a magnificent flight of steps that descends to the beach.

The interior arrangements remind you of the enchanted palaces of the Arabian tales; for what the whole world can produce in costly stuffs, precious woods, and choice workmanship is here to be seen in its perfection.

There are state apartments in the Chinese, Persian, Indian, and European styles, and a garden saloon which is probably unique in its kind, for it not only contains the most beautiful and rare flowers, but even the highest trees. Palms with their rich crowns of leaves rear their majestic heads, intertwining foliage decks the walls, and flowers and blossoms spring up on every side, while the pure air is perfumed with their fragrant breath, and soft swelling divans stand half hidden in leafy bowers; every thing, in short, is combined to produce the most enchanting impression on the senses. The proprietor of this fairy palace, Prince Woronzoff, was unfortunately absent. I had letters to him, and should have been glad to have made his acquaintance, for I heard him spoken of everywhere, by rich and poor, as a most just, noble-minded, and benevolent man. They endeavoured to make me await his return, saying he was only gone for a few days to a neighbouring estate, but my time was too short to allow of my accepting the invitation.

In the neighbourhood of the castle lies a Tatar village, of which there are many in the Crimea. They are distinguished by their flat roofs covered with earth, which are more used by the inhabitants than the interior of the houses, for they do all their work upon the housetop, and when they have done it remain and pass the night upon the same spot. The men are adopting more and more the Russian costume, but the women still dress in the oriental style, though they do not veil their faces. I have nowhere else seen vineyards so beautifully planted and kept so clean as here. The grapes are sweet and full flavoured, the wine light and good, and perfectly adapted to the making champagne which is indeed often done. In the Prince Woronzoff's vineyards there are above a hundred different species of grapes.

When I returned to Yalta I found I had above two hours to wait, as the Russian gentlemen with whom I was to go on board the steamer had not yet finished their drinking bout, and when at length they arrived one of them was so excessively drunk that he could not stand, and was dragged by two others to the shore. Here we found the steamer's boat waiting, but the sailors said it was for the captain, and refused to take us. It became necessary therefore to hire a boat, for which twenty silver copeks was demanded.

The gentlemen did not know that, though I could not speak Russian, I understood it, and one of them said in a half whisper to the other, "I have no money about me, *let the woman pay*," and thereupon the other turned to me, and said, in the French language, "the share that you have to pay is twenty silver copeks." These were persons who considered themselves gentlemen in Russia !

Sept. 29th.—To-day we stopped at the fine and strong fortress of Sevastopol. The fortifications lie partly at the entrance of the harbour and partly within it. The harbour itself is encircled by hills, and is one of the most secure in the world, and so deep that the largest ships of war can come close up to the quays ; these, as well as the sluices, docks, &c., are all built in a style of profuse grandeur and magnificence. The greatest bustle and activity reigned in all parts of them, and thousands of hands were busied in all kinds of work. Among the labourers I was shown many Polish nobles, who have been sent here as a punishment for the last effort (that of 1831) made to free themselves from the Russian yoke.

The fortifications and barracks are capable of containing thirty thousand men. The town is of very recent origin, and lies on a naked and desolate chain of hills. Among the buildings the Greek Church strikes the eye first, as it lies quite alone on a hill, and is built in the style of a Greek temple. The library is highest, a good allegory if it were not a mere accident. There is also a very handsome open hall surrounded by columns, from which a fine flight of steps leads down to the sea-shore, and forms a very convenient landing place ; and, as in all new Russian towns, the streets are broad and clean.

In two days from Sevastopol we reached Odessa, which has a very handsome appearance from the sea, as it lies high, and its really fine buildings, the palace of Prince Woronzoff, the government offices, several large barracks, and stately private houses, can be seen at a glance. The environs are flat and naked, but the numerous gardens and avenues of trees give the town a pleasant aspect, further animated by the forest of masts in the harbour. The greater part, however, lie not here but in the quarantine harbour ; for all vessels coming from any part of the

Turkish dominions have to submit to a fortnight's quarantine, whether any infectious disease has prevailed in them or not.

Odessa is the capital of the government of Cherson, and by its position on the Black Sea and at the mouths of the rivers Dniester and Dnieper, is one of the most important commercial cities of Russia. In the year 1817 it was declared a free port.* Most of the merit of its rapid rise and present prosperity is commonly attributed to the Duke of Richelieu, who, after making in the emigrant corps several campaigns against his native country, was, in 1803, appointed to the governorship of Cherson. On his entering on his office it contained scarcely 5,000 inhabitants; but under his administration it rapidly rose to nearly its present population of 80,000. In acknowledgment of his services his name has been conferred on many of the finest streets, and his statue in bronze is the ornament of a beautiful public walk, planted with trees and commanding a view of the sea. From this boulevard broad flights of steps lead down to the beach; at one end of it lies the Exchange, a building in the Italian style, and surrounded by a garden; and not far off is the Academy of the Fine Arts. The theatre, with its beautiful portico, promises more than its interior fulfils; and next the theatre you find the Palais Royal, with its rows of handsome shops containing abundance of costly goods, but not so tastefully arranged as they might be. In the interior of the town lies what is called the Crown Garden, which, though neither large nor fine, affords recreation to the inhabitants, who assemble there in great numbers on Sundays and holidays to listen to a band of music that plays under a tent in summer and in a simple pavilion in winter. Among the churches the Russian Cathedral is most worthy of notice. It has a high vaulted nave, resting on strong pillars, covered with a polished white substance that resembles marble; and the decorations in pictures, chandeliers, candlesticks, &c. are rich, though not artistically managed. This was the first church in which I saw stoves, and it was really necessary, for the approaching winter was beginning to make itself keenly felt. I had not seen an autumn for several years, and it made a mournful impression on me. I

---

* Odessa is not a perfectly free port, but merchandize is liable to only a fifth of the duty it would pay in any other Russian port, and this fifth is given to the city itself.—Tr.

could almost have envied the dwellers in warm climates, with all the sufferings occasioned by heat. I was not likely, however, to feel much inconvenience from cold in Odessa, for it was my intention to leave it as soon as I possibly could; but it is as difficult to obtain leave to get out of the Russian territories as to get into them. You are required to change again the passport obtained at your entrance; each operation costing you two silver rubles; and, besides this, the traveller must have his name, and his intention of leaving the city, announced three times in the papers, in case he should have any creditors whom he might leave unpaid. These announcements take up at least eight days, and in many cases two or three weeks; and the only way of escaping the delay, let your business be ever so pressing, is to find some one who will be bail for you. This service was rendered to me by our Austrian consul, M. Gutenthal; and joyfully did I, on the 2d of October, bid farewell to the dominions of his Imperial Majesty the Emperor of all the Russias.

CONSTANTINOPLE AND ATHENS.

Constantinople.—Changes.—Conflagrations.—Journey to Greece.—The Qua-
rantine in Egina.—A Day at Athens.—Callimachi.—The Isthmus.—
Patras.—Corfu.

I HAD rejoiced at leaving Russia; but I was still on board a Russian ship, and my good friends had resolved that I should not be too tenderly treated, lest the parting might be quite too hard for me. The night was mild and warm, and I had taken refuge from the close steaming cabin on the deck, and was lying wrapped in my cloak not far from the steersman, and had nearly fallen asleep, when I was awakened *by a kick* from one of the sailors, who desired me to leave the place. I thanked him for his delicate mode of giving the hint, but declined complying with it, and remained where I was. Among the passengers were six English sailors, who had been taking a new ship to Odessa, and were now returning to their own country. I quite won their hearts by talking occasionally with them; and when they noticed that I had no friend with me, they asked me whether I knew enough of Turkish to be able to make any agreement with the boatmen, &c when we got to Constantinople. On my confessing I did not, they offered to manage every thing for me, if I liked to land with them

When we got into the boat, on our arrival, a custom-house officer came in after us, in order to examine the luggage, and to expedite his movements I slipped some money into his hand; but when we got to shore the English sailors would not allow me to contribute any thing to the expenses of the boat, as they said I had paid the custom-house officer for all; and I saw that I should really offend them if I persisted in offering it. These were common English sailors; and the three I mentioned at Yalta were Russian gentlemen.

As I have already described the entrance to the Bosphorus, and what is most remarkable in Constantinople, in my "Voyage to the Holy Land," I will not dwell much on the subject now. I went immediately to my good Mrs. Balbiani, but found, to my great regret, that she had left Constantinople, and given up her hotel; and I was recommended to that of the Four Nations, kept by a gossiping Frenchwoman, who was perpetually singing the praises of her servants, her cook, and her whole estabishment; but I believe few travellers will be inclined to join in the chorus. She charges also four florins a day, and adds in besides a number of "*pour boires*," to make up the account.

Some changes had taken place since I was last here. A new handsome wooden bridge had been thrown over the Golden Horn, the beautiful palace of the Russian embassy was finished, and the Oriental women did not go so closely veiled as on my first visit to Constantinople. Some indeed wore such thin veils that the form of the face could be seen through them; others had only the forehead and chin covered, leaving eyes, nose, and cheeks openly to be seen. The suburb of Pera had a very desolate appearance, for there had been several conflagrations in it, and their number was increased by two more in the three days of my stay.

These two were what are called little fires, since only thirty houses were destroyed by one, and only a hundred and thirty houses, shops, and huts by the other. In general, the numbers on these occasions are reckoned by thousands.

The first fire broke out in the evening, while we were at dinner; and one of the guests offered to take me to it, thinking, that, if I had not yet witnessed such a spectacle, it would interest me. The scene of the occurrence was at a considerable distance from our abode; but we had not gone a hundred yards before we found ourselves in a crowd of people, who all carried paper lanterns, so that the streets were completely lighted.* All were running, and bawling as loud as they could. The people in the houses tore open their windows to ask the amount of their own danger, and watched with fear and trembling the reflection of the flames on the sky. Ever and anon a loud " *Guarda! Guarda!*" resounded through the street, and four men bearing a small water engine, and skins of water on their shoulders, came rushing along, over-turning everything in their way.† Behind them came foot and horse soldiers, and pachas, with their train of attendants, to urge the people to exertion ; but commonly all their efforts are in vain. The fire finds ample nourishment in the wooden and oil-painted houses, and runs with incredible rapidity along whole lines of streets, till it is stopped by some garden or empty space. Very often a thousand houses are destroyed at once, and the unhappy occupants can barely escape with their lives. Those living farther off the danger hastily pack up their goods, and hold themselves in readiness for instant flight. Thieves too, as may be supposed, are not inactive at such times; and only too often the poor burnt-out people lose again, in the throng and tumult, the few things that they have been able to save.

The second fire broke out in the middle of the night, when we were all asleep ; but the fire watchmen stormed through the streets, striking with their iron bound staves upon the doors, and scream-ing till everybody was broad awake.

I sprang from my bed in a fright, ran to the window, and looked out in the direction where the sky was reddened by the fire ; but in a few hours the glow had faded from the sky, and the noise was hushed. They are now beginning to build stone houses, not only in Pera but even in Constantinople.

On leaving the Turkish capital I went to Smyrna, and afterwards passed through the Grecian Archipelago ; but as precisely the same route is described in my former work, before referred to, I shall pass at once to Greece, where I arrived on the 10th of October.

Sailing near the coast, we first caught sight of a lofty promontory

---

* The streets of Constantinople are not lit, and whoever goes about without a lantern is regarded as a suspicious person.

† On account of the unevenness of the streets, and their being often full of holes, it would be impossible to use horse engines.

on which stood twelve great pillars, the remains of a temple of Minerva, and we soon neared the hill on which lies the glorious Acropolis. I was glowing with an enthusiastic longing to tread the soil, which, after that of Rome and Jerusalem, is the most remarkable and interesting in the world. How eagerly my eyes sought the city of Athens, which lies on the same spot as the one of old renown; but a hill concealed it from my view, and before I could have any chance of seeing it we had to go out again, and sail for Egina, where we were compelled to go into quarantine for twelve days, for fear we might bring cholera. Had the fear been of plague it would have been for three weeks.

It was quite dark when we reached the island, and the steamer lowered a boat, and sent us ashore. But neither porters nor waiters were to he seen who could lend us any assistance, and we were obliged to drag along our trunks, boxes, and portmanteaus as well as we could ourselves to the quarantine building, where they at length put us into a small empty room, but did not even allow us a light. Fortunately I had in my pocket a wax taper, which I cut into pieces, and distributed amongst my companions, by which a little relief was afforded; and on the following morning we were informed of the quarantine arrangements; a small perfectly empty room was rated at three drachmas (about 1s. 9d.) a day, and three shillings was charged for board. A small fee to the doctor on our arrival, and another on our departure; and additional charges were made for water, attendance, for every separate article of furniture, and for small matters innumerable.

I cannot conceive how this system can be permitted in an institution established for the sake of public health, and which the poorest cannot escape, and where, consequently, they must suffer more privations than they do at home. They cannot even allow themselves a warm meal, for it costs five or six times what it would do any where else in the country. Some mechanics who came in our steamer lived the whole twelve days on bread, cheese, and dried figs.

What was worse, these men, and a servant girl, were put all into the same room, and after a few days the poor thing begged me for God's sake to take her into mine, as their behaviour towards her was extremely improper. What a situation would she have been in had not a woman been accidentally among the passengers, or if I had refused her request! Is it not injury enough, too, to a poor person to keep them all this time in a state of enforced idleness, without exposing them also to extortion and ill-treatment?

On the second day of our quarantine our cage was opened a little, and we were allowed to promenade within an enclosed space about 150 paces long. On the fourth day we were allowed to fly a little farther, as it might be, at the end of a string ; that is, under the superintendence of a guard, to visit a neighbouring hill ; and at length the joyful hour of freedom arrived. We had ordered, the evening before, a boat, that was to take us early in the morning to Athens ; but my fellow prisoners chose to celebrate their release at a tavern, so that it was eleven o'clock before we set off, and then there was not a breath of wind to fill our sails, the men had to take to the oars, and it was eight o'clock in the evening before we at length landed at the Piræus. Our first visit, of course, was to the health office, where the testimonies we had brought with us from the quarantine at Egina were studied with the deliberation due to such important documents, and there was, unluckily, no one among us who could, by the distribution of a few drachmas, render them more easily intelligible. We were next requested to make a call at the police office ; but the police office was shut, and we were therefore forbidden to leave the quarter that night. I went into a large handsome looking coffee-house, to endeavour to find a lodging for the night, and I was conducted into a room, of which half the windows were broken; but, as the waiter observed, that was of no consequence, as one could close the shutters. The room did not in other respects look so *very* bad, and I went to bed ; but scarcely had I taken possession of my couch than I discovered that it had already so many occupants that I could not think of intruding. I betook myself to the sofa; but there, alas! the population was no less numerous, and I had finally to pass the remainder of the night on a chair.

I had been told before of the condition of the inns at the Piraeus, and warned not to pass a night there ; but the police regulations left me no chance.

The distance from the harbour of the Piræus to Athens is six miles, and the road leads between noted hills and plantations of olives. The Acropolis remains constantly in sight ; but the town of Athens does not come into view till later. I had proposed to myself to stay at least eight days there ; but I had scarcely alighted before I was met by the news of the October revolution of Vienna.

The February revolution of Paris I had heard of at Bombay, and subsequent events at Tabreez and Teflis ; but no news had so completely taken away my breath as this. I knew, too, that my family was in Vienna, and I had not heard from them ; and had it been "possible I would gladly have set off to them that very moment. Fate had really played me a cruel trick. There had I been kept twelve days in quarantine, longing to tread the classic soil of Greece, and now that I was free to do so the ground seemed to burn beneath my feet. The steamer did not, however, start till the following day ; so, in order to pass away the time, I engaged a cicerone to take me to all the most remarkable places.

The original city lay on a rocky hill in the middle of a plain, which consequently became covered with buildings. The upper part was called the Acropolis ; the lower, the Katopolis. Now there is nothing left but a part of the fortress, the renowned Acropolis, on the hill which boasted the finest works of Athenian art. Its principal ornament was the Temple of Minerva, the Parthenon, which still, in its remaining fragments, is the admiration of the world. It was 215 feet long, 97 broad, and 70 feet high ; and here stood the gold and ivory statue of Minerva, by Phidias. Fifty-five columns yet remain of the entrance to the temple, and some enormous blocks of marble resting upon them. Of the Temple of Neptune some beautiful fragments are still to be seen, and it is easy to make out the circuit of the amphitheatre. Outside the Acropolis lie the temples of Theseus and of the Olympian Jupiter ; one on the north and the other on the south side. The first is of Doric structure, and surrounded with thirty-six fine pillars, and the exploits of Theseus are represented in magnificent reliefs upon the metope. The interior is full of beautiful sculptures, most of which, however, have been taken from other temples, and merely placed here. Outside the temple stand several marble seats, brought from the neighbouring Areopagus. Of this nothing more is left than a chamber hewn in the rock, to which a flight of steps, also cut in the rock, leads. Of the Temple of Jupiter Olympus enough of the foundation wall is left to show its proportions, as well as sixteen magnificent columns of fifty-eight feet in height. This temple, which was completed by Hadrian, was the most superb building in Athens. The exterior was adorned with 120 fluted columns 59 feet in height and six feet in diameter, and all three temples were built of the purest white marble. Not far from the

Areopagus is the Pnyx, where the free people of Athens were accustomed to debate ; but all that remains of it is the rostrum for the orators, and the seats for the clerk, which are cut out of the rock. What men have stood and spoken from that spot! And not far off is the rocky prison where Socrates drank the poison· In the new city of Athens there is nothing to be seen of the antiquities but the Temple of the Winds, sometimes called the " Lantern of Diogenes," a small octagonal temple, with fine sculptures, and the monument of Lysicrates, consisting of little more than a pedestal, some columns, and a dome of Corinthian architecture. There are a considerable number of houses in modern Athens, but most of them small and insignificant, though the country houses are pretty, and surrounded by tasteful gardens. The royal palace, of course a quite new building, is of dazzling white marble, and built in the form of a large quadrangle, but without any ornament, and its great walls look so naked that even the splendid milk white of the marble produces no effect, and it is not till you come quite close that you perceive what costly material has been employed in its construction. I was sorry to see such a building on a soil rendered classic, as much by its treasures of arts as by its heroic men. The marble for this, as well as for the glorious edifices on the Acropolis, has been taken from the quarries of the Pentelicon ; yet they are still so rich that whole cities might be built out of them.

As it was Sunday, and a beautiful day, I had the advantage of seeing the whole beau-monde of Athens, and even the court itself, assembled on the public walk. This consists merely of an avenue of trees, at the end of which is a wooden pavilion, and it has neither lawns nor flower-beds to adorn it. Every Sunday a military band plays from five to six o'clock, and the king rides or drives about with his wife, to show himself to the people. This time he came in an open carriage, drawn by four horses ; and though his wife wore the ordinary French costume, he himself had assumed the Greek, or rather Albanian, which is one of the handsomest that can be seen. It consists of a full white tunic, from the hip to the knee ; a closely-fitting waistcoat of coloured stuff, without sleeves ; and over that a jacket of fine red, blue, or brown cloth, with the sleeves left open to display a silk shirt, and the whole profusely decorated with buttons, clasps of gold or silver &c., cords, rings, and tassels. On the head is a scarlet fez, with a

blue silk tassel, and the shoes are mostly of red morocco.   Of the
women, few wear the Greek dress, and even when they do it has
lost much of its original character.   The principal garment is a
French dress, open at the bosom, and over it a closely-fitting
jacket, also open, and the sleeves of which are wide, and something shorter than those of the dress.   On the head they wear a
little fez, wound round with pink or other coloured crape, or gold
and silver embroidered muslin.

I left Athens on the small steamer, of seventy-horse power, the
"Baron Kubeck," which was going to Callimachi, on the Isthmus
of Corinth; and I much regretted, when we arrived there, to be
compelled to change to another, for the captain, Mr. Luitenburg,
was one of the most obliging whom I had ever met with.

The village of Callimachi has not many attractions.   Its few houses
only date from the establishment of steam communications, and
the high mountains on which it leans are for the most part barren,
or covered only with low brushwood.   We took a few walks upon
the isthmus, and climbed some small heights, whence you look
down from one side on the Gulf of Lepanto, and on the other on
the Egean Sea.   Before us rose far above its compeers the mighty
mountain of Akro-Corinth, the summit of which is crowned by a
fortress, in good preservation, used by the Turks in the last war.
The once world-renowned city of Corinth, which gave its name to so
many of the appliances of wealth and luxury in the interior of the
Byzantine palaces, has sunk into a little town of scarcely 1,000
souls, which lies at the foot of the mountain, among vineyards
and gardens, and owes its place in the world's estimation to a
single article of commerce—its small dried grapes, commonly
known in England as *currants*.

No town in Greece possessed so many costly statues of marble
and bronze as Corinth; and here, on this isthmus, which consists
of a narrow gently-sloping mountain ridge, formerly, in great part,
covered with groves, stood the magnificent temple of Neptune,
and here were celebrated the Isthmian games.   How low can
a country and a nation sink from what it once was.   Greece, which
once held the foremost place in all the earth, is now occupied by
one of the last.   I was told I could not think, in Greece, of trusting
myself alone with a guide, as I had done in other countries ; that
I must by no means venture far from the harbour, and must make
a point of returning to the steamer at twilight.   We had to leave

it however in two days, and cross the isthmus, which is at this part about three miles in width.

At Lutrachi, on the other side, we found the steamer Hellenos, and the following day reached Patras, a town which before the breaking out of the Greek revolution in 1821 had 20,000 inhabitants, but now has only 7000. It was formerly an important commercial town, and is protected by three forts; two at the entrance to the harbour, and one on a hill above the town. The streets are narrow and dirty; but the country round is better cultivated than any I have yet seen in Greece, and is rich in vineyards, fields, and meadows. The size and beauty of the grapes tempted me to buy some; but I found them so hard, dry, and tasteless, that I could not even venture to offer them to one of the ship boys, but threw them into the sea.

The next stop we made was at Corfu, at the entrance to the Adriatic. The town (since 1815 under the protection of the English) lies in a much finer and more fertile country than that of Patras, and is defended by two bold romantic rocks, with strong fortifications. On one of them is also a telegraph and a lighthouse. Both are surrounded with moats, crossed by drawbridges; and the whole island is rich in groves of olive and orange trees. At the entrance to the town is a large covered stone hall, on one side of which the butchers, and on the other the fishmongers, expose their wares; and on the open space before it are laid out the choicest vegetables and most tempting fruits. There are many handsome houses and streets, though some of the bye ones are astonishingly crooked, and by no means too clean; and there is a pretty theatre, which, from the character of the stone figures upon it, has certainly at some time served as a church. The principal square, where the palace of the English governor stands, is very fine, being planted with avenues of trees, and having one side open to the sea.

The celebrated church of Spiridion contains many fine oil paintings; but its chief attraction is a little dark chapel in the back ground, where, in a silver sarcophagus, rest the remains of the saint who is held in high veneration by the Ionians. This chapel is constantly filled with devout visitors, who press many fervent kisses on the marble.

On the 29th of October I once more came in sight of the low mountains of Dalmatia; and on the 30th, at break of day, landed at Trieste, whence I hurried in a post-chaise to Vienna; but the city had just been taken by storm, and no one was allowed to enter it.   In the most painful anxiety I waited before it till the 4th of November ; and when I had found all my family safe and well, returned thanks to God for their safety, and for the wonderful protection which had been granted me through so many perils, and I thought with renewed gratitude of the many kind hearts that had lightened for me so often the toils and hardships of my pilgrimage.

My readers I can only entreat to pass a mild judgment on a little book which professes but to describe in the simplest manner what I have myself seen, felt, and experienced, and has no claim on their attention but that of truth,

THE END.

LONDON:
SPOTTISWOODES and SHAW,
New-street-Square.